Science and Theology

Science and Theology

*An Assessment of Alister McGrath's
Critical Realist Perspective*

JAMES K. DEW JR.

WIPF & STOCK · Eugene, Oregon

SCIENCE AND THEOLOGY
An Assessment of Alister McGrath's Critical Realist Perspective

Wipf & Stock
An Imprint of Wipf and Stock Publishers
199 W. 8th Ave., Suite 3
Eugene, OR 97401
www.wipfandstock.com

ISBN 13: 978-1-60899-855-5

Manufactured in the U.S.A.

To Tara, my lovely wife,
Natalie, Nathan, Samantha & Samuel, my wonderful children

Contents

Preface

Prior to the modern era, both theology and science were joined together in a mutual quest for understanding and truth. As history shows, each discipline had its own unique interests, methods, and theories about reality. Nevertheless, they worked together, trying to gain a coherent grasp of the nature of reality. The seventeenth century, however, brought about a significant shift. Rene Descartes developed a theory of knowledge based solely on human reason, and Francis Bacon offered a new method for scientific investigation, and the gap between theology and science widened, leading to an ultimate split between the two disciplines. Initially, science seemed to gain the upper hand. During the Enlightenment, religion was pushed aside and marginalized in western culture. The church still played a part in human life, but certainly not the part it once did. As science moved forward with investigation and made discoveries about the physical world, the church seemed to wrestle with age-old questions without coming to any certainties. Thus modernity taught that science was about knowledge and religion was about belief. The victory and power of science seemed absolute. Based on investigation and human reason, men felt they could solve the world's problems without reference to theology or religion. Men spoke of inevitable progress and developed political systems that promised utopia. Indeed, the prospects of the future seemed bright.

However, the western world would see yet another significant ideological shift. Modernity, which once seemed so victorious and absolute, would be knocked from its influential high horse. The causes of the shift were subtle and began to emerge within the modern period itself. Kant's influence here is noteworthy. With his Copernican Revolution, he made the mind central in the acquisition of human understanding, making way for an influential distinction between noumena and phenomena. Modern thinkers tended to see the mind as passive in the acquisition of knowledge. As such, they naively assumed that their apprehension of reality was accurate and completely reliable. From Kant forward, however, the mind would be viewed as active, acting as a constructor of knowledge from the raw data of the senses. Implicitly, this would suggest that we likely do not see things as they actually are. Reality, as postmoderns would say, is mind dependant.

Other important developments helped shake the influence of modernity. The rise of Romanticism, Existentialism, and Pragmatism further eroded pre-modern and modern notions of truth. Moreover, in the twentieth century, the western world also experienced two world wars and a sexual revolution. With all this, it was difficult to affirm modern notions about epistemological objectivity, inevitable progress, and the possibility of gaining a reliable metanarrative. Towards the end of the twentieth century, the intellectual, as well as cultural, condition of the western world was labeled postmodernity. Modernity, with its high confidence in human reason and modern science, was called into question and appeared to be more problematic than beneficial. Postmodern thinkers rejected all metanarratives, whether religious or scientific, and were suspicious of all truth claims. Science, like religion and theology before it, was pushed aside by postmodern thinkers.

Postmodernism shed some much needed light on the problems with modernity. Unfortunately, however, it offered no solutions to the problems of the world and failed to account for the actual accomplishments of modern science. As such, it is widely rejected by most contemporary intellectuals from all disciplines, even if it still holds a certain cultural appeal in the western world. Intellectually speaking, postmodernism was short lived.

Where things go from here is hard to predict. The successes of the natural sciences suggest that there is a reality independent from the mind, and that this reality can be known and represented. At the same time, however, a simple return to modernity seems unwise. Modernity, with natural science as its most valuable tool, has given much to the modern world. Yet, natural science has not resolved all the difficulties of this world, and it seems impossible that it will be able to resolve them in the future. There are certain issues that surpass the grasp of natural science and call for philosophical or theological investigation. To give an adequate account of the whole of reality, both science and theology must play a part.

But exactly what part will each play, and what is the nature of their relationship? Is it possible to highlight areas of common ground between them, where one can encourage and stimulate the other, while at the same time maintaining their distinct interests, methods, and commitments? These questions highlight the value and importance of Alister McGrath's work. Among other things, his work offers one of the most comprehensive examinations of the relationship between science and theology to date. McGrath has spent more than thirty years investigating the relationship between science and theology and holds earned doctorates in both fields. After several preliminary works on the subject, he gave his fullest and most comprehensive treatment of this relationship in his seminal collection, entitled *A Scientific Theology*, and subtitled *Nature*, *Reality*, and *Theory*, respectively. These volumes were followed up with a briefer work entitled *The Science of God*.

The following book offers a critical assessment of McGrath's approach to the relationship between science and theology. It argues that a critical realist perspective, like McGrath's, offers the philosophical basis for a relationship between the two disciplines, and provides a viable alternative to a modern or postmodern perspective. As such, science is a helpful *ancilla theologia* (handmaiden of theology).

Chapter 1 presents the historical background for understanding McGrath's contribution. It shows that

1. Prior to the seventeenth century, science and theology were joined in a mutual quest to understand and explain reality

2. This relationship was radically changed by the philosophical developments of modernity and postmodernity

3. Both modernism and postmodernism are inadequate paradigms for the pursuit of knowledge

Chapter 2 offers a summary of McGrath's scientific theology (ST), showing how he responds to modernity and postmodernity by developing a theological method similar to the scientific method. This chapter gives special attention to his work on *Nature*, *Reality*, and *Theory*. Chapter 3 focuses on some areas of ambiguity relating to McGrath's ST. It gives special attention to McGrath's view of revelation, possible connections to methodological naturalism, natural theology, and a few other minor issues. Here the book argues that these concerns might call for more development of clarification, but not for the rejection of his ST. Chapter 4 offers an assessment of McGrath's ST. It argues that McGrath's work makes a valuable contribution to evangelical theology in at least three different ways:

1. It develops a theological method in a critical realist perspective.

2. It shows how the Christian doctrine of creation is beneficial to both theology and science.

3. It recasts and reclaims natural theology as a legitimate aspect of Christian theology.

In chapter 5, the book offers a final assessment of McGrath's ST. Here, it presents a number of areas that call for additional study, but concludes by commending McGrath's ST to evangelicals as a legitimate theological method, since his ST

1. Accepts the valuable lessons of modernity and postmodernity without falling prey to the dangers of either

2. Bridges the divide between theology and science with the doctrine of creation

3. Shows how a revised natural theology gives Christian theology apologetic appeal

1

The History of Dialogue in Theology and Science

THIS CHAPTER PRESENTS THE historical context for understanding Alister E. McGrath's scientific theology (ST). It shows how, prior to the modern period, science and theology were joined in the effort of giving a unified explanation of reality and how this situation changed with the rise of modernity, which separated faith and reason and left the western world in a state of epistemological unsettledness. To show this, the chapter begins with a brief discussion of the different ways the relationship between theology and science has been portrayed, concluding that Warfare and Friendship theses are overly simplistic. After this, it considers the relationship of science and theology prior to the seventeenth century. Here it shows how theology and science, despite certain challenges, mutually encouraged one another. The chapter ends with a discussion of the philosophical developments of the modern and postmodern periods, which describes the various challenges that McGrath's ST attempts to overcome. In later chapters, the book argues that McGrath's theological method rectifies the epistemological problems incurred by modernity and postmodernity, and offers evangelicals an appropriate way to integrate science and theology.

THEOLOGY AND SCIENCE
PRIOR TO THE SEVENTEENTH CENTURY

Regarding the relationship between science and theology, two perspectives surface most frequently in the literature:

1. That theology and science are bitter enemies of each other, with theology being a serious obstacle to the progress of modern science, or

1

2. That theology and science enjoy a deep friendship, with theology giving rise to modern science.

The first perspective is typically referred to as the Warfare Thesis, and has numerous advocates within both disciplines. John William Draper's well-known *History of the Conflict between Religion and Science* and Andrew Dickson White's *A History of the Warfare of Science with Theology* serve as the most popular examples of this view.[1] To make their cases, Draper and White, and others, point to the church's response to Galileo, Darwin, and the Scopes Trials. Today, however, scholars are more skeptical of this perspective, as it does not account for times and places where Christianity did helpfully influence modern science. Moreover, Nancy Pearcey and Charles Thaxton point out that this understanding of the relationship between science and religion is a fairly recent development, which, according to them, stems from a desire to marginalize Christianity. In their view, this understanding comes from the influence of Thomas H. Huxley, who tried to make the scientific worldview more prominent or acceptable by disassociating it from Christianity.[2]

The second view, sometimes referred to as the Friendship Thesis, emerged in the first half of the twentieth century. Robert K. Merton, for example, argued that Puritanism made significant contributions to the rise of modern science.[3] Vincent Carroll and David Shiflett also take this position. They argue that Christianity may have been one of the leading factors in the rise of modern science. They note, "Far from being an eternally heavy weight on intellectual progress, Christianity has frequently been its inspiration and spur. After all, if Christianity is so irredeemably hostile to intellectual inquiry, how is it that modern science sprang from the one civilization on earth grounded in the Christian worldview and habits of mind?"[4]

Like the first, this view also has difficulties. In particular, it does not give an adequate account of the counter evidence. In spite of the positive contributions theology has made to the sciences at times, the church has

---

1. See Draper, *Conflict*, and White, *Warfare*. Others could be cited who adopt this view. For a brief sample of these authors, see Sarton, *History of Science*; Dampier, *History of Science*; Singer, *Religion and Science Considered*; Bernal, *Science in History*; and Goldstein, *Dawn of Modern Science*.

2. Pearcey and Thaxton, *Soul of Science*, 19.

3. Merton, "Science, Technology and Society," 4:432–34.

4. Carroll and Shiflett, *Christianity on Trial*, 57.

had its moments of embarrassment such as the Scopes Trials of 1925. Likewise, those holding this view often fail to account properly for the other factors that gave rise to modern science.[5] For example, one should be careful to note that factors such as growth in commerce, developments and advancements of technology, the establishment of scientific institutions, and the circulation of journals were also great factors that fueled the scientific revolution.

In truth, it seems that both views are overly simplistic. The relationship between theology and science has had its challenges, but there is good reason to suggest that the two were mutually enhanced by their working relationship, as each sought to explain reality. In fact, as the rest of this chapter will argue, prior to the seventeenth century, science and theology were joined together in a mutual quest to understand and explain creation. At least part of the reason for this is that they were often practiced by the same individuals. As Lindberg notes:

> Scholars who made scientific beliefs their business and scholars who made religious or theological beliefs their business were not rigidly separated from one another by disciplinary boundaries . . . all medieval scholars were both theologically and scientifically informed, and all understood that theological beliefs necessarily entailed scientific consequences and conversely. Indeed, the scientist and the theologian were often the very same person, educated in the full range of medieval disciplines—capable of dealing with both scientific and theological matters and generally eager to find ways of integrating theological and scientific belief.[6]

He later adds, "In short, the interaction between science and religion in the Middle Ages was not an abstract encounter between bodies of fixed ideas but part of the human quest for understanding."[7]

Thus, prior to the modern period, it seems that science and theology enjoyed a complex, yet rich, working relationship as both sought a unified explanation of reality. Because of this, there was considerable interaction between the disciplines. In the following pages, a brief treatment of this relationship is given, which begins with Augustine and goes through the sixteenth century and the Protestant Reformation.

5. Lindberg, "Medieval Science and Religion," 63.

6. Ibid., 58.

7. Ibid., 59.

Fifth Century

St. Augustine stands out as one important thinker regarding the relationship of theology and science (natural philosophy) in the early medieval period. In his works, one can find statements that suggest a hostile view toward natural philosophy as well as positive statements about its usefulness as a handmaiden to theology. For example, in *Christian Doctrine*, Augustine harshly condemns the pursuit of astronomical knowledge. Here, Augustine's rejection seems to be in reference to the zodiac. In his mind, such knowledge is of little value in aiding biblical interpretation and, since it was so closely tied to "the very pernicious error of the diviners of fates," it should be avoided altogether.[8] Likewise, in *Confessions*, he appears to downplay the value of natural philosophy when it is pursued for the sake of knowledge itself.[9]

This does not, however, tell the whole story of Augustine's view of natural philosophy. To begin with, Augustine felt that Christians should possess scientific knowledge in order to avoid ignorance. While speaking about the need to know astronomy, biology, zoology, and geology in his *Literal Meaning of Genesis*, he says it "is a disgraceful and dangerous thing for an infidel to hear a Christian . . . talking nonsense on these topics; and we should take all means to prevent such an embarrassing situation, in which people show up vast ignorance in a Christian and laugh it to scorn."[10] But this is not the only reason Augustine values natural knowledge. As he explains in *On Christian Doctrine*, such knowledge is helpful in illuminating Christian thought. He says, "If those who are called philosophers, especially the Platonists, have said things which are indeed true and are well accommodated to our faith, they should not be feared; rather, what they have said should be taken from them as from unjust possessors and converted to our use."[11] Lindberg notes how Augustine's approach was helpful exegetically. He says:

> [Augustine] acknowledged that the temporal could serve the eternal by supplying knowledge about nature that would contribute to the proper interpretation of Scripture and the development of Christian doctrine. And in his own works, including his theo-

8. Augustine, *Christian Doctrine*, 2:550.

9. Augustine, *Confessions*, 242. Here he suggests that these pursuits were only valuable when they gave aid to the exegesis of Scripture.

10. Augustine, *Meaning of Genesis*, 41:42–43.

11. Augustine, *Christian Doctrine*, 75.

logical works, Augustine displayed a sophisticated knowledge of Greek natural philosophy. Natural philosophy, like philosophy more generally, was to serve handmaiden functions.[12]

Thus, one should be careful not to overemphasize Augustine's negative comments regarding natural philosophy. In fact, Augustine appears to encourage the use of science when and where it serves a theological purpose.

The Twelfth Century

Alister McGrath points to the twelfth century as one of the most important periods of interaction between science and theology in premodern times. While theologians continued to use natural philosophy for the exegesis of Scripture, there were a number of other significant contributions to the relationship of theology and science that developed during this time. As McGrath explains, there are at least three important aspects of this period in the relationship between the two: the translation of Aristotle into Latin, the establishment of great universities and institutes of higher education, and the development of natural theology in support of theology.[13] McGrath refers to this first development as simply the translation of important Greek and Arabic documents. Nevertheless, the important documents here deal primarily with Aristotle's works.

TRANSLATION OF ARISTOTLE'S WORKS INTO LATIN

Up until the twelfth century, much of the ancient Greek writings on natural philosophy were unavailable to Christendom. During the medieval period, however, these works were reintroduced to the western world when they were translated into Latin. As A. C. Crombie notes, "The new science which began to percolate into Western Christendom in the 12th century was largely Arabic in form, but it was founded on the works of the ancient Greeks. The Arabs preserved and transmitted a large body of Greek learning, and what they added to its content themselves was perhaps less important than the change they made in the conception of the purpose for which science ought to be studied."[14] Once these works were reintroduced, Christendom quickly saw the need to harmonize its

12. Lindberg, *Beginnings*, 150–51.

13. McGrath, *Science & Religion*, 2–3.

14. Crombie, *Science*, 1:33.

theology with the thought of the Greeks, including their work in natural philosophy. For example, when Plato's *Timaeus* was translated into Latin, the church went to great lengths to harmonize his view of the creator with the Genesis account of creation.[15] According to Crombie, however, the most important of these recently translated works came from Aristotle, who he argues provided the basis for natural philosophy.[16] Edward Grant seems to agree with this assessment:

> Aristotle's treatises on physics, metaphysics, logic, cosmology, the elements, epistemology, and the nature of change furnished the Middle Ages with its conception of the structure and operation of the physical world . . . For approximately 450 years, from 1200 to 1650, the universities of Western Europe emphasized a philosophical and scientific curriculum based on the works of Aristotle, whose logic and natural philosophy were studied by all who received the master of arts degree. Since the latter was usually a prerequisite for entry into the higher faculty of theology, most theologians were well acquainted with contemporary science.[17]

This does not mean, however, that Aristotle's teaching fit naturally with the theology of the church. As Grant observes, "By 1255, Aristotle's works had been adopted as the official curriculum at the University of Paris . . . Nevertheless, some influential theologians in Paris, specifically those at the university, were deeply concerned about the potential dangers that Aristotelian natural philosophy posed for the faith."[18] Elsewhere, he says:

> Where Plato's creation account in the *Timaeus*, which featured a creator God who sought to share his goodness by fabricating a world from preexistent and coeternal matter and form, was reasonably compatible with Christianity, Aristotle's cosmic system, which assumed a world without beginning or end and a deity who had no knowledge of that world, was not. When to these difficulties were added those concerning the soul (it apparently perished with the body) and a strong tendency to employ naturalistic and even deterministic modes of explanation, it becomes obvious that the Aristotelian world system was not readily reducible to the status of a theological handmaiden.[19]

---

15. Lindberg, "Medieval Science and Religion," 62.

16. Crombie, *Science*, 48.

17. Grant, "Science and Theology," 52.

18. Grant, "Aristotle and Aristotelianism," 44.

19. Grant, "Science and Theology," 52–53.

In the end, the church saw some of Aristotle's views on natural philosophy to be quite objectionable. Because of this, Lindberg notes, "in 1210 and again in 1215, the teaching of Aristotle's natural philosophy in the faculty of arts was banned, first by a council of bishops and subsequently by the papal legate. A papal bull (and subsequent letter) issued by Gregory IX (b. 1147, p. 1227–41) in 1231 acknowledged both the value and the dangers of Aristotelian philosophy, mandating that Aristotle's writings on natural philosophy be 'purged of all suspected error.'"[20] Within two or three decades, however, these bans had completely lost their force.[21] Nevertheless, this situation points to the rise of hostility between science and theology that becomes more pronounced within a few centuries.

ESTABLISHMENT OF UNIVERSITIES

Another significant factor of the twelfth century was the establishment of major universities, which allowed for the exploration of nature to a greater degree and by more people.[22] According to McGrath, this is a major development. He says:

> [Universities] would prove to be of central importance in the development of the natural sciences. Courses in logic, natural philosophy, geometry, music, arithmetic, and astronomy were prescribed for all those wishing to gain any qualification from a typical medieval university. The introduction of natural philosophy into the medieval university curriculum ensured that a significant number of scientific issues were addressed as a routine part of higher education.[23]

Thus, as others have already noted, the theologian and natural philosopher were often the same person and the two disciplines were developed and explored alongside each other. However, according to Grant, it was the theologian, not the master of arts student, who was allowed to apply the sciences to theology and vice versa.[24] In other words, the task

20. Lindberg, "Medieval Science," 66.

21. Ibid.

22. Justo Gonzalez notes that during the twelfth century, the universities of Paris and Oxford were of great importance, especially for theology. For those specializing in medicine, the universities of Montpelier and Salerno were important. For law, on the other hand, one might study at Ravenna, Pavia or Bologna. See Gonzalez, *Story of Christianity*, 1:315.

23. McGrath, *Science & Religion*, 2.

24. Grant, "Science and Theology," 69.

of synthesizing the two subjects was given to the theologians and not to the arts majors. McGrath believes that this explains why it is difficult to see a sharp division between theology and science during this period. He says the fact that "medieval theologians combined extensive and intensive training in both natural philosophy and theology, and possessed exclusive rights to interrelate the two, may provide a key to explain the absence of a science-theology conflict in the extensive medieval commentary literature on the Sentences and Scripture. For the host of issues they regularly confronted, the medieval theologians / natural philosophers knew how to subordinate the one discipline to the other and how to avoid conflict and confrontation."[25]

Development of Natural Theology

Though its high point within the medieval period technically took place in the thirteenth century, the development of natural theology arises out of the university context of the twelfth century, where natural philosophy and theology were studied alongside each other. That they were studied alongside each other does not mean hostilities or tensions were never present. It simply means they were often considered together and by the same people. The most notable example of one who developed and made such great use of natural theology is Thomas Aquinas. With his famous proposal in his *Summa Theologica*, he suggests that there are five ways God's existence can be proved or demonstrated.[26] That Aquinas speaks of these five ways as proofs or demonstrations does not mean he places reason about revelation. Rather, when considered in the overall context of his work, it seems Aquinas is simply attempting to show how belief in God's existence is consistent with what can be known through nature and reason. McGrath says "there are excellent reasons for suggesting that Aquinas regards natural theology as a demonstration, from the standpoint of faith, of the consonance between that faith and the structures of the world. In other words, natural theology is not intended to prove the existence of God, but presupposes that existence; it then asks, 'What should we expect the natural world to be like if it has indeed been created by such a God?'"[27] Nevertheless, though he does not elevate nature above Scripture, Aquinas does believe that nature reveals

---

25. McGrath, *Science & Religion*, 69–70.

26. Aquinas, *Summa Theologica*, 1:1.2.3.

27. McGrath, *Science of God*, 81.

the existence of God.[28] Aquinas felt that natural philosophy, instead of contradicting the church's theology, could be used to clarify and demonstrate its claims. As McGrath notes, this explains why "many of the greatest names in the world of medieval natural science—such as Robert Grosseteste, Nicolas Oresme, and Henry of Langenstein—were all active theologians who did not see a contradiction between their faith and the investigation of the natural order. "[29]

Thus, in the twelfth century, a number of developments occurred pertaining to the relationship between theology and science. Aristotle's works were translated into Latin, which forced the church to interact with his works on natural philosophy. Likewise, universities were established where theology and natural science were often explored by the same individuals. Finally, beginning in the twelfth century, natural theology was developed, and reached a high point in the writings of Aquinas. These developments presented both challenges and benefits to the relationship between theology and science.

The Sixteenth Century

In the sixteenth century, theologians like Martin Luther and John Calvin rearticulated biblical doctrines that had been lost or corrupted in the previous centuries. But the Protestant Reformation did much more than simply re-shape the religious landscape of the western world. Jacques Barzun believes that it is one of the most, if not the most, important periods in western history because of its far-reaching influence.[30] Regarding the relationship between theology and science, it is important to remember that the rise of modern science took place around the same time and in the same place as the Reformation. This is not to say that scientific developments took place only in this period and in this region. Other developments can be noted during the Renaissance and in other parts of the world. Nevertheless, as will be shown momentarily, there were a number of significant developments in this region and during this period that were encouraging to the rise of modern science. Thus, it is important to discuss the Reformation's theological benefits, for modern science as well as for the important protestant scientists working in this period.

---

28. Aquinas, *Summa Theologica*, 1.2.2. For his thoughts on the limitations of natural revelation see 1.1.1.

29. McGrath, *Science & Religion*, 3.

30. Barzun, *Dawn to Decadence*, 3–20.

THEOLOGICAL BENEFITS OF THE REFORMATION FOR THE RISE OF MODERN SCIENCE

Andrew White and Bertrand Russell criticize Martin Luther, Philip Melanchthon, and John Calvin as being obstacles to the rise of modern science.[31] Nevertheless, their claims have been thoroughly refuted by a number of historians of science.[32] Among other things, their criticism fails to account for the positive contributions these theologians made for the rise of modern science. In the case of Melanchthon, for example, one could point to his influence in mathematics in the German universities. As Robert Westman explains, Melanchthon "believed that mathematics (and thus astronomy) deserved a special place in the curriculum because through study of the heavens we come to appreciate the order and beauty of the divine creation. Furthermore, mathematics was an excellent subject for instilling mental discipline in students."[33] Edward Davis and Michael Winship agree, saying, "Although Melanchthon never accepted the hypothesis of the earth's motion, he positively encouraged the teaching of mathematics (and its sub-discipline, astronomy) at Lutheran universities in Germany."[34] As a result, "a powerful tradition of mathematical astronomy developed at Wittenberg from the late 1530s and spread throughout the German and Scandinavian universities."[35]

Moreover, White and Russell fail to recognize how the reformers highly respected nature's ability to reveal the glory of God. As R. Hooykaas notes, "What strikes one most about the early Protestant scientists is their love for nature, in which they recognize the work of God's hands, and their pleasure in investigating natural phenomena."[36] Calvin, for example, makes very strong claims about the revelatory capacity of creation. In the *Institutes*, he says, "Upon his individual works [God] has engraved unmistakable marks of his glory, so clear and so prominent that even unlettered and stupid folk cannot plead the excuse of ignorance."[37] He goes on to

---

31. White, *History of Warfare*, 126; and Russell, *History of Western Philosophy*, 528.

32. See Dillenberg, *Protestant Thought*, 37; Gerrish, "Reformation and Rise," 244–55; Davis and Winship, "Protestantism," 121; Westman, "Copernicans and Churches," 82, Reid, "Calvin's View," 247; and Hooykaas, *Religion and Rise*, 117.

33. Westman, "Copernicans and Churches," 82.

34. Davis and Winship, "Protestantism," 121.

35. Westman, "Copernicans and Churches," 82.

36. Hooykaas, *Religion and Rise*, 105.

37. Calvin, *Institutes*, 1:1.5.1.

suggest that, "wherever you cast your eyes, there is no spot in the universe wherein you cannot discern at least some sparks of his glory."[38]

Furthermore, Calvin encouraged the study of nature by saying, "There is no doubt that the Lord would have us uninterruptedly occupied in this holy meditation; that, while we contemplate in all creatures, as in mirrors, those immense riches of his wisdom, justice, goodness, and power, we should not merely run over them cursorily, and, so to speak, with a fleeting glance; but we should ponder them at length, turn them over in our minds seriously and faithfully, and recollect them repeatedly."[39] Elsewhere, he suggests that there "are innumerable evidences both in heaven and on earth that declare his wonderful wisdom; not only those more recondite matters for the closer observation of which astronomy, medicine, and all natural science are intended, but also those which thrust themselves upon the sight of even the most untutored and ignorant persons, so that they cannot open their eyes without being compelled to witness them."[40] In his commentary on Genesis, Calvin also says, "For astronomy is not only pleasant, but also very useful to be known: it cannot be denied that this art unfolds the admirable wisdom of God. Wherefore, as ingenious men are to be honored who have expended useful labor on this subject, so they who have leisure and capacity ought not to neglect this kind of exercise."[41] Thus, it seems that Calvin had an admiration for creation and encouraged its meditation and exploration through science.

R. Hooykaas and W. Stanford Reid note the significance of Calvin's influence. Hooykaas contends that Calvin's words "implied the right, and even the duty, for those who had the talents, to study Scripture without depending on the authority of tradition and hierarchy, together with the right and the duty to study the other book written by God, the book of nature, without regard to the authority of the fathers of natural philosophy."[42] Likewise, Reid says, "In summing up Calvin's view of natural science, therefore we see that he believed that we are called upon to understand nature . . . Furthermore, he believed that there were certain people who were called to do this work. In this way God's cre-

38. Ibid., 1.5.1.
39. Ibid., 1.14.21.
40. Ibid., 1.5.2.
41. Calvin, *Genesis*, 1:86.
42. Hooykaas, *Religion and Rise*, 109.

ative and providential activity would be made apparent to mankind."[43] Understanding nature in this way had a great effect on the natural sciences. Theologians could encourage science because it gave evidence of God's wisdom, power, and goodness.

Thus, the reformers, especially Calvin, seem to have given a theological stimulus to the study of nature. The reformers' recognition that nature displayed the glory of God meant that it was worthy of study and exploration. Perhaps this is why a majority of the scientists during this period came from Protestant countries. G. B. Deason notes a great disparity between Roman Catholic and Protestant scientists in Europe during the period of reformation. He states:

> An imbalance between numbers of Protestants and Roman Catholics belonging to the French Academy of Science from its founding in the early seventeenth century until the end of the nineteenth century. Whereas the proportion of Protestants to Roman Catholics in the general population averaged 6 to 27, Protestants outnumbered Roman Catholics 6 to 4 in the Academy. In Switzerland during the same period, Protestants and Roman Catholics contributed none. In southern Belgium during the same period, Protestants were a very small minority of the population, but they comprised a large majority of the scientists.[44]

This disparity alone suggests that something significant was taking place in the Reformation that was encouraging to modern science.

PROTESTANT SCIENTISTS

Finally, any treatment of the relationship between theology and science during the Reformation would be incomplete without a brief consideration of some of the Protestant scientists of the period. Two of the most important include Georg Joachim Rheticus and Johannes Kepler.

Georg Joachim Rheticus was a famous Protestant scientist who helped popularize Copernicus's famous work, *On the Revolutions of the Heavenly Bodies*. This work would cause great debate in the sixteenth century, but would later be verified by Galileo. According to Westman, "Rheticus himself was Copernicus's first major disciple."[45] As Davis and

---

43. Reid, "Calvin's View," 247–48.

44. Deason, "Protestant Reformation," 38:223–24.

45. Westman, "Copernicans and Churches," 81.

Winship point out, Rheticus aided Copernican teaching by introducing it at the university in Wittenberg. By doing so, this helped spread the teaching of Copernicus throughout Protestant circles. Moreover, Rheticus was influential because he was the one to encourage Copernicus to publish his work in the first place.[46] Due to Copernicus's fear of being accused of heresy, he was hesitant to put his theory of the heliocentric universe into print. Recognizing the value of this theory, however, Rheticus urged him to publish it under a false name. As Owen Gingerich sees it, "It is quite possible that Copernicus would never have published his hypotheses except for the persuasive intervention of a young Lutheran astronomer from Wittenberg, Georg Joachim Rheticus. Rheticus's initial account of Copernicus's ideas, *Narratio prima* (First Narrative [1540]), did not create the opposition Copernicus feared, so the Polish astronomer gave him permission to take a manuscript of *De Revolutionibus* to Nuremberg for publication."[47]

Another important Protestant scientist was Johannes Kepler. As Van Doren points out, "His greatest contribution was a set of three laws of planetary motion that solved the problem of epicycles and eccentric orbits once and for all. The three laws are still valid and are called by his name."[48] Russell offers this explanation of Kepler's laws: "His first law states: The planets describe elliptic orbits, of which the sun occupies one focus. His second law states: The line joining a planet to the sun sweeps out equal areas in equal times. His third law states: The square of the period of revolution of a planet is proportioned to the cube of its average distance from the sun."[49] Many modern science textbooks speak of Kepler and his laws without mentioning his religious convictions and motivations. Yet, his religious beliefs played an enormous role in his thinking. As Richard Westfall argues, "In Kepler's religious thought Christianity remained intact, harmoniously interwoven with his science and scarcely altered by it. His personal piety furnished the background to his work, forcing itself as it were onto the printed page, as though he were unable to contain it."[50] He adds that for Kepler, God "had revealed his wisdom in the act of creation, and Kepler's primary theological inter-

---

46. Davis and Winship, "Early Modern Protestantism," 121.

47. Gingerich, "Copernican Revolution," 97.

48. Van Doren, *History of Knowledge*, 198.

49. Russell, *History of Western Philosophy*, 530.

50. Westfall, "Rise of Science," 219.

est centered on the wisdom of God . . . Kepler not only redirected the focus of Christian thought but also elevated nature as a revelation of God to a status equal to that of the Bible."[51]

Pearcey and Thaxton also note the religious influence in Kepler's thought. They argue that "Kepler was attracted to a heliocentric astronomy at least in part because he attached religious significance to the sun. He appears to have thought of the sun as the physical seat of God's presence in the world."[52] They explain that the sun fulfilled three roles in Kepler's system. "It was the mathematical center in describing the motions of the planets; it was the physical center in its exertion of force upon the planets to keep them in their orbits; and it was the metaphysical center as the temple of the deity."[53] Moreover, Kepler also believed that the universe itself was spherical, representing the triune nature of God. As Westman puts it, "The ultimate union of Christianity and science in Kepler's mind, however, lay in a further feature of his conception of nature, a feature possible only because his universe remained an ordered cosmos. Wherever he looked, and he looked everywhere, Kepler saw a universe organized in triads, and not just ordinary triads, but triads that are at the same time unities. It was not by accident that Kepler's universe remained finite, finite and spherical, because to him the sphere represented an embodiment of the Trinity."[54] Thus, with Kepler, one finds an example of a protestant believer working within the realm of natural science. Like Calvin, Kepler believed that God had revealed himself in nature and saw the need to give nature careful study. His discoveries and theories would have a great influence on Galileo and Newton.

PHILOSOPHICAL DEVELOPMENTS
OF THE MODERN PERIOD

As the previous half of this chapter argued, in the premodern period, science and theology were joined in a mutual quest of understanding and explaining reality. In the second half of the chapter, however, it will be shown that this relationship suffered greatly in the modern period, beginning with the philosophical developments of the seventeenth cen-

---

51. Ibid., 220.

52. Pearcey and Thaxton, *Soul of Science*, 66.

53. Ibid.

54. Westfall, "Rise of Science," 222.

tury. From this time forward, thinkers such as René Descartes, Francis Bacon, and Immanuel Kant developed epistemologies that forever changed the western world. It is not the purpose of this book to give a complete philosophical analysis of the modern period. Nevertheless, it is necessary to give a brief outline of the period's key philosophical developments that led to the separation of science and theology. This separation left the western world in a state of epistemological turmoil.

Key Philosophical Developments

The modern period, often referred to as the Enlightenment, is a time when human reason achieved an unprecedented authority. There are many aspects of this that might be mentioned. Nevertheless, there are a number of specific developments that are of major importance. These include:

1. The quest for absolute epistemological certainty

2. The establishment of classical foundationalism

3. The assumption that complete objectivity was possible

4. The emergence of metaphysical naturalism[55]

THE QUEST FOR ABSOLUTE CERTAINTY

One defining feature of the modern period is the belief that it is both possible and necessary to gain absolute certainty on a given matter before one could consider it knowledge. As Esther Meek observes, from the modern period forward, westerners assumed that for "knowledge to be knowledge, it has to be characterized by certainty and infallibility, necessity, universality."[56] Likewise, Tim Morris and Don Petcher suggest that one could "see the Enlightenment Project emerging as an attempt to find a way toward certain knowledge through human faculties, those of reason and experience."[57]

Charles Van Doren suggests that this quest for certainty began with René Descartes. He says Descartes sought a "scientific methodology that would revolutionize not only science but also the way mankind lives

---

55. While the first point entails the second and third, I delineate them for the sake of clarity.

56. Meek, *Longing to Know*, 32.

57. Morris and Petcher, *Science & Grace*, 25.

in the world."[58] John Feinberg agrees, saying, "With Descartes things changed, because Descartes wanted to know that what he believed about anything could be supported by evidence and argument. So he called into question everything he had believed, for the purpose of ascertaining whether there was anything he claimed to know that could not reasonably be doubted."[59]

Descartes himself says that he would "reject as absolutely false everything in which I could imagine the slightest doubt and to see, as a result, if anything remained among my beliefs that was completely indubitable. Thus, because our senses sometimes deceive us, I decided to assume that nothing was the way the senses made us imagine it."[60] Consequently, the quest for absolute certainty began to emerge with Descartes.

Though not as pronounced as it is with Descartes, the search for certainty can also be found in Francis Bacon. He describes his approach, early on in the *Novum Organum*, when he says that he hopes to develop an "account of a better and more perfect use of reason in the investigation of things and the true aids of the intellect, so that (despite our humanity and subjection to death) the understanding may be raised and enlarged in its ability to overcome the difficult and dark things of nature."[61]

Thus began the quest for certainty in the seventeenth century, and it continued throughout the modern period and into the present. As Meek observes, "We have thought that knowing something means that what we claim to know can't be wrong or we cannot doubt—that it is *infallible*, or *certain*. For knowledge to *be* knowledge at all, it must be infallible or certain."[62] She then says, "It is still very much a part of the Western philosophical tradition to accept as knowledge only those statements that can be fully justified, and thus to try to determine what kind of justification would be foolproof."[63] Daniel Taylor agrees, saying, "Still, the feeling is very widespread that the goal of reasoning is certainty and that, if we can simply think clearly and logically enough, we can solve

---

58. Van Doren, *History of Knowledge*, 203.

59. Feinberg, *No One Like Him*, 85.

60. Descartes, *Discourse*, 24.

61. Bacon, *New Organon*, 15.

62. Meek, *Longing to Know*, 26.

63. Ibid., 33.

our individual and collective problems and get on with the business of being happy."[64]

THE EMERGENCE OF CLASSICAL FOUNDATIONALISM

Closely associated with the quest for absolute certainty is the method used by philosophers to achieve this certainty. Philosophers, theologians, and historians point to classical foundationalism as the defining epistemological method of the modern period. Millard Erickson describes this by saying:

> Classical foundationalism contended that in the knowing process there are certain unshakable starting points. These are not justified by any other propositions. They are simply immediately justified. They possess a character such that they are indubitable (they cannot be doubted) and incorrigible (it is not possible to be mistaken about them). In the rationalist form of foundationalism, such as that of Descartes, such a foundation is known rationally, or by pure thought, while for an empiricist like Locke, the foundation is sense data.[65]

Likewise, Morris and Petcher describe it as "an attempt to build the whole system on certain foundational axioms that can (supposedly) not be doubted and upon a procedure that would allow deductions from the foundations to further knowledge."[66] W. Jay Wood offers a similar description. He says:

> The root idea suggests that each of us holds some beliefs "basically" or "immediately," while we hold other beliefs "nonbasically" or "mediately." Nonbasic or mediate beliefs receive their support from other beliefs we hold. For example, I believe that insects attacked my garden during the night; this belief is based on my belief that there are holes in the leaves of the plants. Basic or immediate beliefs do not receive their support from other beliefs we hold but are based directly on experiences or the "self-evident deliverances of reason," to cite two commonly alleged sources of basic belief. I believe there is a chair under me, not on the basis of other beliefs but because of experiences I am having. So on the

---

64. Taylor, *Myth of Certainty*, 78.

65. Erickson, *Truth or Consequences*, 252.

66. Morris and Petcher, *Science & Grace*, 22.

foundationalist view, some beliefs are justified even though they are not based on other beliefs we hold.[67]

Finally, using architecture as an analogy for the concept of foundationalism, Ronald Nash says, "The key analogy in the foundationalist picture of knowledge is a structure such as a building where various upper levels or stories are supported by lower stories."[68] He then adds: According to foundationalism, then, noetic structures should be thought of as hierarchies in which every belief is either basic or derivative (Nonbasic). Derivative beliefs are those that are grounded on or dependent in some way on more basic beliefs. Basic beliefs are those not derived from or dependent on other beliefs. In order for a belief to be rational, it must either be a basic belief or be justified by its relation to a basic belief.[69]

As with the quest for certainty, historians of philosophy point to Descartes as the initiator and prime example of this project. As noted, he began by doubting everything until he found something that simply could not be doubted. Once such a belief was identified, using the same methods of mathematics and geometry, this belief would serve as the basis or foundation of all other knowledge. In the *Meditation*, Descartes describes his approach:

> The long chains of inferences, all of them simple and easy, that geometers normally use to construct their most difficult demonstrations had given me an opportunity to think that all the things that can fall within the scope of human knowledge follow from each other in a similar way, and that as long as one avoids accepting something as true which is not so, and as long as one always observes the order required to deduce them from each other, there cannot be anything so remote that it cannot eventually be reached nor anything so hidden that it cannot be uncovered.[70]

Whereas Descartes developed his foundationalist approach through rationalism, Bacon—another example of foundationalism—developed a similar approach by way of empiricism. In his mind, if science could make any progress at all, a new method would be required. Thus, Bacon combined experimentation and observation with induction in the development of the empirical method. Comparing his new approach with the deductive method of ancient and medieval philosophy, Bacon says:

67. Wood, *Epistemology*, 78.

68. Nash, *Faith and Reason*, 80.

69. Ibid., 81.

70. Descartes, *Discourse*, 16.

And so the order of demonstration also is completely reversed. For the way the thing has normally been done until now is to leap immediately from sense and particulars to the most general propositions, as to fixed poles around which disputations may revolve; then to derive everything else from them by means of intermediate propositions; which is certainly a short route, but dangerously steep, inaccessible to nature and inherently prone to disputations. By contrast, by our method, axioms only at the very end; and the most general axioms come out not as notional, but as well defined, and such as nature acknowledges as truly known to her, and which live in the heart of things.[71]

As such, one sees in Bacon an attempt to develop a method aimed at gaining sure and certain knowledge. He says, our method, though difficult to practice, is easy to formulate. It is to establish degrees of certainty, to preserve sensation by putting a kind of restraint on it . . . [and] to open and construct a new and certain road for the mind from the actual perceptions of the senses.[72] Hicks offers a helpful summary of Bacon's influence when he notes how

[Bacon] suggested a more rigorous program of observation and experimentation, which, he claimed, would give us certain knowledge. Scientists, he said, must work slowly and thoroughly, keeping careful records . . . they must make a study of anything that appears to contradict them or only partially supports them. After patient and careful observation, a preliminary hypothesis may be formed, which is then tested by carefully planned experiments. Once one hypothesis has been established, others should be added until a comprehensive system of laws has been established.[73]

Thus, in the seventeenth century, Descartes, with rationalism, and Bacon, with empiricism, developed an epistemology that sought to ground all knowledge on sure and certain foundations. One may observe, then, that foundationalism can operate within the perspective of rationalism, empiricism, or a combination of the two. As Fienberg explains, "Whereas for Descartes the ultimate foundation was something rational, the empiricists emphasized sense impressions as the most basic beliefs that form the foundations of our knowledge. Kant combined both rational (the mind's categories that allow it to structure reality) and

71. Bacon, *New Organon*, 16–17.

72. Ibid., 28.

73. Hicks, *Journey So Far*, 239.

empirical (data from observation) as foundational."[74] What is important to note, however, is that regardless of whether or not it was rationalist or empiricist, foundationalism seems to have dominated the modern period. As Fienberg goes on to say, "Reason was deemed capable of grasping and interacting correctly with the world, and it was held that this is true for all people. Just as Descartes wanted to find an indubitable foundation on which to base his knowledge, so others after him thought this was both necessary and possible."[75]

The Assumption of Objectivity

Another defining feature of the modern period is the assumption that one could be completely objective in his view and representation of reality. Put another way, philosophers in the modern period felt that one could prevent subjective factors from clouding his view of the world, making it possible for him to come to a completely accurate understanding of reality. Feinberg notes how there was a wide spread assumption that a "universal perspective on reality was possible through reason, and belief in everyone's ability to find the truth made it possible in every discipline of study to know truth and error and to convince others, if one thought their views were wrong."[76]

Likewise, Douglas Groothuis suggests that "modernism exaggerated these basic truths to the point of falsehood: it was believed that human reason could be completely objective, that scientific study defines the limits of knowledge."[77] Paul Hiebert explains how this was especially important to the development of natural science. He says, "Science is based on the assumption that scientists, by means of instruments and senses, can gain an accurate, objective knowledge of reality . . . scientific knowledge is seen as a photograph or literal picture of reality in which information is additive (the whole is the sum of the parts), and scientific statements correspond one-to-one to reality."[78] Because of this, natural science seemed to gain a huge advantage over religion. Feinberg notes how philosophers in the modern period believed that "objectivity is possible, and is most clearly seen in science. The fact that science works with

---

74. Feinberg, *No One Like Him*, 88.

75. Ibid., 87.

76. Ibid.

77. Groothuis, *Truth Decay*, 41.

78. Hiebert, *Missiological Implications*, 11.

data of the tangible world and uses an observational method that everyone can use to confirm or disconfirm scientific conclusions seemed to guarantee objectivity."[79]

THE RISE OF NATURALISM

With the philosophical developments mentioned thus far, the natural sciences gained a significant advantage over Christian theology. Where religion seemed to falter, science began to thrive. The claims of theology were considered biased and unprovable, meaning one could not be certain about such claims. Science, on the other hand, was seen to be objective and was able to produce empirical evidence to support its claims. Thus, the claims of science could be held with certainty. Groothuis explains how this gave rise to naturalism. He says, "Modernism, especially in its later stages, is based on the worldview of naturalism . . . God and all other concepts having to do with values, morality, spirituality and supernatural/immaterial realities became only concepts. They are mere linguistic signifiers."[80] This is further explained when he says:

> The modernist vision presupposed the power of rationality to discover objective truth. They desired a rational, scientific worldview over the perceived irrationality and acrimony stemming from religion, and the possibility of progress through humanity's emancipation from received dogma and superstition. Some Enlightenment thinkers did not entirely reject belief in God but replaced Christian theism with deism—belief in a Creator without revelation or providence or incarnation—but this evisceration of theism naturally led to naturalism. God readily went from being once removed to being absent entirely.[81]

Albert Mohler seems to agree. He thinks that the "problem with the Enlightenment was the totalitarian imposition of the scientific model of rationality upon all truth, the claim that only scientific data can be objectively understood, objectively defined, and objectively defended. The loss in the wake of this modernist agenda was huge. It left Western culture with little more than a materialist worldview."[82] Thus, naturalism seems to be closely related to the quest for certainty, classical foundationalism, and the empirical method.

79. Feinberg, *No One Like Him*, 89.
80. Groothuis, *Truth Decay*, 41.
81. Ibid., 35.
82. Mohler, "Truth and Culture," 56.

Consequences of the Modern Period

As mentioned briefly in the previous section regarding the rise of naturalism, the philosophical developments of the modern period had serious consequences for the relationship between science and theology. To name just a few, one can observe: a separation between science and theology, the marginalization of religious belief, and the decline of natural theology.

THE SEPARATION OF SCIENCE AND THEOLOGY

One well-documented consequence of the philosophical developments of the modern period is a radical division between science and theology. As J. Wentzel van Huyssteen puts it, "The dialogue between theology and the sciences has been forced into a rather radical conflict, a kind of modernist 'duel' where 'objective', universal scientific claims were starkly contrasted to conflict with subjective, 'irrational' theological beliefs, resulting in a relentless pressure toward the absolute polarization of religion and science."[83] Hiebert notes this as well and says, "Modernity is the division of reality into two separate and largely unrelated realms, natural and supernatural. On the one hand there is the spiritual realm in which God and other spirit beings live and act. This is the world of religion. On the other hand there is the natural realm—the material world of science . . . the latter became public facts, taught to everyone; the former was increasingly a matter of private faith."[84] Morris and Petcher make a similar observation, saying, "In the Modern landscape right from the beginning, science and theology have been assumed to be two distinct trees of human knowledge. In this Modern mind-set, each tree is rooted in its own distinctive type of soil, each grows by different processes, and each bears its own sort of fruit."[85]

An example of this is found with Stephen Jay Gould. In his mind, the separation between science and theology is so distinct that the two disciplines have nothing to say to each other. He says:

> If religion can no longer dictate the nature of factual conclusions residing properly within the magisterium of science, then scientists cannot claim higher insight into moral truth from any superior knowledge of the world's empirical constitution. This mutual

83. van Huyssteen, *Duet or Duel?*, 2.

84. Hiebert, *Missiological Implications*, 16.

85. Morris and Petcher, *Science & Grace*, 8.

humility leads to important practical consequences in a world of such diverse passions . . . I may, for example, privately suspect that papal insistence on divine infusion of the soul represents a sop to our fears, a device for maintaining a belief in human superiority within an evolutionary world offering no privileged position to any creature. But I also know that the subject of souls lies outside the magisterium of science. My world cannot prove or disprove such a notion, and the concept of souls cannot threaten or impact my domain.[86]

One will notice here that scientific claims are classified as factual conclusions, and religious claims merely deal with moral considerations. Although theologians and philosophers are beginning to see this division as problematic, some theologians have been willing to embrace it. Langdon Gilkey is a case in point. By affirming a rigid separation between science and religion, he says, "Science is not a threat to Christianity—but then religious theory is limited to its proper arena, namely, to talking about God in relation to nature, and not about the sequences of natural causes in and of themselves. There is theological discourse about God, but there is no theological astronomy, physics, geology, or biology."[87] Thus, as Ted Peters notes, "Up until now, theologians have made themselves feel reasonably secure by hiding behind the Kantian split between theoretical and moral knowledge and by consigning science to the former while reserving privileged access to the latter. Even if natural scientists exclude God from their worldview, theologians have thought they could earn an honest living by appealing to the realm of value and morality."[88]

The split between science and theology can be easily traced back to Descartes. Epistemologically speaking, he felt that theological inquiry should be separated from all other forms of inquiry and not subjected to his method of systematic doubt. This is not to say that the split begins with Descartes, but only that this split is clearly seen in his thinking. He says, "I respected our theology and hoped, as much as anyone else, to get to heaven. But once I learned, as something which is very certain, that the path to heaven is just as open to the most ignorant as to the most learned, and that the revealed truths which lead there are beyond

---

86. Gould, "Domains," 556.

87. Gilkey, *Creation on Trial*, 52.

88. Peters, Introduction to Pannenberg, *Theology of Nature*, 2.

our understanding, I did not dare subject them to the feebleness of my reasoning, and thought that one needed to have some extraordinary assistance from heaven and to be more than human in order to study them successfully."[89] Later, he says, "Having convinced myself of these maxims and having set them to one side, together with the truths of faith that have always been among my primary beliefs, I thought I could begin freely to rid myself of all my other views."[90]

The division of science and theology, however, becomes very clear with Immanuel Kant. After David Hume leveled such strong arguments against the notion of cause and effect relationships, both theology and science had been called into question. But here Kant made an observation. He noted that Hume was partially right and partially wrong, since science was having such great success and metaphysics had never made much progress. This helped establish scientific knowledge but left metaphysical and theological knowledge in a vulnerable situation. Kant says, "Respecting these sciences, as they do certainly exist, it may with propriety be asked, how they are possible?—for that they must be possible, is shown by the fact of their really existing. But as to metaphysics, the miserable progress it has hitherto made, and the fact that of no one system yet brought forward, as far as regards its true aim, can it be said that this science really exists, leaves anyone at liberty to doubt with reason the very possibility of its existence."[91]

Noting the successes of natural science and the failures of theology and metaphysics, Kant developed a system that made a clear distinction between the *noumena* and the *phenomena*. That is, Kant believed it necessary to distinguish between the appearance of a thing and the thing-in-itself. The *phenomena* could be known through scientific investigation, but the *noumena* could only be believed or asserted by faith. The end result of this was that theology and science now belonged to two different epistemological groups. Science dealt with empirical data, which could yield certain knowledge, but theology belonged in the arena of faith, and could not be classified as knowledge at all. To expect more of theology was a great error. As Richard Tarnas observes:

---

89. Descartes, *Discourse*, 9.

90. Ibid., 22.

91. Kant, *Critique of Pure Reason*, 13.

> In Kant's view, the attempt by philosophers and theologians to ra-
> tionalize religion, to give the tenets of faith a foundation by pure
> reason, had succeeded only in producing a scandal of conflict,
> casuistry, and skepticism. Kant's restriction of reason's author-
> ity to the phenomenal world thereby freed religion of reason's
> clumsy intrusion. Moreover, by such a restriction, science would
> no longer conflict with religion . . . Kant thus held that although
> one could not know that God exists, one must nevertheless be-
> lieve he exists in order to act morally. Belief in God is therefore
> justified, morally and practically, even if it is not certifiable. It is
> a matter of faith rather than knowledge. Ideas of God, the soul's
> immortality, and the freedom of the will could not be known to
> be true in the same way that the laws of nature established by
> Newton were so known.[92]

Thus, in the modern period, one sees that science and theology are separated into two distinct epistemological groups. This split arose with the
quest for absolute certainty and the establishment of classical foundationalism. This division is clearly seen in the thinking of Descartes, but
becomes even more pronounced in the writings of Immanuel Kant.

THE MARGINALIZATION OF RELIGIOUS KNOWLEDGE

One of the most serious consequences of the philosophical development of modernity is that, epistemologically speaking, claims of religious knowledge were now considered inferior to claims of scientific
knowledge. This is a direct consequence of the split between science and
theology, where scientific claims were held to be verifiable by empirical investigation and religious claims were simply a matter of faith that
required no justification at all. Intellectually speaking, then, theological
claims were denied the status of knowledge. As Meek notes:

> One automatic, unfortunate consequence of saying that we ac-
> cess God in some way other than knowledge, by faith as opposed
> to reason, for example, is that faith and its objects inevitably get
> discredited as something inferior. Reason trumps faith . . . After
> all, if words and rationality lie on the side of ordinary knowledge,
> these tools cannot be used to say anything about religious experi-
> ence. Who would not be compelled, in the name of survival, to
> anchor most of his or her efforts on the side of the rational?[93]

92. Tarnas, *Passion of the Western Mind*, 349.
93. Meek, *Longing to Know*, 43.

As Hiebert observes, "Many people argue that whereas science is a matter of facts and truth, religion is a matter of feelings and is the source of deep personal experience. Others assert that religion has to do with morality; it provides people with values that regulate their behavior and so make corporate life possible."[94]

Similarly, Peters explains how in modern thought "science provides all the knowledge we need to know. There is but one reality, the finite reality of nature, and the natural sciences provide the only methods for giving us the truth. Religion does not provide us with knowledge of reality. It provides us only with pseudo-knowledge, that is, false knowledge about nonexistent fictions."[95] Clark notes this as well, saying, "When science becomes the supreme instance—the paradigm—of rational thinking, theology must either concede the field of culture to science or play by science's rules to gain rational standing. The default position in our culture (although this is eroding in our postmodern time) is that science has the rational upper hand, that science is the only (or at very least preferred) path to knowledge."[96]

The famous physicalist John Searle also notes the marginalization of religious belief. In *Mind, Language and Society*, he dismisses the "God question" altogether as unimportant and distasteful. He says, "In earlier generations, books like this one would have had to contain either an atheistic attack on or a theistic defense of traditional religion. Or at the very least, the author would have had to declare a judicious agnosticism . . . Nowadays nobody bothers, and it is considered in slightly bad taste to even raise the question of God's existence. Matters of religion are like matters of sexual preference: they are not to be discussed in public, and even the abstract questions are discussed only by bores."[97] He goes on to say:

> What has happened? I think that most people would suppose there has been a decline of religious faith among the more educated sections of the population in Western Europe and North America . . . I believe that something much more radical than a decline in religious faith has taken place. For us, the educated members of society, the world has become demystified. Or rather,

---

94. Hiebert, *Missiological Implications*, 16.

95. Peters, *Cosmos as Creation*, 14.

96. Clark, *To Know and Love God*, 269.

97. Searle, *Mind, Language and Society*, 34.

to put the point more precisely, we no longer take the mysteries we see in the world as expressions of supernatural meaning. We no longer think of odd occurrences as cases of God performing speech acts in the language of miracles. Odd occurrences are just occurrences we do not understand. The result of this demystification is that we have gone beyond atheism to a point where the issue no longer matters in the way it did to earlier generations. For us, if it should turn out that God exists, that would have to be a fact of nature like any other.[98]

The populist atheist Sam Harris is even more brazen in his description of the situation. He says:

The conflict between science and religion is reducible to a simple fact of human cognition and discourse: either a person has good reasons for what he believes, or he does not . . . While believing strongly, without evidence, is considered a mark of madness or stupidity in any other area of our lives, faith in God still holds immense prestige in our society. Religion is the one area of our discourse where it is considered noble to pretend to be certain about things no human being could possibly be certain about.[99]

According to Harris, genuine knowledge comes from science, not theology, and the latter is seen to be intellectually inferior to the former.

This elitist idea is often referred to as scientism. J. P. Moreland and William Lane Craig describe it well by saying, "If something does not square with currently well-established scientific beliefs, if it is not within the domain of entities appropriate for scientific investigation, or if it is not amenable to scientific methodology, then it is not true or rational. Everything outside of science is a matter of mere belief and subjective opinion, of which rational assessment is impossible. Science, exclusively and ideally, is our model of intellectual excellence."[100] In the end, it is easy to see how claims of religious knowledge were seen to be inferior to scientific beliefs. Science could give knowledge, religion could only speculate. This becomes even more evident with the emergence of Darwinian evolution and the decline of natural theology.

---

98. Ibid., 34–35.

99. Harris, *Letter*, 66–67.

100. Moreland and Craig, *Philosophical Foundations*, 346–47.

THE DECLINE OF NATURAL THEOLOGY

Another negative consequence of these philosophical developments for the relationship between theology and science was that natural theology came to be seen as impossible or illegitimate. With the division between theology and science in place, it is easy to see why David Hume's philosophical critique of the design argument and Charles Darwin's theory of evolution were so effective in undermining natural theology. In Hume's famous work, entitled *Dialogues Concerning Natural Religion*, the reader finds a debate among three friends named Cleanthes, Demea, and Philo. The particular argument that Hume critiques is defended by the character Cleanthes. He says:

> Look round the world. Contemplate the whole and every part of it. You will find it to be nothing but one great machine, subdivided into an infinite number of lesser machines, which again admit of subdivisions, to a degree beyond what human senses and faculties can trace and explain. All these various machines, and even their most minute parts, are adjusted to each other with an accuracy, which ravishes into admiration all men, who have ever contemplated them. The curious adapting of means to ends, throughout all nature, resembles exactly, though it much exceeds, the productions of human contrivance; of human design, thought, wisdom, and intelligence. Since therefore the effects resemble each other, we are led to infer, by all the rules of analogy, that the causes also resemble; and that the author of nature is somewhat similar to the mind of man; though possessed of much larger faculties, proportioned to the grandeur of the work, which he has executed. By this argument *a posteriori* and by this argument alone, do we prove at once the existence of a deity, and his similarity to human mind and intelligence.[101]

For the remainder of the work, Hume presents a multifaceted critique of this argument. Though Hume's objections are not presented in chronological fashion, Stephen T. Davis distinguishes at least five different criticisms leveled at Cleanthes' design argument. These include

1. The who designed God objection

2. The coherent universe objection

---

101. Hume, *Dialogues*, 53. This argument has great resemblance to the argument of William Paley, approximately twenty-five years later, which used the analogy of a watch and a watchmaker. See Paley, *Natural Theology*, 7.

3. The insufficient evidence objection

4. The problem of evil objection

5. The weak analogy objection[102]

Thus, by the time Hume was finished, natural theology had been presented with a major philosophical challenge.

Charles Darwin also played a part in undermining natural theology. In 1859, he published his famous work *On the Origin of Species* and radically changed the trajectory of science from his day forward. With his theory of natural selection, Darwin offered what appeared to be a workable option for the question of origins. Up until this, naturalistic explanations tended to rely on chance to account for the diversity of animal life. He believed that nature was just as good, if not better, at producing functioning life forms. He says, "As man can produce and certainly has produced a great result by his methodical and unconscious means of selection, what may not nature effect? Man can act only on external and visible characters: nature cares nothing for appearances, except in so far as they may be useful to any being. They can act on every internal organ, on every shade of constitutional difference, on the whole machinery of life."[103]

Neal Gillespie notes that it "has been generally agreed (then and since) that Darwin's doctrine of natural selection effectively demolished William Paley's classical design argument for the existence of God. By showing how blind and gradual adaptation could counterfeit the apparently purposeful design . . . Darwin deprived their argument of the analogical inference that the evident purpose to be seen in the contrivances by which means and ends were related in nature was necessarily a function of mind"[104] Anna Case-Winters agrees with this evaluation. Design arguments, as she notes, lost much credibility. She says:

> With the publication of Charles Darwin's *On the Origin of Species* in 1859, the argument from design met a truly formidable challenge to its credibility. In the theory of evolution, a genuine alternative explanation for apparent design in organisms came to the fore. Mere chance and intelligent design were no longer the

---

102. Davis, *God, Reason & Theistic Proofs*, 101–6. I have worded these objections differently than Davis.

103. Darwin, *Origin of Species*, 83.

104. Gillespie, *Charles Darwin*, 83–84.

only possibilities. Organic structures come to be what they are through development from simpler forms through purely natural processes of mutation and natural selection over an extended period of time. No intelligent designer was needed to design the eye for sight.[105]

Thus, with Darwin, natural theology faced a serious scientific objection that seemed to make design arguments obsolete. This further established the split between science and theology because, once again, theological claims were left with no way of empirically validating their claims.

Assessment of the Consequences

The philosophical developments of the modern period had enormous consequences for the relationship between science and theology and the intellectual merit of religious knowledge claims. By splitting the two disciplines into two epistemological groups, the modern period placed theology in a vulnerable position. It was seen as second rate and intellectually inferior to scientific knowledge, as it did not qualify as knowledge in the first place. And, as a consequence, natural theology suffered a serious blow, which meant theology was left with no means of justifying its claims for the modern mind. Thus, the working relationship that existed in premodern times between science and theology was now being eroded in the modern period.

PHILOSOPHICAL DEVELOPMENTS OF POSTMODERNITY

In the last half of the twentieth century, the western world experienced a shift from modernism to postmodernism. As Erickson notes, "Gradually at first, but more rapidly of late, there has been a growing dissatisfaction with this modern way of viewing things. A sense has arisen that the modern approach has failed to accomplish that which it purported to do or that which needed to be done."[106] Morris and Petcher agree, saying, "Although the Enlightenment Project had auspicious beginnings, and often with motivations that seemed very much in line with Christian commitments, the Project as envisioned by many has failed. The Modern pretense that autonomous human reason and objective method on their own can penetrate the ultimate truth and bring order and fulfillment

---

105. Case-Winters, "Argument From Design," 74.

106. Erickson, *Christian Theology*, 164.

to humans has been exposed as a false hope."[107] A number of philosophers were important to the rise of postmodernity including Ludwig Wittgenstein, Jacques Derrida, Thomas Kuhn, Michel Foucault, Martin Heidegger, Richard Rorty and Jean-François Lyotard.[108] Nevertheless, Tarnas contends that "by all accounts the central prophet of the postmodern mind was Friedrich Nietzsche, with his radical perspectivism, his sovereign critical sensibility, and his powerful, poignantly ambivalent anticipation of the emerging nihilism in Western culture."[109] Once again, space prohibits a treatment of Nietzsche and the other important philosophers of postmodernism. It is necessary, however, that a brief treatment of the major themes of postmodernity be given.

Key Philosophical Developments of Postmodernity

J. P. Moreland and William Lane Craig note the difficulty of defining postmodernism, since it "is a loose coalition of diverse thinkers from several different academic disciplines."[110] Moreover, this difficulty also arises from the fact that postmodernism might be thought of as both modernity's logical extension and its antithesis. Groothuis, for example, notes the logical connections between modernity and postmodernity when he says, "Postmodernism is so often presented as a radical departure from modernism that it is easy to miss the insight that postmodernism is, in many ways, modernism gone to seed, carried to its logical conclusion and inevitable demise."[111] Mohler seems to agree. He says, "For modernism has been replaced by postmodernism—or if not replaced, then at least joined, for postmodernism, I will argue, is nothing more than the logical extension of modernism in a new mood."[112]

Edward O. Wilson, however, notes the radical differences between modernity and postmodernity. He says, "Postmodernism is the ultimate polar antithesis of the Enlightenment. The difference between the two extremes can be expressed roughly as follows: Enlightenment thinkers

---

107. Morris and Petcher, *Science and Grace*, 47.

108. See Moreland and Craig, *Philosophical Foundations*, 145. Also see Erickson, *Truth or Consequences*, 113–84.

109. Tarnas, *Passion of the Western Mind*, 395.

110. Moreland and Craig, *Philosophical Foundations*, 144.

111. Groothuis, *Truth Decay*, 40.

112. Mohler, "Truth and Contemporary Culture," 57.

believe we can know everything, and radical postmodernists believe we can know nothing."[113]

Nevertheless, Moreland and Craig think that it is still "possible to provide a fairly accurate characterization of postmodernism in general, since its friends and foes understand it well enough to discuss the view."[114] As Tarnas puts it, "What is called postmodern varies considerably according to context, but in its most general and widespread form, the postmodern mind may be viewed as an open-ended, indeterminate set of attitudes that has been shaped by a great diversity of intellectual and cultural currents."[115] Some of the major attitudes or themes of postmodernity include denial of objective realism, denial of truth, rejection of foundationalism, and rejection of metanarratives.

DENIAL OF OBJECTIVE REALISM

Whereas philosophers in the modern period assumed that one could be completely objective in his view of reality, postmodern thinkers have denied this assumption altogether. Instead, postmodern thinkers suggest that everyone views reality from a socially constructed perspective which means that all of what humans claim as knowledge is mediated in some way and in some degree. Thus, there is no single correct and neutral view of reality. As van Huyssteen explains, the "modernist notion of universal rationality can also be described as taking for granted not only that all rational persons conceptualize data in one and the same way, but also that—because honest observers are allegedly able to put aside or rise above the prejudices of prior commitment to belief—they would report the same data, the same facts, in the same way."[116]

Tarnas elaborates on this further, saying, "All human knowledge is mediated by signs and symbols of uncertain provenance, constituted by historically and culturally variable predispositions, and influenced by often unconscious human interests."[117] He later adds, "Basic to this perspective is the thesis that all human thought is ultimately generated and bound by idiosyncratic cultural-linguistic forms of life. Human knowledge is the historically contingent product of linguistic and social

---

113. Wilson, *Consilience*, 42.

114. Moreland and Craig, *Philosophical Foundations*, 145.

115. Tarnas, *Passion of the Western Mind*, 395.

116. van Huyssteen, *Alone in the World?*, 5.

117. Tarnas, *Passion of the Western Mind*, 397.

practices of particular local communities of interpreters, with no assured 'ever-closer' relation to an independent ahistorical reality."[118] Feinberg, a realist who differs considerably from postmoderns like Tarnas, also acknowledges the mediated nature of human knowledge when he says, "Even if sense organs are functioning perfectly, and even if people have exactly the same vantage point, there is no guarantee that they will report seeing the same thing. Their conceptual framework, formed by their life experiences and by the linguistic and cultural community in which they were raised, is a major determining factor in how people view things and in what they actually perceive."[119]

Thus, postmodernism builds on the now widely noted acknowledgement that human knowledge is at least partially mediated. It strongly rejects the notion that a person can gain an objective understanding of reality. Though this criticism can certainly be directed at modernist theologians, Hiebert suggests that it can also be directed at the scientist. He says:

> The social sciences, when applied to the study of scientists and science, showed that scientists are deeply influenced by their historical and cultural contexts. Psychologists destroyed the notions of unbiased observation, and of the mind either as a passive recipient and reflector of sensory information or as an observer with innate mental categories with which to organize sense experiences. Linguists . . . showed us that the language in which we encode knowledge is itself a cultural creation . . . By the 1940s and 1950s, the idea of a neutral observation language had been discarded. It was taken as self-evident that every body of knowledge, including every scientific theory, has its own language.[120]

Furthermore, Hiebert also notes how anthropologists and sociologists "showed that scientists are influenced by the scientific communities of which they are a part, and there is no value-free or power-free knowledge. Anthropologists demonstrated that scientists themselves are molded by their own cultural and historical contexts. In other words, there can be no culture-free human knowledge—no transcendental knower who is able to know without affecting the known."[121]

---

118. Ibid., 399.
119. Feinberg, *No One Like Him*, 99.
120. Hiebert, *Missiological Implications*, 30.
121. Ibid., 30–31.

Moreland and Craig suggest that the postmodern rejection of Enlightenment objectivity leads to an antirealist conception of reality. They say:

> Postmodernism involves an antirealist rejection of these realist commitments. According to postmodernism, "reality" is a social construction. Language creates reality, and what is real for one linguistic group may be unreal for another. Thus, God exists relative to Christians but does not exist relative to atheists. Further, the basic laws of logic are Western constructions, and in no way are they to be taken as universally valid laws of reality itself.[122]

Robert Greer seems to agree. He suggests that, committed to antirealism, postmodernism "insists that the really real (the thing-in-itself) cannot be known in any definitive cultural and historical moments, from which we look at reality from afar."[123] As van Huyssteen observes, then, with the rise of postmodernism the western world rejected objective realism and affirmed that "all our inquiry, whether scientific or theological, is highly contextual and already presupposes a particular theoretical, doctrinal, or personal stance and commitment."[124]

Denial of Truth

Closely associated with the postmodern denial of objective realism is its denial of absolute truth. Since it is impossible for a person to gain an objective understanding and view of reality, there simply cannot be absolute truth. As Mohler explains, "While most arguments throughout history have been disputes between rival claims to truth, postmodernism rejects the very notion of truth as a fixed universal, or objective absolute."[125] He then says, "According to postmodern theory, truth is not objective or absolute at all, nor can it be determined by any commonly accepted method. Instead, postmodernists argue that truth is socially constructed, plural, and inaccessible to universal reason, which itself does not exist anyway."[126] Andreas Köstenberger agrees, suggesting that the "notion of truth has largely become a casualty of postmodern

---

122. Moreland and Craig, *Philosophical Foundations*, 145.

123. Greer, *Mapping Postmodernism*, 124.

124. van Huyssteen, *Alone in the World?*, 6.

125. Mohler, "Truth and Contemporary Culture," 58.

126. Ibid.

thought and discourse . . . Hence truth is simply one's preferred, culturally conditioned, socially constructed version of reality."[127]

Feinberg notes how, not surprisingly, postmodernists also reject a
correspondence theory of truth. He says, "They wish they could say that
their beliefs correspond to the world, but the human condition is such
that we are in no position to know this through either our senses or
reason . . . Thus, postmoderns typically adopt some form of the coherence theory of truth . . . [where] what is true is the set of sentences that
fit together without contradicting one another."[128] Erickson also believes
that the rejection of a correspondence theory of truth leads most postmoderns to accept a coherentist view of truth.[129] Moreland and Craig,
however, suggest that postmoderns prefer a pragmatic understanding
of truth. They say, "Postmodernists reject the correspondence theory of
truth. Some eschew any talk of truth at all, while others advance a coherentist or, more frequently, pragmatist notion of truth. The important
thing is that truth is relative to a linguistic community that shares the
same narrative . . . There is no objective truth, no God's eye view of
things."[130] In the end, the important thing to note is that, along with
their denial of objective realism, postmoderns also reject the notion of
absolute truth.

Rejection of Foundationalism

Stanley Grenz and John Franke suggest that a postmodern understanding
of rationality "entails the rejection of epistemological foundationalism."[131]
Though a more detailed critique of foundationalism is offered in chapter
4, a few reasons for its rejection should be briefly noted here. Erickson
suggests that one problem with foundationalism is that it does not actually establish a foundation for knowledge. That is, it does not satisfy the
problem of epistemic regress. He says, "This is the question of how we
justify some item of belief or knowledge, and then, how we justify the
justifier. If I say that I believe *j*, and then am asked why, my answer is that
I believe *j* because of *k*. The further question may then be pressed, how-

---

127. Köstenberger, *Whatever Happened to Truth*, 9.

128. Feinberg, *No One Like Him*, 100.

129. Erickson, *Truth or Consequences*, 255.

130. Moreland and Craig, *Philosophical Foundations*, 146.

131. Grenz and Franke, *Beyond Foundationalism*, 23.

ever, as to why I consider *k* to be adequate justification for *j*."[132] Likewise, Moreland and Craig note how postmodernism rejects foundationalism since it "represents a quest for epistemic certainty, and it is this desire to have certainty that provides the intellectual impetus for foundationalism … But there is no such certainty, and the quest for it is an impossible one. Further, that quest is misguided because people do not need certainty to live their lives well."[133] Thus, the denial or rejection of foundationalism is a major aspect of the postmodern movement.

Rejection of Metanarratives

A natural result of the postmodern rejection of truth and objectivity is a rejection of metanarratives. As Feinberg suggests, "Postmoderns, drawing out the logical conclusions of their views, answer that there is no grand story, no 'meta-narrative' that will somehow make sense of everything."[134] Erickson agrees, saying, "One of the most characteristic themes of postmodernism has been its aversion to metanarratives, or inclusive theories. For a number of reasons, these are regarded as either impossible, undesirable, or both. At best, we can hope to construct petit narratives, local theories or stories."[135] Groothuis further explains:

> In a nutshell, postmodernism holds that truth is not determined by its connection with objective reality, but by various social constructions devised for different purposes. Put another way, various cultures have their own "language games," which describe reality very differently. However, we cannot adjudicate which language game or which linguistic "map" correlates more correctly with reality, since we cannot get beyond our own cultural conditioning. There is no objective reality apart from our languages and concepts. To say we know the objective truth is to set up a "metanarrative" that is intrinsically oppressive and exploitative.[136]

Once again, this aspect of postmodern thought is leveled against theological as well as scientific explanations. As Mohler explains, "Modernist thinkers had earlier rejected revelation as a source of truth and, confident

132. Erickson, *Truth or Consequences*, 254.

133. Moreland and Craig, *Philosophical Foundations*, 146–47.

134. Feinberg, *No One Like Him*, 101.

135. Erickson, "Theological Fog," 343.

136. Groothuis, "Truth Defined and Defended," 70.

that their approach would yield objective and universal truths by means of autonomous human reason, had attempted to establish truth on the basis of inductive thought and scientific investigation. Postmodernists reject both these approaches, arguing that neither revelation nor the scientific method is a reliable source for truth."[137]

Assessment of the Consequences

In the modern period, theology was seriously challenged by the philosophical developments previously discussed. With the rise of postmodernism, however, both theology and science are called into question. Commitments to absolute and objective truth have been abandoned and the idea that truth is relative is now pervasive throughout culture. Thus, postmodernism undermines both theology and science. As Hiebert observes, science, like theology, has been taken "from its privileged vantage point outside and above history and culture, and [placed] squarely in the middle of human subjectivity."[138] Morris and Petcher also make this point. They note:

> Modern science is a cultural achievement that has demonstrated many successes, mostly for the good of mankind. But modern science also has its down side, and partly as a consequence, in the Postmodern world science has come under suspicion in various ways. Not only has science been knocked off its pedestal of being the source for objective truth in the world, but science is also seen by many as a potent enabler of evil.[139]

With theology and science both called into question, the western world became skeptical to all truth claims, and relativism ensued. As Moreland and Craig note, postmodernism "represents a form of cultural relativism about such things as reality, truth, reason, value, linguistic meaning, the self and other notions."[140] Groothuis makes a similar observation, saying, "Modernist theology set the ball rolling with the assertion that the Bible is a collection of myths, as are religions in general. Since morality is grounded in religion, the next development was relativizing moral values. In the modern era, moral relativism was adopted

137. Mohler, "Truth and Contemporary Culture," 58.

138. Hiebert, *Missiological Implications*, 32–33.

139. Morris and Petcher, *Science & Grace*, vii.

140. Moreland and Craig, *Philosophical Foundations*, 145.

primarily by the cultural elite, while common folk continued to hold on to a vestigial Christian morality. In the postmodern era, nearly everyone believes moral values are relative—that is, constructed by cultures, not ordained by God."[141] Köstenberger agrees. He says, "In much of contemporary culture, truth has been supplanted by a kind of paranoia that is so skeptical toward any finality of knowing that it is prone to believe conspiracy theories, no matter how far-fetched (witness the *Da Vinci Code* phenomenon). All of this contributes to a sense of uncertainty that holds that all knowledge is provisional and subject to constant revision as new facts surface that need to be considered."[142] Likewise, Hiebert says, "Postmodern philosophy takes subjectivism to its logical limits . . . it gives priority to emotions, intuition, personal experience, the particular, and mystical experience. Ultimately, its goal is not to formulate an alternative set of assumptions but to register the impossibility of establishing any such underpinning for knowledge."[143]

Thus, with the rise of postmodernism, the notion of truth itself is in question, and theology and science alike are viewed with suspicion. If postmodernism is correct, it is difficult to see how either discipline could be practiced with any intellectual credibility. Nevertheless, there is the very large question of whether or not postmodernism is valid that needs to be answered.

POSTPOSTMODERNISM

At the beginning of the twenty-first century, postmodernism is being challenged by many in the natural sciences and questioned by a growing number of philosophers and theologians. In fact, James Parker III observes, "While one theologian after another is rushing to turn out books and articles about some aspect or implication concerning the end of modernism or about the implications of postmodernism, it can be plausibly argued that postmodernism is overrated and that it will come to a certain (and perhaps soon) demise—or at least will be relegated to the realm of the curious but passé."[144] D. A. Carson made this observation as far back as 1996, when he said, "I should acknowledge that

---

141. Groothuis, *Truth Decay*, 41.

142. Köstenberger, *Whatever Happened to Truth*, 131.

143. Hiebert, *Missiological Implications*, 52.

144. Parker III, "Requiem," 307.

some avant-garde intellectuals are already announcing the impending death of postmodernity. Certainly there are some individuals who have passed through postmodernity and emerged on the other side, casting about gamely for another worldview."[145] A classic example of this can be found among scientists in the Humanist Manifesto 2000, where Paul Kurtz—along with 141 other scientists—says:

> There has emerged in many Western countries a so-called postmodernist ideology that denies the objectivity of science, deplores the use of modern technology, and attacks human rights and democracy. Some forms of postmodernism counsel defeatism: at best, they offer no program for resolving the world's problems; at worst, they deny that solutions are either possible or achievable. The effects of this philosophical-literary movement are counterproductive, even nihilistic. We think it profoundly mistaken because science does offer reasonably objective standards for judging its truth claims. Indeed, science has become a universal language, speaking to all men and women no matter what their cultural background.[146]

Parker seems to agree with this assessment of postmodernism. He suggests that it "commits epistemological suicide" by asserting "that truth is merely a social construct—or as one postmodernist puts it, truth is whatever your colleagues let you say."[147] He then says, "If that is the case, then postmodern thought is also just another social construct and has neither universal nor normative force. Therefore, there is no reason that one should be compelled to let it be a normative criterion to shape and determine one's beliefs."[148] Thus, according to a growing number of scientists and philosophers, postmodernism is an unacceptable epistemological position that must be rejected.

But if postmodernism has already been rejected, what will take its place? In 1996, Carson said, "At the moment there is no pattern on the horizon to replace postmodernism, and as far as I can see the giant wave of the movement has not yet crested, or even come close."[149] Today, how-

---

145. Carson, "Gagging of God," 79.

146. Kurtz, *Humanist Manifesto 2000*, 22. Some of the notable naturalists to sign this document include Arthur Clarke, Alan Cranston, Richard Dawkins, Daniel Dennett, Richard Leakey, E. O. Wilson and Michael Martin.

147. Parker, "Requiem," 308.

148. Ibid.

149. Carson, "Gagging of God," 79.

ever, this is no longer true. Erickson, who also finds problems with modernism, suggests that postmodernism "has passed its peak, or at least that the rate of its growth has declined, and that there are some early signs of the rise of a postpostmodernism."[150] Parker agrees with Erickson's call for a new epistemological approach, but prefers the term transmodernism to Erickson's postpostmodernism. He says, "Transmodernism would indeed constitute a rejection of both the overreaching claims of modernism and the nihilistic absurdity of postmodernism, while benefiting from the positive contributions of both."[151] He goes on to explain:

> A new transmodern vision seems to be emerging from diverse disciplines. This vision is neither uniform nor monolithic—nor is it necessarily theistic. But what it has in common is the rejection of the philosophical naturalists' or materialists' claims of modernism (viz., autonomous reason and unjustified progressive optimism) and the rejection of the fundamental assertions of postmodernism (viz., that truth is a community fiction, morals are social constructs, and tradition and classical influence are undesirable and illegitimate). Transmodernists affirm objective and normative truth without capitulating to a naturalistic scientism, and they affirm true moral values and virtues. They hold out beauty, harmony, and wisdom as real possible entities. Cynicism based on modernistic naturalism and postmodern fictions are replaced by hope—a hope that is based on the very nature of things. While one might hesitate to predict the future of this movement (if indeed it can be called a movement), developments on the horizon appear to indicate that a significant (or even monumental) cultural shift is in the offing.[152]

According to Parker and Erickson, what is necessary to move forward is an epistemological approach that walks a middle path between the extremes of modernity and postmodernity.

Fortunately, a recently emerged epistemological system called critical realism seems to do just this. Hiebert describes this approach by saying, "Ontologically, it is a form of realism, for it assumes a real world that exists independently from human perceptions or opinions of it. It is critical, for it examines the processes by which humans acquire knowledge and finds that this knowledge does not have a literal one-to-one

---

150. Erickson, *Truth or Consequences*, 320.

151. Parker, "Requiem," 310.

152. Ibid., 320–21.

correspondence to reality."[153] Or, as Kees van Kooten Niekerk explains, "Critical realism presupposes metaphysical realism. That is, it assumes that the world we meet in normal sense experience (as distinguished from dreams, hallucinations, etc.) exists as a real physical world independently of our experience."[154] He goes on to explain:

> The recognition of the role of sensation and conceptualization leads critical realism to the rejection of the naïve realist claim that experience conveys a precise reflection of a real, external world. On the other hand, it interprets the experiential constraints upon the mental world as the impact of an external world. Therefore, it regards it as possible to acquire valid knowledge of that world. It is, in other words, a form of epistemological realism. But according to critical realism, valid knowledge of the external world can only be acquired in and through a critical attitude, which attempts to distill the real from the mental.[155]

Thus, critical realism attempts to walk a middle path between modernity and postmodernity by affirming the existence of objective reality while at the same time denying the naiveté of the Enlightenment, which assumed that one could be completely objective in his view of reality.

Today, critical realism is being applied to a multitude of disciplines with the hope that it may yield genuine knowledge of reality while avoiding the detrimental aspects of modernity and postmodernity. If critical realism is found to be a reliable epistemological method, then it will rectify the epistemological crisis brought about by the philosophical developments outlined in this chapter. Thus, the legitimacy of critical realism, especially with regard to theology, is a major issue throughout the remainder of this book.

CONCLUSION

Prior to the modern period, science and theology were joined in a mutual quest to explain reality. In many cases, science and theology were even practiced by the same individuals. As Padgett notes, "In the late Middle Ages, the relationship between theology and natural philosophy (or science) was understood as that of a queen to her handmaidens."[156]

153. Hiebert, *Missiological Implications*, 69.

154. van Kooten Niekerk, "Critical Realist Perspective," 52.

155. Ibid., 57–58.

156. Padgett, *Science and Study*, 1.

With the rise of modernity, however, a radical division separated the two disciplines, which resulted in the marginalization of Christian theology. Then, as the western world shifted from a modern to a postmodern outlook, the notion of truth was lost altogether. As a result, people grew skeptical of truth claims and relativism became all pervasive.

More recently, however, philosophers and theologians are suggesting that postmodernism is misguided. As Meek puts it, "If we are being asked to settle for skepticism, I believe our search for a workable model of human knowing must still be continued, for we are being asked to settle for that which is untrue to our very selves."[157] Nevertheless, Meek contends that the goal of this search is to find a method that avoids the dangers of both modernity and postmodernity. In her view, just as it is irresponsible to deny objective truth, one must also understand that it is not "possible to avoid personal and communal responsibility in knowing. What we need to see is that personal and communal responsibility in knowing is the sole vehicle for profoundly accessing the objectively real."[158]

A Scientific Theology by Alister E. McGrath is an attempt to do just that. By applying critical realism to theological method, McGrath offers an approach that may hold great promise for evangelical theology, in that it allows one to embrace the valuable lessons of modernity and postmodernity and, at the same time, to avoid their dangers. The book now turns to examine his project.

---

157. Meek, *Longing to Know*, 34. Some of the problems of postmodernism are given full treatment in chapters 2 and 4.

158. Ibid., 148.

2

Alister E. McGrath's Scientific Theology

ALISTER E. MCGRATH'S COMPLETION of the trilogy *A Scientific Theology* represents one of the most significant treatments of the relationship between theology and science by an evangelical in recent time.[1] According to Elmer M. Colyer, McGrath's work is "possibly the most systematic and extended exploration of the relation between theology and natural science to date."[2] He goes on to say, "No Evangelical theologian has attempted, much less successfully completed, anything close to McGrath's work in terms of immersion in the natural sciences and encyclopedic interaction with intellectual currents of the Enlightenment and postmodernity, all aimed at developing a comprehensive scientific theological method in service of a future scientific dogmatics. This is the most significant work devoted to theological method to come into print in a long time."[3] John J. Roche agrees, suggesting that McGrath has "read everything of relevance in the history of science, in contemporary science, in the history of philosophy and in the history of the philosophy of science, in historical and in current theology, in the history of science and religion, and also in the current field. And in each of these fields he brings a professional competence to bear. This is rare indeed."[4]

In McGrath's mind, a scientific theology (ST) is based on the contention that "the relationship of Christian theology to the natural sciences is that of two fundamentally related disciplines, whose working methods reflect this common grounding in responding to a reality which lies beyond them, of which they are bound to give an ordered

---

1. McGrath, *Scientific Theology.*

2. Colyer, "Scientific Theology 3," 233. By *ancilla theologia*, McGrath is suggesting that science is the handmaiden of theology.

3. Ibid., 240.

4. Roche, "Scientific Theology Project," 34.

account."[5] As such, he believes that "the natural sciences can serve as a dialogue partner to the theological enterprise."[6]

To better understand his contribution to this important issue, this chapter will present a review of the major elements of his theological method developed in *A Scientific Theology*. Beginning with a concise biographical sketch of McGrath, it gives special attention to his theological commitments. After this, the chapter offers a summary of each volume of *A Scientific Theology*, which gives the context necessary for the assessments appearing in chapters 3 and 4.

BIOGRAPHY

Alister E. McGrath was born January 23, 1953 in Belfast, Ireland, but spent the first thirteen years of life in Downpatrick, Ireland. During his high school years, he considered himself to be an atheist who was deeply influenced by the thinking of Karl Marx and A. J. Ayer.[7] Thus, by the time McGrath began his collegiate studies, he was "convinced that the future lay with atheism, and that religion would either die of exhaustion or be eliminated by resentful humanity within [his] lifetime."[8] The major passion for McGrath during this time was natural science. Specifically, his initial interests were in biology and he seriously considered a career in medicine.[9] Nevertheless, during his time at Methodist College from 1966 to 1971, he was quickly attracted to mathematics, chemistry, and physics.[10]

As his time at Methodist College came to a close, McGrath prepared to continue his studies at Oxford. "Having obtained top grades in these subjects at A level," he says, "I stayed on at the Methodist College for an additional year, in order to sit for the Oxford entrance examinations."[11] Believing that he had done poorly on his interview with the college's three major chemistry professors, McGrath was delighted to learn that he had been accepted at Oxford and granted a major scholarship. He accepted this scholarship and began his studies at Oxford in the fall of

---

5. McGrath, *Scientific Theology*, vol. 1, xvii–xix.

6. Ibid., xvii.

7. Ibid., xii.

8. McGrath, *Science of God*, 3.

9. Ibid., 2.

10. McGrath, "Contributors," 333.

11. Ibid., 334.

1971.[12] It was at this point that McGrath's life and career took an un-expected turn. He says, "By the end of my first term at Oxford, I was in a state of mental flux. I had suffered the immense inconvenience of discovering that Christianity could not be dismissed as easily as I had thought. In fact, it seemed to have rather a lot going for it."[13] Specifically, he says:

> I began to discover that Christianity was much more exciting than I had realized. While I had been severely critical of Christianity as a young man, I had never extended that same critical evaluation to atheism, tending to assume that it was self-evidently correct, and was hence exempt from being assessed in this way. During October and November 1971, I began to discover that the intel-lectual case for atheism was rather insubstantial. Christianity, on the other hand, seemed rather more interesting . . . I also discov-ered that I knew far less about Christianity than I had assumed. It gradually became clear to me that I had rejected a religious stereotype.[14]

Thus, by the end of his first full term at Oxford, McGrath had con-verted to Christianity, believing it to be "both intellectually persuasive and personally fulfilling."[15] As one might expect, this conversion brought a significant change in the direction of his life. He says, "I was converted to Christianity in November 1971, and found myself having to rethink countless questions, not least that of what I should do with the rest of my life."[16] On first thought, he considered abandoning the natural sciences and switching to Christian theology, but was "dissuaded from this, and in the end completed [his] first degree in chemistry and went on to gain a doctorate from Oxford in molecular biophysics."[17] In fact, he says the "conclusion that I came to was quite simple. I would complete my stud-ies in chemistry. In fact, I would do more than that: I would undertake research in some aspect of the natural sciences. And then I would switch to theology, and try to establish the connection between them."[18]

12. McGrath, *Science of God*, 3.
13. McGrath, *Scientific Theology*, vol. 1, xiv.
14. McGrath, *Science of God*, 4.
15. McGrath, *Scientific Theology*, vol. 1, xiv.
16. McGrath, "Contributors," 334.
17. McGrath, *Scientific Theology*, vol. 1, xiv.
18. McGrath, *Science of God*, 4.

The motive to make this connection was brought about in part by the realization that the relationship between science and theology had been misrepresented. He says, "Having previously thought, in rather uncritical terms which I now realize to have been shaped by Andrew Dickson White's hostile and inaccurate account of the relation of Christianity and the sciences, that the natural sciences were the enemy of religion, I now began to realize that the situation was rather more complex (and interesting), demanding a more nuanced and informed response."[19] Thus, in the summer of 1976 while working at the University of Utrecht in the Netherlands, this idea was crystallized. He says:

> I cannot recall quite how the idea came into my mind; it was as if a mental bolt of lightning flashed across my consciousness, eclipsing my thoughts on how best to apply Fourier Transforms to study the time resolved anisotropy of a fluorescent probe that I had developed for studying lipid viscosity in biological membranes and their models. The idea that shot through my mind was simple: explore the relation between Christian theology and the natural sciences, using philosophy and history as dialogue partners. It would be grounded in and faithful to the Christian tradition, yet open to the insights of the sciences. This would be more than a mere exploration of a working relationship; it would be a proposal for a synergy, a working together, a mutal [sic] cross-fertilization of ideas and approaches—in short, a scientific theology.[20]

This, of course, meant that McGrath would need to embark on a more serious and detailed engagement of Christian theology. But this was more complicated than one might think. How exactly would he be able to finish his scientific studies and begin studying theology on a more serious level at the same time? The answer came in the form of a scholarship from Merton College, which allowed him to continue the study of molecular biophysics while also studying for a second undergraduate degree. McGrath used this opportunity to begin studying theology at Oxford.[21] By 1978, McGrath received a doctorate in molecular biology as well as first class honors in theology. Moreover, due to his excellent theological performance, he was awarded the Denyer and Johnson Prize

---

19. McGrath, *Scientific Theology*, vol. 1, xvi.

20. Ibid., xi.

21. McGrath, "Contributors," 334–35.

in theology. This in turn brought an invitation by an editor at Oxford University Press to write a book responding to Richard Dawkin's book *The Selfish Gene*. McGrath gave this careful consideration, but decided he must further immerse himself in the study of theology before taking on such endeavors.[22]

With that in mind, McGrath moved to Cambridge, where he was granted the Naden Research Studentship in Theology at St. John's College. Here he "chose to study one thinker (Martin Luther), one doctrine (justification) and one historical period (the Reformation, set against its later medieval context) in detail, and found this an invaluable preparation for serious theological reflection."[23] Shortly after, he was ordained into the Church of England and moved to Nottingham to serve in a suburban parish. As a result of this ministry, McGrath's commitment to evangelicalism was strengthened.[24]

Thus, McGrath's exploration of the relationship between theology and science comes from an evangelical who places high priority on the testimony of Scripture. In his view, "Christian theology is under an obligation to pay respectful and obedient attention to the biblical testimony and allow itself to be shaped and reshaped by what it finds expressed there."[25] To be clear, he "insists that theology must be nourished and governed at all points by Holy Scripture, and that it seeks to offer a faithful and coherent account of what it finds there."[26] Therefore, McGrath's ST attempts to offer an evangelical theological method.

MCGRATH'S SCIENTIFIC THEOLOGY

Having earlier delayed his writings on the relationship between theology and science, in 1998, McGrath published what would be his first major work on the subject: *The Foundations of Dialogue In Science & Religion*.[27] In his view, much of the available material at that time continued to perpetuate a dangerous misunderstanding of how theology and science related to each other. In particular, each discipline had great hostility

22. Ibid., 335.
23. Ibid.
24. Ibid., 336.
25. McGrath, "Engaging the Great Tradition," 140.
26. McGrath, *Scientific Theology*, vol. 1, xix.
27. McGrath, *Foundations of Science*.

toward the other.[28] In addition, he sensed that certain philosophical shifts brought about the demise of philosophical foundationalism, and the rise of postmodernism brought new opportunities for considering the issue.[29] Thus, McGrath felt the need for a fresh examination of the relationship between theology and science, and claimed his intention to "explore the areas in which science and religion can be seen to converge, and those in which they diverge, believing that this illuminates the distinctive characteristics of each, without in any way compromising their integrities."[30] In his mind, such an exploration would enrich both fields. From *The Foundations of Dialogue in Science & Religion*, all the way through his later works on ST, McGrath makes it clear that the central issue to be explored is the issue of methodology. In other words, his primary intention is not to focus on questions that theology and science both explore, such as evolution, creation, or ethics. Rather, his focus is epistemological in nature. He says, "Systematic engagement with the issues just noted rests upon a prior substantial engagement with questions of method—including such issues as the way in which knowledge is gained and confirmed, the manner in which evidence is accumulated and assimilated, and particularly the manner in which the world is represented."[31] That is, one cannot deal with issues like evolution, creation, and ethics, until he has considered the epistemological assumptions of theology and the natural sciences. Thus, a central concern of this work, as with the latter trilogy of *A Scientific Theology*, is to show the similarities in methodology between theology and science. As Roche observes, McGrath understands how "the sciences and theologies are distinct chiefly in terms of their subject matters, their methodologies and their historical developments. Nevertheless, each of these features of both fields overlaps, and it is inappropriate to try to force them into isolated compartments. This overlap undoubtedly creates difficulties, but it also means that they can mutually stimulate and illuminate each other at various points."[32] But how exactly do they overlap and illuminate? Roche explains McGrath's thinking by saying:

28. Ibid., 7.

29. Ibid., 9.

30. Ibid., 33.

31. Ibid., 29.

32. Roche, "Scientific Theology Project," 41–42.

Both the scientific and theological communities can be thought of as wrestling with the ambiguities of experience, of very different kinds and in very different ways, of course, but in ways that are not totally different. Both disciplines generate theories that are highly complex and often counter-intuitive, and both view these theories as consistent with, even demanded by, the 'phenomena.' Science is by no means raw experiment: it is interpretation, it is theorizing and it involves theory-change . . . Very similar features can be identified in theology: God, for example, could reasonably be inferred as the best explanation of the way the world is. These structural parallels—although by no means complete—are not surprising, since both scientific and theological theorizing are the products of minds that have been schooled in a richly connected cultural milieu for 2000 years.[33]

Although McGrath develops this idea more fully in *A Scientific Theology*, he had already given preliminary consideration to this issue in *The Foundations of Dialogue in Science & Religion*. Nonetheless, methodology is not the only issue that surfaces in his earlier work. One can also find preliminary discussions on

1. The doctrine of creation

2. Critical realism

3. Modes of representation for science and religion[34]

Though many of the issues dealt with here are discussed in McGrath's earlier works, this chapter focuses primarily on his later, more fully developed works found in the trilogy *A Scientific Theology* and in the smaller, more concise treatment of the subject, *The Science of God*.

Prolegomena

The first major section of volume 1 sets out the prolegomena, which is essential to McGrath's ST. To begin, he gives further clarification regarding the nature of his project by reminding the reader that his central concern is methodology.[35] He says, "There are often significant similarities in the issues faced by both Christian theology and the natural sciences as they go about their respective tasks. It is therefore of consid-

33. Ibid., 47.

34. In McGrath's *Foundations of Dialogue*, chapters 2–5.

35. McGrath, *Scientific Theology*, vol. 1, 45.

erable interest to ascertain whether these disciplines might have any-thing to learn from each other."[36] Thus, one must realize that McGrath is not primarily concerned with how the different theories and claims of theology and science fit together. Rather, he contends that the basis for dialogue between the two comes from the epistemological assumptions that they share. But this raises an important question. As important as methodology may be, is there no place for considering how the different theories and claims of theology and science fit together? In other words, what role should the theories and claims of the natural sciences play in theological development?

McGrath provides an answer. In his view, the specific discoveries of the natural sciences help the church in the constant process of evaluating its theological claims so that it is not blinded by outdated scientific as-sumptions of previous generations. He says, "The natural sciences . . . offer an important resource to Christian theology, in that they invite the church continually to reconsider its present interpretations of Scripture, in order to ensure that the settled scientific assumptions of earlier generations— now known or suspected to be incorrect— have not inadvertently been incorporated into the teachings of the church. The importance of this role of the natural sciences is recognized by many theologians, including the influential evangelical writer Benjamin B. Warfield."[37]

Not surprisingly, then, McGrath presents the natural sciences as the ideal *ancilla theologiae*: that is, the handmaiden of theology. As he notes, the church has a long-standing tradition of making use of various disci-plines outside of Christianity, when they serve as helpful tools for theo-logical inquiry.[38] While previous generations made use of Platonic and Aristotelian philosophy, McGrath believes that the natural sciences are now the preferred dialogue partner for theology. In his view, he says:

> No philosophy has ever gained global acceptance. Yet the working methods of the natural sciences come very close to representing a globally valid and acceptable means of encountering reality, not least because those methods seem independent of culture, race and gender. Indeed, many natural scientists would argue that the scientific method is the nearest thing to a universally accepted and valid way of thinking that has ever been known. The natural

36. Ibid., 3.
37. Ibid., 64.
38. McGrath, *Science of God*, 18.

sciences, when rightly understood, thus represent an obvious and credible dialogue partner for Christian theology. The task facing a scientific theology is thus to encourage and facilitate a respectful and positive dialogue between Christian theology and the natural sciences, without the latter overwhelming the former.[39]

McGrath admits that this approach includes some risks. In particular, if one allows the natural sciences to play such a large role in theology, there is the danger of compromising the distinct integrity of Christian theology. [40] In order for science and theology to maintain their distinct integrities, the natural science must not be placed over theology as its judge. As Roche explains, because McGrath's use of science allows it "to function in a ministerial rather than in a magisterial capacity the integrity of theology as a discipline can be maintained without too much difficulty."[41] As McGrath would himself explain, "To permit the natural sciences to act in this matter is to allot them a certain privilege, and it must be understood from the outset that its role is limited, circumscribed and above all supportive. The natural sciences neither prove nor disprove Christianity; they are, however, a most profitable dialogue partner."[42] When used in this fashion, McGrath argues that the natural sciences can be very profitable for theology. He argues that this approach was first adopted by Augustine, who "laid the foundation for the assertion that whatever was good, true or beautiful could be used in the service of the gospel. It was this approach which would prove dominant in the western church, providing a theological foundation for the critical appropriation by Christian writers of philosophical ideas and literary genres whose origins lay outside the church."[43]

Practically speaking, McGrath sees the natural sciences as a profitable dialogue partner for theology. But this is hardly his major reason for attempting this dialogue. As he makes clear, the greatest reason for this comes from the ontological imperative found in the doctrine of creation. In fact, one "fundamental assumption of a scientific theology is that, since the ontology of the natural world is determined by and reflects its status as God's creation, the working methods and assumptions of

39. Ibid., 20–21.

40. Ibid., 18.

41. Roche, "Scientific Theology Project," 69.

42. McGrath, *Scientific Theology*, vol. 1, 7–8.

43. Ibid., vol. 1, 15.

the natural sciences can stimulate and inform the working methods and assumptions of a responsible Christian theology."[44] In short, he argues that the "Christian doctrine of creation demands a unitary approach to knowledge, while being responsive to diversity within that creation. If God made the world, which therefore has the status of being 'creation' as well as 'nature,' it is to be expected that something of the character of God might be disclosed through that creation."[45] At this point, one will discern a Christological connection between science and theology. As Colyer notes, "Theology and the natural sciences are fundamentally related as human inquiries whose working methods reflect a common grounding as respective responses to the realities they investigate and have an ultimate connection rooted in a correlation between the Logos incarnate in Jesus Christ and the logos of the natural world."[46] Indeed, McGrath says, "The Christological dimensions of the doctrine of creation are such that the divine rationality—whether this is conceptualized as logos or as ratio—must be thought of as being embedded in creation and embodied in Christ . . . Creation and Christ ultimately bear witness to the same God, and the same divine rationality."[47]

In bringing theology and science together, McGrath's ST takes a significant step toward developing a unified theory of knowledge. The need for this arose in the wake of modernity when theology and science were split into what might be thought of as two epistemological circles. As a result, both "the natural sciences and the arts have fallen into the habit of deploying a rhetoric of autonomy, insisting upon their intellectual independence."[48] Though McGrath does not think that the warfare paradigm is an accurate way of understanding the relationship of theology and science, he does acknowledge that this is the common perception among many today. He says, "Whatever the origins of the perceived divide between the natural sciences and the humanities may be, and however valid this perception may be, there is no doubt that precisely this perception remains deeply embedded in western academic life and culture. As C. P. Snow pointed out in his 1959 Rede Lecture, the gulf between the arts and sciences had by then become so pronounced that

44. McGrath, *Science of God*, 22.

45. McGrath, *Scientific Theology*, vol. 1, 21.

46. Colyer, "Scientific Theology, vol. 1," 227.

47. McGrath, *Scientific Theology*, vol. 1, 24–25.

48. Ibid., 31.

it was necessary to speak of two distinct and non-interactive cultures in western society."[49] In response to this, McGrath bridges the gulf between the natural sciences and theology. He says, "One of the underlying concerns of a scientific theology is to lay a foundation for bringing together the various aspects of the long human quest for wisdom and authenticity within the framework set out by the Christian tradition."[50]

Before leaving McGrath's "Prolegomena," one other feature should be mentioned. Here McGrath introduces an element of his ST that will be quite significant for the project at hand. He explains that his theological method is committed to a form of realism. He says, "A scientific theology adopts a realist perspective, affirming that its task is to offer an *a posteriori* account of what it encounters or is made known to it. One of the most important working assumptions of the natural sciences is that there exists a reality, independent of the human mind, of which some account may be given. This commitment within the natural sciences to some form of realism is of immense importance to this investigation."[51] In fact, "the most fundamental and significant perspective adopted by this study is its undisguised and unapologetic commitment to a realist position. Theology is to be viewed as a discipline which offers an account of reality."[52] In McGrath's view, realism is the appropriate ontological perspective to be adopted because it is assumed by theology and the natural sciences alike. He notes, "Both Christian theology and the natural sciences understand genuine knowledge to have ontological foundations in objective reality. Any responsible intellectual discipline—including both the natural sciences and Christian theology—is thus under an intrinsic obligation to give an account of that reality."[53] Thus, McGrath's ST focuses on the common epistemological and ontological assumptions that make a dialogue between theology and the natural sciences possible.

49. Ibid., 33.

50. McGrath, *Science of God*, 23.

51. McGrath, *Scientific Theology*, 1:71.

52. Ibid., 74.

53. Ibid., 76.

Nature

After making a case for his ST project in the "Prolegomena," McGrath turns his attention to the concept of nature. For the remainder of the first volume, he deals with four major issues:

1. Nature as a socially constructed concept

2. The Christian doctrine of creation

3. The implications of the doctrine of creation

4. The nature and function of natural theology

In what follows, each of these sections will be treated in detail.

NATURE AS A SOCIALLY CONSTRUCTED CONCEPT

For McGrath, discussing the issue of nature is the most logical place to begin since natural theology and natural law rest on the concept of nature.[54] More importantly, McGrath argues that the concept itself is ambiguous because each group uses its own socially constructed ideas to understand the concept. Thus, from one group to the next, the term *nature* may be employed with different meanings in mind, leading to great confusion and equivocation. "Nature," McGrath says, "is an extremely elusive concept, which possesses different meanings for different interest groups."[55] McGrath demonstrates this by pointing to the various ways *nature* has been used in the last two thousand years. One brief example of this comes from the twentieth century. As he points out, the various twentieth-century ways of viewing the term include

- Nature as a mindless force, causing inconvenience to humanity, and demanding to be tamed

- Nature as an open-air gymnasium, offering leisure and sports facilities to affluent individuals who want to demonstrate their sporting prowess

- Nature as a wild kingdom, encouraging scuba-diving, hiking and hunting

- Nature as a supply depot—an ageing and increasingly reluctant provider that produces (although with growing difficulty) minerals, water, food, and other services for humanity[56]

---

54. Ibid., 81.

55. McGrath, *Science of God*, 35.

56. Ibid., 38.

McGrath also shows how *nature* was viewed as a mindless force by the Presocratics, as feminine or motherly by the medievals, as mechanistic during the Enlightenment,[57] as a stage by Shakespeare and the poets, and as a book by Pierre Viret and Francis Bacon.[58] Hence, McGrath contends that the concept of nature is:

> profoundly ambivalent, reflecting the aspirations, longings and fears of those who appeal to it. These values, hopes and longings have been projected onto the essentially neutral canvas of "nature." In the absence of a strong ontology, which affirms that certain things are intrinsically true of nature, the concept has become what its champions choose it shall be. It is thus potentially meaningless to speak of nature—along with cognate notions such as "natural" and "naturalism"—unless there are reasons for supposing that it is more than a free construction of human minds which are at liberty to create what they please.[59]

With this in mind, McGrath draws on the postmodern observation that a given concept may be socially constructed.

At this point, a word of clarification is in order. As a realist, McGrath certainly affirms the existence of objective reality. Thus, his claim that there is "no self-evidently correct" way of viewing nature should not be taken as an antirealist claim. The mere fact that volume 2 is devoted to advocating a realist perspective is enough to make this clear. Rather, he is simply saying that the *concept* of nature is socially constructed and thus subjective. Here McGrath makes a distinction between the object and the representation of that object through concepts. It is the conception of nature, as opposed to nature itself, that he is critiquing in the first volume. Though McGrath finds postmodernism to be a deficient view of reality, he does believe it is useful for critiquing socially constructed concepts.

One might not immediately see the value in McGrath's use of postmodernism to critique the assumption that there is one correct and universal way of viewing what is often referred to as nature. Nevertheless, the significance is seen when the criticism is set against the naturalist who often claims to have *the* correct view of nature. Understanding that nature is a socially constructed concept is, according to McGrath, very

---

57. Ibid., 37–38.

58. McGrath, *Scientific Theology*, vol. 1, 103.

59. Ibid., 86.

helpful in countering the attitude of epistemological elitism often suggested by naturalists. For the naturalist, reality must be "defined as that which may be known through the methods of natural sciences."[60] Not surprisingly, then, since God is not observed by the natural sciences, naturalists conclude that God simply does not exist. Thus, the naturalist assumes, but does not prove, the non-existence of God, and views theologians as being epistemologically inferior, if not altogether deceived. Yet, as McGrath rightly asks, "How do we know that the world which may be known by the senses is the whole of reality?"[61] Therefore, the naturalist is no better off than anyone else, since his notion of nature is also socially constructed and hence limited. Quite the opposite of what the naturalist might assume, if the concept of nature "is socially mediated—to whatever extent—it cannot serve as an allegedly neutral, objective or uninterpreted foundation of a theory or theology. Nature is already an interpreted category."[62]

In McGrath's view, the overall effect of this observation is that the playing field has now been leveled. In other words, no particular definition of nature is self-evidently correct. In light of this, McGrath believes that the Christian has just as much right to propose his view of nature as anyone else, as long as it is not contrary to the evidence. As James Keating puts it, "If the natural sciences are seen as offering interpretations of nature, and not the single fundament upon which all must build, nothing prevents Christians from asserting their particular interpretation of nature as God's creation and entering into dialogue with the sciences on an equal footing."[63] Or, as McGrath explains, if "there is no autonomous character to creation, which forces humanity to see it in one way, to the exclusion of all others, then Christianity is free to reassert its distinctive understanding of nature . . . There is, after all, a distinctive Christian way of looking at nature—as creation."[64] Thus, in the early part of volume 1, McGrath offers an important critique of the concept of nature. This critique is necessary to his project as he lays the groundwork for the Christian concept of creation as a preferable alternative to nature in both theology and science.

60. Ibid., 127.
61. Ibid., 130.
62. Ibid., 113.
63. Keating, "Natural Sciences," 129–30.
64. McGrath, *Science of God*, 44.

The Christian Doctrine of Creation

McGrath's proposal of viewing "nature as creation" is not arbitrary. He defends this view because it is faithful to the Christian tradition and provides the appropriate ontological basis for the natural sciences to build upon. As he aptly puts it:

> Unless the potentially meaningless or conceptually fluid notion of "nature" is given an ontological foundation through the more rigorous Christian doctrine of creation, the continued appeal to "nature" is without intellectual justification or merit. The Christian doctrine of creation is perhaps the only viable means by which the notion of "nature" may be salvaged, and placed on a sustainable intellectual foundation. Without an ontological foundation, "nature" is simply one person's construction and projection, and what is "natural" is a restatement of that person's own moral vision, which has been read into—and not out of —an ethically and philosophically amorphous world.[65]

As one might expect, McGrath devotes considerable space to the origins and development of the doctrine of creation. As important as the doctrine of creation is for the Old Testament, McGrath notes two important features of the doctrine contained in the New Testament that make it especially important: (1) the Christological dimension to the doctrine of creation, and (2) the doctrine of creation *ex nihilo*.[66] To demonstrate how the Christian idea is distinct from non-Christian ideas, McGrath notes how the Patristics took these two ideas from the New Testament and developed them. In contrast to Greek thinkers, such as Plato, who thought of the universe as being made of preexisting matter, the early church fathers argued for creation *ex nihilo*. As McGrath clarifies, against "any idea that the natural order was chaotic, irrational or inherently evil (three concepts which were often regarded as interlocking), the early Christian tradition affirmed that the natural order possessed a goodness, rationality and orderedness which derived directly from its creation by God."[67] Given this understanding of creation, McGrath explains the double significance for a scientific theology:

---

65. McGrath, *Scientific Theology*, vol. 1, 87.

66. Ibid., 155.

67. McGrath, *Science of God*, 51.

1. The doctrine of creation *ex nihilo* is primarily concerned with the ontological dependence of the cosmos upon its creator.

2. The doctrine affirms that God, in creating the universe, was not constrained by the limitations of the already-existing stuff from which that universe was to be fashioned, but was free to bring into existence a universe in which the divine will was recognizably embodied and enacted.[68]

Moreover, McGrath sees this understanding of creation to be in keeping with the creeds, as well as the thinking of Aquinas and Calvin.[69]

IMPLICATIONS OF THE DOCTRINE OF CREATION

McGrath believes that the doctrine of creation has significant implications for his ST. In particular, he thinks it shows an important link between God and the universe and thus explains why traces of orderliness can be found in the universe, making natural theology possible. He says:

> The Christian understanding of creation leads directly to the conclusion that there is a correspondence—the degree of which requires clarification—between the works of God and the being of God . . . For the Christian, the creation is not divine, but bears the hallmarks of divine crafting. The fundamental assumption of a responsible natural theology . . . is that we are authorized by Scripture to seek a partial disclosure of the glory of God through the works of God in creation. God is rendered in and through the creation.[70]

If God is the supreme rationality, and creation bears marks of its creator, then one should expect to observe traces of this rationality in creation.

The rationality contained in creation, however, is only part of the equation. Another major factor that makes it possible for mankind to discern order is the fact that man was created in the *imago dei*.[71] He goes on to say that the "Christian tradition has always insisted that Christ is the true image of God (Colossians 1:15), and that humanity has been created according to this image. To use the language and conceptualities of the Alexandrian theology of the fourth century, the divine *logos* is

---

68. Ibid., 52.

69. McGrath, *Scientific Theology*, vol. 1, 167–81. A more brief treatment can be found in McGrath, *Science of God*, 53.

70. Ibid., 193.

71. Ibid., 197.

the prototype which God used in the creation of humanity; Christ is thus the archetype of what it is and means to be human."[72] Because of this, McGrath notes that there is a great deal of correspondence between divine and human rationality. Thus, the marks of the creator in creation, along with humanity being created in the image of God, allow man to find order within the natural. McGrath considers this to be critical for his ST, noting that it "makes a particular appeal to the intrinsic resonance between the structures of the world and human reasoning, which it grounds in the doctrine that humanity is created in the 'image of God' (*imago Dei*)."[73]

For McGrath, these two points have enormous significance for natural science. He says, "there is something about the world—and the nature of the human mind—which allows patterns within nature to be discerned and represented."[74] In other words, since God created both the natural world and human beings—leaving traces of divine rationality within both—then human beings will be able to discover truth about the physical world. Instead of seeing this as a threat to their work, McGrath thinks that natural scientists should be open to the Christian doctrine of creation, since one "of the fundamental dilemmas of natural science . . . is that it cannot be proved that there is order in the world, in that such proof would imply the prior assumption of precisely such an order."[75] The Christian doctrine of creation, however, provides the proper foundation on which the natural sciences may operate. McGrath explains, saying, "What the natural sciences are forced to assume . . . the Christian understanding of 'wisdom' allows to be affirmed on the basis of divine revelation, and correlated with the existence of a transcendent creator God, responsible both for the ordering of the world and the human ability to grasp and discern it."[76] Therefore, according to McGrath, the Christian doctrine of revelation has positive implications for theology and the natural sciences by providing an important source of revelation for the theologian, and an ontological basis for scientific inquiry.

72. Ibid., 199.

73. McGrath, *Science of God*, 59–60.

74. McGrath, *Scientific Theology*, vol. 1, 218.

75. Ibid., 221.

76. Ibid., 222.

The Nature and Function of Natural Theology

Moving from the doctrine of creation to the issue of natural theology, McGrath distinguishes his approach from more recent versions. For example, unlike William Alston, who defines natural theology as "the enterprise of providing support for religious beliefs by starting from premises that neither are nor presuppose any religious beliefs,"[77] McGrath argues that natural theology is the practice of looking at the world in such a way that one can find support for the preexisting belief in God. He defines natural theology "as the enterprise of seeing nature as creation, which both presupposes and reinforces fundamental Christian theological affirmations."[78]

In contrast to Alston, McGrath sees his understanding of natural theology as having two major strengths. First, he believes his approach has a strong biblical basis whereas Alston's does not.[79] Second, McGrath believes his approach is more in line with various expressions of natural theology throughout church history. In particular, he looks at how nature was understood by Aquinas, Calvin, as well as the Gallic and Belgic confessions.[80] In this, McGrath believes himself to be fully in line with the premodern approach to natural theology. He says, "Natural theology—as this notion would now be understood—is actually a recent invention, and is best seen as a response to upheavals in the intellectual world in England during the seventeenth and eighteenth centuries."[81] As he explains, the modern version of natural theology "saw a rational appeal to the natural order, without reference to revelation, as a means of defending the Christian faith at a time of intellectual ferment."[82]

As history shows, when used the way Alston describes it, natural theology has had numerous objectors. In *A Scientific Theology*, McGrath concerns himself with two in particular: the philosophical objection of

77. Alston, *Perceiving God*, 289.

78. McGrath, *Science of God*, 113.

79. Ibid., 77.

80. McGrath, *Scientific Theology*, vol. 1, 273–77.

81. McGrath, *Scientific Theology*, vol. 1, 242. McGrath identifies four important factors: (1) the rise of biblical criticism; (2) a growing impatience with and dislike of ecclesiastical authority; (3) a dislike of the pomposity of organized religion and the apparent complexity of Christian doctrines; (4) the continuing successes of the mechanical worldview. See Ibid., 244.

82. McGrath, *Science of God*, 76.

Alvin Plantinga and the theological objection of Karl Barth. In short, McGrath notes that Plantinga sees all natural theology from Aquinas forward as an example of classical foundationalism. [83] In other words, Plantinga feels that natural theologians try to use natural theology as the rational basis for belief in God. McGrath, however, argues that with Aquinas and other premodern theologians, "natural theology is not intended to prove the existence of God, but presupposes that existence; it then asks, 'What should we expect the natural world to be like if it has indeed been created by such a God?' The search for order in nature is therefore intended not to demonstrate that God exists, but to reinforce the plausibility of an already existing belief."[84] Thus, McGrath sees Plantinga's objection as having greater weight when put against modern versions of natural theology, but missing the mark with regard to Aquinas and other premodern approaches to natural theology.

The second objection came from Karl Barth, who suggested that natural theology is opposed by the reformed tradition itself. Barth, McGrath notes, mounted "a theologically informed and responsible critique of certain approaches, which he regards as perpetuating the human quest for autonomy, which reached its high water mark in the culture of the Enlightenment. For Barth, 'natural theology' represents a concerted human attempt to subvert revelation, by declaring that what needs to be known about God can be determined without recourse to divine self-disclosure."[85] To begin with, it should be noted that McGrath takes Barth's concerns regarding "the human quest for autonomy" quite seriously. Nevertheless, he does not follow Barth in disregarding natural theology altogether. Instead, he advocates a form of natural theology that is subject to special revelation. He explains his position by saying that Barth's concerns "can be met fully and fairly by a refocusing of the category of natural theology, which grounds it in divine revelation rather than autonomous human reflection on the natural order. This lays a foundation for the development of a responsible natural theology as a means for offering the Christian tradition a significant means of justifying its own claims to universality, while affirming that it is anchored in a series of particularities."[86] As Charles Gutenson suggests, "For McGrath,

---

83. McGrath, *Science of God*, 81. See Plantinga, "Reformed Objection," 187.

84. Ibid., 81.

85. Ibid., 74.

86. Ibid., 75.

it is clear that, when understood as he proposes, natural theology is an important and complimentary source of divine revelation."[87]

Moreover, with regard to Calvin and the reformed tradition, McGrath argues that there "is a growing feeling within the theological community that Barth's theology marks an over-correction of the Reformed theological position, and that an informed recovery of an older position is overdue."[88] With that in mind, McGrath argues that, going well beyond Calvin, Barth actually deviates from the reformed tradition. To be clear, Calvin thought that all people know something of God by way of creation. At the same time, McGrath is careful not to take Calvin too far. He says, "Calvin does not regard natural theology as offering an autonomous route to a full and saving knowledge of God, and it is of particular importance to avoid reading his statements on 'knowledge of God the creator' as if they were framed with the eighteenth-century discussion of the matter in mind. Calvin's primary concern is to explicate Paul's insistence (Romans 1:18–21) that all of humanity has an awareness of the existence of God, and is thus responsible for any failure to respond properly to the demands of the creator upon the creatures."[89] It appears that McGrath presents a well-balanced portrayal of Calvin's position on natural theology. On the one hand, he sees Calvin, in his insistence that something of God can be known from the world, as having a much more liberal view of natural theology than Barth. In Keating's words, "McGrath accuses Barth of imposing his agenda on Scripture and of misleading an entire generation of Protestant students about their own history, and emphasizes the need to liberate theology from its 'Barthian captivity.'"[90]

One further point is worth noting about his natural theology. Simply put, McGrath sees natural theology as a bridge between theology and science. He says, "Perhaps most significantly, natural theology enables the Christian tradition to engage in discourse in the public arena."[91] Instead of using natural theology as a proof for God's existence, McGrath uses it to show the resonance between theology and the natural sciences. In his mind, natural theology can be used to offer an epistemological com-

87. Gutenson, "McGrath," 164.

88. McGrath, *Science of God*, 82.

89. McGrath, *Scientific Theology*, vol. 1, 275–76.

90. Keating, "Natural Sciences," 133.

91. McGrath, *Science of God*, 90.

mon ground with the nonbeliever. He says, "The question of whether there can be a legitimate natural theology is of considerable apologetic importance, through the recognition that, if God has indeed created the world and allowed this world to bear witness to its creator, the Christian evangelist will have a number of 'points of contact' for the gospel within the created order."[92]

To summarize McGrath's development of ST thus far, one should note several features. First, he begins with a strong critique of the assumption that there is one neutrally universal way to define nature and suggests that each community develops its own socially constructed notion of this concept that serves its own purposes. Second, if this is true, then theologians are not obligated to adopt a view of nature from outside their own tradition. In fact, the Christian theologian is as justified as any other in his view that nature is God's creation. Third, McGrath explores the implications of the doctrine of creation and rejects the concept of nature suggesting that creation is the only acceptable concept for the Christian in talking about the universe. If the universe is the creation of God, then McGrath believes there will be great continuity between the divine logos and the rationality found in the human mind and the ordered structures of the universe. Thus, there is a link between theology and the natural sciences. Finally, McGrath reclaims the premodern understanding of natural theology as "the enterprise of seeing nature as creation, which both presupposes and reinforces fundamental Christian theological affirmations."[93]

Reality

Turning from the issue of nature to the related issue of reality, McGrath responds to the ontological/epistemological dilemma left by the development and downfall of modernity and postmodernity. To orient the reader, McGrath says, "The themes of this second volume are to be set against the backdrop of radical changes in western philosophy and theology resulting from the collapse of the Enlightenment project, and the consequent fragmentation of intellectual discourse."[94] McGrath believes that one can recognize the strengths of an Enlightenment and postmod-

---

92. McGrath, *Scientific Theology*, vol. 1, 299.

93. McGrath, *Science of God*, 113.

94. McGrath, *Scientific Theology*, vol. 2, xi.

ern approach to reality without falling prey to the extremes of either perspective. That is, one may affirm that there is such a thing as objective reality while at the same time recognizing that it may be comprehended in a socially constructed way. He argues that a "realist approach to the world is not called into question through the recognition of socially constructed aspects of the explanations offered by the natural sciences."[95] It is here that McGrath finds the natural sciences to be most helpful since they offer insight on how to navigate between the strengths and weaknesses of modernity and postmodernity.

Volume 2, *Reality*, covers the following issues:

1. Rationality and knowledge in theology and the natural sciences

2. Natural theology and the trans-traditional rationality of the Christian tradition

3. The foundations of realism in the natural sciences

4. Critical realism: engaging with a stratified reality

5. The encounter with reality: the contours of a scientific theology[96]

RATIONALITY AND KNOWLEDGE IN THEOLOGY AND THE NATURAL SCIENCES

From the outset of volume 2, McGrath makes it clear that epistemology lies at the heart of his ST. He says, "A scientific theology is concerned with knowledge of God and the world. So how is such knowledge to be acquired and confirmed?"[97] He then explains that he adopts a realist perspective, saying that volume 2 "defends the view that knowledge arises through a sustained and passionate attempt to engage with a reality that is encountered or made known."[98] This approach navigates between modern and postmodern perspectives. That is, he admits the objective nature of truth while allowing for its subjective reception and human representation. He says, "While the place of human language, social location and traditions of discourse and reflection in this process of engagement must be fully acknowledged, realism insists that there exists an extra-linguistic reality which must be allowed to act as the ultimate

95. Ibid., xiv.

96. Ibid., vii–x.

97. Ibid., 3.

98. Ibid., 3–4.

foundation and criterion of responsible human thought."[99] With this, one might summarize McGrath's approach thus far as an effort to distinguish his perspective from three different epistemological perspectives:

1. Classical foundationalism of René Descartes

2. Post-liberal coherentism of George Lindbeck

3. Postmodern anti-realism of Richard Rorty

McGrath contends that foundationalism arises with René Descartes, who thought that true knowledge "would be infallible, incorrigible and indubitable. Its axioms would be generated by the human mind, and shown to be immune from error, refutation and doubt. Other propositions could then be derived from these basic axioms of reason, which served as a foundation (hence 'foundationalism') of all knowledge."[100] In spite of its popularity during the Enlightenment, foundationalism has been abandoned by many in more recent times. As McGrath notes, "The search for such indubitable foundations of knowledge had failed. As has often been pointed out, foundationalism has now been rejected by virtually every major epistemologist and philosopher of science of the last half of the century, from the later writings of Ludwig Wittgenstein through Karl Popper, W. F. Sellars and W. V. O. Quine. The belief that foundationalism is philosophically indefensible is the closest thing to a philosophical consensus there has been for a very long time."[101] At least part of the reason that foundationalism has been rejected is that foundationalists typically argued in favor of a neutrally universal rationality that could be known by any person so long as he was thinking properly. Today, however, many are highly skeptical of this idea. Following Alasdair MacIntyre, McGrath opposes the foundationalist perspective, suggesting that "Christianity possesses a distinct yet rational understanding of reality."[102] Thus, while McGrath affirms the objective nature of reality, he is careful to distinguish himself from a foundationalist perspective and insists that foundationalists fail to acknowledge the subjective component of human perception.

---

99. Ibid., 4.

100. McGrath, *Science of God*, 97.

101. Ibid., 99.

102. Ibid., 111.

After his critique of foundationalism, McGrath goes on to further distinguish himself from the post-liberal coherentist view of George Lindbeck. As McGrath explains, Lindbeck attempts to avoid a foundationalist approach to theology, which "de-emphasizes the intellectual content of a doctrinal statement in order to stress its formal function. It is not what a doctrine appears to say that matters, but its place and function within the overall fabric of the Christian faith."[103] In this case, theology is focused on formulating a coherent belief system, whether or not it says anything about who and what God actually is.[104] For McGrath, Lindbeck's approach also has significant problems. He says, "The reason that it 'seems odd' is that it is not what the Christian tradition has understood itself to be doing, despite Lindbeck's attempts to redirect it or reinterpret it on this point. Applied consistently, Lindbeck's approach renders doctrine incapable of making any cognitive, propositional or even intelligible statements about God."[105] In addition to this, "Lindbeck does not explain how doctrines are grounded in, or related to, reality."[106] Overall, McGrath's critique of Lindbeck's coherentist approach is that it is insufficient by itself as a test for truth. Coherentism, by itself, may show a system to be consistent, but will fail in determining if the system is actually true. Simply put, a system of belief cannot be true unless it genuinely reflects the way things actually are.[107] By contrast, McGrath's approach seeks for both internal consistency and grounding in the real world. Put another way, it "aims to achieve extra-systemic correspondence with intra-systemic coherence, regarding both these criteria as of fundamental importance."[108]

McGrath further distinguishes himself from postmodern anti-realism with a strong critique of thinkers such as Richard Rorty who rejects the idea of there being "some objective reality, standing above history and culture, which the human mind is able to grasp and represents."[109] Instead, Rorty argues "human communities create their own values and

---

103. Ibid., 102.

104. Ibid., 103.

105. Ibid., 103.

106. Ibid., 104.

107. McGrath, *Scientific Theology*, vol. 2, 19.

108. Ibid., 56.

109. McGrath, *Science of God*, 95.

ideas, without any need to refer to, engage with or feel accountable to an alleged 'external reality.'"[110]

McGrath argues that the failure of postmodernity is demonstrated by the success of the natural sciences. In short, if postmodern anti-realism were true, science and mathematics would be impossible.[111] But this is not all. McGrath also believes that postmodernity undermines itself. He says, "Postmodernity has defeated itself, by deploying weapons that could be used more effectively against it than in its support. As the credibility of postmodern accounts of natural sciences wanes, an increasingly vigorous critique of its assumptions and methods is gaining momentum."[112] As Myers summarizes, McGrath's approach to theology is "able to appropriate the valid insights of both Enlightenment objectivism and postmodern social constructivism, without capitulating to the one-sidedness of either."[113] Thus, McGrath's approach can be distinguished from modern foundationalism, post-liberal coherentism, and postmodern anti-realism.

NATURAL THEOLOGY AND THE TRANS-TRADITIONAL RATIONALITY OF THE CHRISTIAN TRADITION

Having distanced himself from classical foundationalism, post-liberal coherentism, and postmodern anti-realism, in volume 2, McGrath revisits the issue of natural theology. His purpose is to give further clarification to the role of natural theology in his ST. Here, McGrath makes one of his most important contributions to natural theology by placing it squarely within the life of the church. He suggests:

> Natural theology gains its plausibility and derives its intellectual foundations from within the Christian tradition. Its roots lie *intra muros ecclesiae*, even if its relevance extends *extra muros ecclesiae*. It is not a tradition-independent or autonomous intellectual discipline, in that its legitimation rests upon a Christian doctrine of creation—including the related concepts of the contingent ordering of the created world, and the epistemic and spiritual capacities of human nature.[114]

110. Ibid., 95.

111. McGrath, *Science of God*, 107. For an example of some scientists who make the same point, see Kurtz, *Humanist Manifesto 2000*.

112. McGrath, *Scientific Theology*, vol. 2, 192.

113. Myers, "McGrath's Scientific Theology," 10.

114. McGrath, *Scientific Theology*, vol. 2, 74. That is, natural theology arises inside

With this, McGrath distinguishes his approach from Alston and others who see natural theology as "the enterprise of providing support for religious beliefs by starting from premises that neither are nor presuppose any religious beliefs."[115] He does not think that natural theology must begin from neutral grounds and establish God's existence. Instead, a theologian can begin from within the framework of the Christian worldview while developing his natural theology. If this is done, however, an important question arises. How does this approach to natural theology have any apologetic value?

McGrath explains how the insights of MacIntyre function in answering this question. According to McGrath, MacIntyre denied the need for a universal reality in adjudicating between different traditions.[116] For MacIntyre, there are two criteria for evaluating competing traditions. First, each tradition must examine its own claims for internal consistency. Second, one must see which tradition is most comprehensive. McGrath sees the second of these two criteria as most important and explains its significance for natural theology. He says:

> Can questions which cannot be answered by tradition A be answered by tradition B? In other words, can tradition A recognize that tradition B is able to answer a question that tradition A has been unable to answer satisfactorily in its own history? The Christian doctrine of creation is thus of meta-traditional significance. The scientific tradition, for example, finds itself having to presuppose the uniformity and ordering of creation; Christian theology offers an account of this. The scientific tradition recognizes that the natural world has a rationality which human rationality can discern and systematize; Christian theology, however, offers an explanation of why this is the case.[117]

McGrath thinks that natural theology "offers us an interpretative grid by which other traditions may be addressed on the common issues of existence, enabling the coherence and attractiveness of the Christian vision to be affirmed."[118] Put another way, with McGrath's proposal, natural theology is "able to offer important insights as to why rival traditions exist,

---

the walls of the church, but its significance extends beyond the walls of the church.

115. Alston, *Perceiving God*, 289.

116. McGrath, *Scientific Theology*, vol. 2, 64.

117. Ibid., 75.

118. Ibid., 75.

especially in offering a coherent explanation of why certain themes are common to most traditions."[119] Thus, within ST, McGrath believes that natural theology plays a significant role of explaining other traditions.

THE FOUNDATIONS OF REALISM IN THE NATURAL SCIENCES

One might summarize the next section of McGrath's work as a defense of a realist perspective. By realism, McGrath is referring to "a family of philosophical positions which take the general position that there exists a real world, external to the human mind, which the human mind can encounter, understand and represent, at least in part. There is an objective world, quite apart from the human thinker, which exists independently of our thoughts, fears, longings and musings."[120] The easiest way to defend a realist perspective is by pointing to the success of the natural sciences. Simply put, McGrath says, "*Realism works . . .* the credibility of realism arises directly from the experimental method."[121] McGrath then notes the success of the natural sciences to show the appropriateness of realism for theological enquiry. He explains, "If a realist approach applies to the study of the works of God, how much more so must it apply to their ultimate ground?"[122]

McGrath continues with his defense of realism by responding to two possible objections: (1) radical theory change and (2) underdetermination theory.[123] He believes both of these objections are dependant upon anti-realism and responds by turning the objection against those who use them. He says, "If anti-realism is to be 'proved,' or the social constructivist or postmodern approach is to be shown to be the 'science of science,' then a case must be made from the available evidence, including historical case studies."[124] He further explains, "As many scholars have pointed out, this inevitably means that such theories are themselves underdetermined by the evidence, and hence can never hope to have

---

119. McGrath, *Science of God*, 113.

120. McGrath, *Scientific Theology*, vol. 2, 126.

121. Ibid., 123.

122. McGrath, *Science of God*, 126.

123. Radical change theory refers to the fact that dominant scientific theories of one day are often overturned in the next generation. Due to this constant cycle of change, some have suggested that a realist perspective is implausible. The underdetermination theory simply suggests that the evidence is never sufficient to fully justify realism. See McGrath, *Scientific Theology*, vol. 2, 161–66, and McGrath, *Science of God*, 132–33.

124. McGrath, *Scientific Theology*, vol. 2, 170.

the explanatory power and appeal which are essential to their gaining acceptance."[125]

CRITICAL REALISM: ENGAGING WITH A STRATIFIED REALITY

From the preceding discussion, it is clear that McGrath believes realism to be an appropriate accounting of the way things really are.[126] Nevertheless, he does see the need to clarify his realist position. Taking the lessons of modernity and postmodernity, McGrath believes it is possible to develop a theological method that takes the positives of both traditions while at the same time avoiding their weaknesses. He notes that "a realist approach to the world is not called into question through the recognition of socially constructed aspects of the explanations offered by the natural sciences."[127] He believes that this is possible by adopting a critical realist perspective. He describes this by noting how "the term 'critical realism' has come to be used within theological circles to designate a style of realism which is sensitive to the historically situated and personally involved character of theological knowledge, while resolutely declining to let go of the ideals of truth, objectivity and rationality."[128]

In order to help distinguish critical realism from other epistemological perspectives, McGrath provides the following descriptions:

1. Naïve realism: Reality impacts directly upon the human mind, without any reflection on the part of the human knower. The resulting knowledge is directly determined by an objective reality within the world.

2. Critical realism: Reality is apprehended by the human mind which attempts to express and accommodate that reality as best it can with the tools at its disposal—such as mathematical formulae or mental models.

3. Postmodern anti-realism: The human mind freely constructs its ideas without any reference to an alleged external world.[129]

By adopting a critical realist perspective, McGrath believes one can safely avoid the pitfalls of modernity and postmodernity. According to McGrath,

---

125. McGrath, *Science of God*, 133–34.

126. McGrath, *Scientific Theology*, vol. 2, 197.

127. McGrath, *Science of God*, 137.

128. McGrath, *Scientific Theology*, vol. 2, 195.

129. Ibid., 195.

the critical realist is able to affirm objective reality, while at the same time acknowledging that human perception and representation of that reality could be socially constructed.[130] This approach affirms objective truth even while at the same time noting the role played by the individual.[131]

McGrath makes clear throughout the project that he is heavily reliant on Roy Bhasker's formulation of critical realism. For one thing, "Bhaskar explicitly recognizes the importance of ontology in the philosophy of science. Any theory of knowledge, he argues, ultimately presupposes and rests upon an ontological commitment concerning the objects of that knowledge, whether this is explicitly acknowledged or not."[132] Because of this, McGrath sees Bhasker's form of critical realism as useful for ST. Furthermore, Bhasker believes realism underlies the natural science as well as the social science. If this is true, then the natural sciences are not the exclusive keepers of knowledge. According to Bhasker, the social sciences have something to contribute as well. Moreover, McGrath thinks that Bhasker's form of critical realism allows for disciplines, such as religion and history, to be viewed in a similar fashion as the natural sciences.

As such, Bhasker is "stridently opposed to any form of reductionism—the rather crude and wooden approach which seems to collapse everything into one allegedly fundamental level."[133] Each field of inquiry has a unique character and should be investigated accordingly. This is in contrast to reductionists such as Edward O. Wilson, who says, "We are approaching a new age of synthesis, when the testing of consilience is the greatest of all intellectual challenges. Philosophy, the contemplation of the unknown, is a shrinking dominion. We have the common goal of turning as much philosophy as possible into science."[134]

To avoid reductionism, Bhasker argues for a stratified view of reality. As Bhasker explains, his approach affirms a methodological unity between the natural and social sciences, "but it does not deny that there are significant differences in these methods, grounded in real differences in their subject-matters and in the relationships in which their sciences stand to them . . . it is the nature of the object that determines the form

---

130. Ibid., 195–96.

131. McGrath, *Science of God*, 142.

132. McGrath, *Scientific Theology*, vol. 2, 210–11.

133. McGrath, *Science of God*, 147. See Bhaskar, *Realist Theory*, 113.

134. Wilson, *Consilience*, 10.

of its possible science."[135] McGrath notes how in Bhasker's view, there is only one single reality, and that this reality exists at different levels or strata which have their own distinct character and integrity. One may study reality from a natural, historical, moral or theological perspective. Though one level may be dependent on another, this does not mean that the two levels are identical and able to be reduced into the same level in terms of methodological investigation. Because of this, the methodology for investigating each level will be different as the nature of the object determines how and what can be known of the object studied.[136] McGrath notes that Bhasker's approach is important because it "demands that the different levels of reality be fully acknowledged. It is impossible to reduce reality to one ontological level, or to insist that what is 'real' is determined by whether it can be 'known.'"[137] In McGrath's view, Bhasker's approach to critical realism has at least two significant implications for ST:

1. "A scientific theology may legitimately be regarded as a response to an existing reality, whose existence is independent of the actuality or possibility of human observation.

2. Each intellectual discipline must adopt a methodology which is appropriate to, and determined by, the ontology of its specific object. Its methodology is thus determined *a posteriori* rather than *a priori*."[138]

Thus, for McGrath, "the stratification of reality is one of the most distinctive features of a scientific theology."[139] That is, the nature of the object determines what can be known about the object and how it can be known.

THE ENCOUNTER WITH REALITY: THE CONTOURS OF A SCIENTIFIC THEOLOGY

McGrath devotes the remainder of volume 2 to outlining the major features of ST. To begin, McGrath notes that ST is to be understood as a response to reality as that which exists objectively.[140] That is, ST is a re-

---

135. Bhasker, *Possibility of Naturalism*, 3.

136. McGrath, *Science of God*, 148.

137. McGrath, *Scientific Theology*, vol. 2, 225.

138. McGrath, *Science of God*, 151.

139. McGrath, *Order of Things*, 101.

140. McGrath, *Science of God*, 153.

sponse to all the strata of reality. Given his realist perspective, McGrath believes the scientific theologian is under the "obligation to give an account of that world on the basis of how that world is experienced and encountered."[141] With this, McGrath believes he takes a step toward a unified approach to knowledge. He says:

> One of the most important themes of a scientific theology is its vision of the unity of reality . . . The Christian vision of reality is such that knowledge of creator and creation, redeemer and redeemed, are interlocked. Perhaps different methods of investigation are appropriate for different purposes; yet the fundamental Christian vision is that of a creator, redeemer and creation which are all possessed of the same intrinsic rationality through the act of creation itself.[142]

Second, McGrath presents ST as an *a posteriori* discipline.[143] In other words, the scientific theologian does not decide in advance what may be known of God and how it can be known. Noting Descartes as an example, McGrath says that the *a priori* approach "lays down certain beliefs as axiomatic, and proceeds to deduce a series of theological propositions from these axioms."[144] McGrath, however, denies the viability of an *a priori* approach and uses the natural sciences to show why an *a posteriori* approach should be preferred. From Bacon forward, science has operated via induction, which places an emphasis on the particular details of creation and then draws its conclusions from there.

Theologically speaking, McGrath believes that the history of particular doctrines supports his *a posteriori* approach. For example, it seems that the doctrine of the Trinity developed, not by deduction from *a priori* axioms, but through the church's response to the person of Christ and the word of God, using philosophy and tradition as guides. If this is true, then McGrath believes one "cannot do theology in advance of, and independent of, an engagement with the reality which we are under obligation to explore and represent."[145] Instead, he argues that theology must work hard to deal with the narrative of Scripture and the

---

141. McGrath, *Scientific Theology*, vol. 2, 248.

142. Ibid., 247–48.

143. McGrath, *Science of God*, 94.

144. McGrath, *Scientific Theology*, vol. 2, 269.

145. McGrath, *Science of God*, 161.

incarnation of Christ to inform and guide its theological affirmations.[146] Thus, one might suggest that the *a posteriori* nature of ST is derived from McGrath's affirmation of realism and a correspondence theory of truth. If so, one can discern the following movement in his thought: realism → correspondence → a posteriori formulation. McGrath explains saying that ST "seeks to apply to theology the same general approach found in the natural sciences—namely, that theories and hypothesis must be constantly checked out against what they purport to represent or describe."[147]

Third, McGrath offers ST as an approach that sees theology as a response to its distinctive object. Because of this, his approach differs sharply from an Enlightenment approach, which prescribed one universal method to all disciplines. He says, "The Enlightenment tended to assume that all sciences were committed to using the same working methods and assumptions; a scientific theology insists that the distinctive identity of the object of a science is reflected in its response to that object."[148] Yet, from all that has been said, McGrath thinks it is clear that there is no "generalized scientific methodology which can be applied without variance and uncritically to all sciences."[149] Instead, each discipline develops its own vocabulary and methods of investigation that are consistent with the nature of their object.[150]

Fourth, McGrath suggests that ST offers an approach aimed at giving an explanation of reality. In McGrath's view, this is one important area of common ground between theology and the natural sciences, since both "attempt to offer explanations of reality, by disclosing the way things truly are, so that the correlations established by observation may be accounted for, and additional observations and correlations proposed, so that they may be subjected to the appropriate validatory processes."[151]

Before moving forward, McGrath makes one final proposal. As a postulate, McGrath argues that ST is, and should be, Christocentric.[152] If ST is to be Christian, McGrath contends that it "can be so only when it focuses on Christ, as it is in Christ that the fullness of the God who

---

146. McGrath, *Scientific Theology*, vol. 2, 273.

147. Ibid., 277.

148. Ibid., 280.

149. McGrath, *Science of God*, 162.

150. McGrath, *Scientific Theology*, vol. 2, 280.

151. McGrath, *Science of God*, 166.

152. McGrath, *Scientific Theology*, vol. 2, 246.

is known partially through the created order is to be encountered (Colossians 2:9)."[153]

In volume 2, McGrath thus articulates and defends a critical realist understanding of reality. Drawing on Roy Bhaskar's notion of a stratified reality, McGrath shows how the individual disciplines of human inquiry can be maintained without resulting in reductionism. Moreover, volume 2 outlines the basic structure of his ST.

Theory

As McGrath brings volume 2 to a close, he offers a concise preview of the third volume, which deals with the issue of theory. He summarizes the third volume as "a direct convergence between the way in which the scientific and theological communities develop, formulate and confirm their theories as to how reality is to be grasped and represented. Both the natural sciences and theology propose that development in theory is governed by attentiveness to reality, so that it is the same ultimate reality that is expressed and conceived in different ways at different times."[154] McGrath's treatment of theory is broken into four major sections, each contained in a single chapter: (1) the legitimacy of theory within a scientific theology; (2) the representation of reality in a scientific theology; (3) the place of explanation in a scientific theology; and (4) the place of metaphysics in a scientific theology. As with the treatment of previous volumes, each section will be briefly considered.

THE LEGITIMACY OF THEORY WITHIN A SCIENTIFIC THEOLOGY

One could view the first major section of volume 3 as a defense of the theological enterprise itself. Here, McGrath argues for the legitimacy of theory formulation, whether in scientific or theological circles. Theory is something common to both disciplines, but in the case of theology is typically referred to as *doctrine*.[155] While some may see the development of theory (doctrine in the case of theology) as illegitimate, McGrath would strongly disagree. He says, "Theory arises precisely because human beings are rational creatures, and feel impelled, both morally and intellectually, to give an account of things. The natural sciences and

153. Ibid., 313.
154. Ibid., 315.
155. McGrath, *Science of God*, 177.

Christian theology are both rooted in human experience and culture; yet they also aspire to transcend the particularities of time and place to yield truths that claim a more universal significance."[156] As such, any attempt at Christianity not doctrinal in nature is not natural.[157] Therefore, McGrath says, it is "ultimately quite irresponsible for Christianity to fail to give an intellectual account of itself in this way."[158]

Once again, McGrath looks to the natural sciences as a model for theological development. He thinks they help show the inevitability of theory. Noting theoretical development in biology, physics, and the human sciences, McGrath claims there "is thus a theoretical imperative built into the patterns of human thought . . . The same fundamental impulse lies behind philosophy, theology and the natural sciences—the desire to see the 'big picture' which the natural world somehow reflects. The demand to eliminate or avoid theory ultimately amounts to a demand that humans should cease thinking. Theory arises precisely because human beings are rational, inquisitive and exploratory."[159] Therefore, the church simply cannot avoid doing theology.

As an example of how this takes place within church history, McGrath points to the development of Christology, by which the church sought to properly understand the person and nature of Jesus Christ. Realizing the dangers of misunderstanding and misrepresenting Christ, the church wrestled for centuries to make sure its conclusions were accurate.[160] In the end, certain theories were formulated and affirmed, while others were strongly rejected as false. For McGrath, theories have a place within ST. Though he believes the concept of dogma to be legitimate and important, McGrath thinks that the term *doctrine* will be of better service for theology.[161] He provisionally defines doctrine as the "communally authoritative teachings regarded as essential to the identity of the Christian community, in which the community tells itself and outsiders what it has seen, and what it has become in response to this vision. Christian doctrine may be regarded as the present outcome of that long

---

156. Ibid., 9.

157. Ibid., 10.

158. McGrath, *Science of God*, 174.

159. McGrath, *Scientific Theology*, vol. 3, 14.

160. Ibid., 23.

161. McGrath, *Science of God*, 177.

growth of tradition in which the Christian community has struggled to arrive at an interpretation of its foundational traditions."[162]

Some might object to theory formulation by suggesting that theories are reductionist and that they rob "reality of its wonder."[163] McGrath notes this concern but suggests that theory formulation is simply inevitable. Moreover, he suggests that this reductionistic concern is resolved by keeping theories accountable to the particulars of human experience. He says, "Theory is obliged to leave things out, to deliberately overlook, to systematically truncate. The redeeming of particularities is an essential antidote to the universalization implicit in theoretical approaches."[164] Epistemologically speaking, placing an emphasis on particulars helps prevent theory from becoming overly reductionistic and leads to a more thorough engagement with reality. As Myers explains, general theories "must be grounded *a posteriori* in the world of particularities, and must arise through a comprehensive engagement with the whole stratified reality of the world."[165]

The fact that theories never fully depict reality raises the important issue of closure. McGrath wonders in "what way and at what point can the right interpretation of a set of particulars be regarded as being settled? How can a specific theory be regarded as having secured 'closure' of an issue, when the particularities it claims to represent are more open-ended than this closure suggests?"[166] Is it possible to find closure on a given theological issue, or are postmoderns such as Hillary Lawson correct who view such attempts as premature and illegitimate.[167] McGrath suggests that there are typically two general responses given to this question. In an Enlightenment model, there is but one universal way of looking at reality and closure is a genuine possibility.[168] In a postmodern model, there is no universal model for apprehending reality, and thus closure is never possible.[169]

162. McGrath, *Scientific Theology*, vol. 3, 28–29.

163. Ibid., 29.

164. Ibid., 31.

165. Myers, "McGrath's Scientific Theology," 15.

166. McGrath, *Scientific Theology*, vol. 3, 43.

167. See Lawson, *Closure*.

168. McGrath, *Science of God*, 186.

169. McGrath, *Scientific Theology*, vol. 3, 46.

McGrath, however, thinks there is a third option, which recognizes that it is possible, given the particular nature of the object under consideration, to gain closure on certain issues while leaving others open to further consideration. He explains that "a scientific theology takes a markedly different approach, insisting, as we have seen, that *ontology determines epistemology*—in other words, that the degree of theoretical closure that may be secured for any aspect of reality is determined by its intrinsic nature. We are thus obliged to think in terms of a range of possibilities of closure, depending on which stratum of reality is being encountered and represented in this manner . . . meaning cannot be totally determined by any one writer or era."[170] As he explains, this approach recognizes the nature of theory and allows for continued discussion on how best to articulate a particular doctrine, but also maintains the essential commitments of the faith. He says, "Traditionally, Christian doctrine has been well aware of its limits, and has sought to avoid excessively confident affirmations in the face of mystery. Yet at the same time, Christian theology has never seen itself as totally reduced to silence in the face of divine mysteries."[171]

After considering the delicate but important issue of closure, McGrath moves to defend further the theological enterprise against those who wish to propose a non-dogmatic form of Christianity. In light of arguments against doctrine arising from the religious wars and the Hellenistic influences on Christianity, McGrath makes three important points. First, he suggests that this non-dogmatic form leads to an intellectually weakened faith. "Instead of encouraging Christians to think about their faith," he says, "it represents a demand that they suspend use of their intellectual faculties in any matters to do with God, Christ or human destiny." Second, he says that a non-dogmatic Christianity is relativistic in nature. Third, he notes that the demand for a non-dogmatic Christianity confuses the tone and substance of Christian doctrine.[172] Thus, noting the difference between tone and substance, McGrath welcomes the development of Christian dogmatics, but distances himself from an uncritical approach to theology.

Finally, McGrath further defends the theological enterprise by pointing to the social function of doctrine. Doctrine, he says, "plays

170. McGrath, *Science of God*, 187.
171. McGrath, *Scientific Theology*, vol. 3, 49.
172. Ibid., 59–61.

an important role in distinguishing the Christian community from the world around it, thus aiding its preservation as a distinct entity in the face of assimilationist pressures from its cultural environment. Doctrine came to be of increasing importance in distinguishing the Church from secular culture at large, and increasing a sense of identity and cohesion within its ranks."[173]

With these considerations, McGrath's ST argues for the legitimacy of theory in both natural science and theology. As he contends, the formation of theories is an inevitable result of human inquiry.

THE REPRESENTATION OF REALITY IN A SCIENTIFIC THEOLOGY

Having offered a defense for the theological enterprise, McGrath then considers the way in which reality is verbally represented in ST. First, McGrath shows how words are used to represent theological aspects of reality. As human knowledge and exploration of an issue grows, there is a corresponding need to develop a new vocabulary to accommodate advancement. This is found within the theological and scientific realms. Although theologians have occasionally created new terms such as *homoousious* to articulate certain ideas, McGrath contends that the more common practice of theologians is to borrow an existing term and reinterpret it "in a manner which is consonant with the Christian vision of God, as expressed in the economy of salvation."[174]

McGrath also spends a considerable amount of time on how imagery is used in representing reality within ST. This is of significant importance given his view of creation in volume 1, whereby something of the creator may be known from creation. Here, however, McGrath is careful to explain that any representation of reality that comes by way of analogy is always partial and never complete.[175] According to McGrath, analogies are helpful and sometimes necessary in this process. He follows Aquinas by affirming the *analogia entis* and insists that "a Christian doctrine of creation entails an analogical mode of argumentation. The created correspondences between humanity, the world and their divine creator entail the use of analogies in both scientific and theological explanation."[176] Because of this, McGrath can argue that something of

---

173. McGrath, *Science of God*, 192.

174. McGrath, *Scientific Theology*, vol. 3, 87.

175. Ibid., 100.

176. Ibid., 108.

God can be known from creation. McGrath is careful, however, to account for the concerns of Karl Barth's *analogia fidei*.[177] With Barth, the central concern is to determine who authorizes an analogy to represent God.[178] As McGrath notes, Barth believed that the "ultimate grounds of any analogical mode of speaking about God are not *creavit Deus* but *dixit quoque Deus*. Analogies rest upon a covenant, not upon nature."[179] In other words, the authority of an analogy resides not in what God has created, but in what God has said. Here Barth demonstrates his hesitancy with the notion of general revelation and natural theology. For him, revelation was found in Jesus Christ, the Bible, and the preaching of the church, but not from nature.

On the face of it, Barth's *analogia fidei*, and Aquinas's *analogia entis* appear to be at great odds with each other. McGrath, however, argues that the two actually work together. At the root of Barth's object to the *anologia entis*, and thus natural theology, is a concern that it will allow human reason to run autonomously apart from special revelation. In McGrath's model, however, this cannot happen. He says, "A responsible *analogia entis* . . . cannot be conceived as an assertion of human epistemological autonomy, but is rather to be seen as reflecting a desire to follow through the implications of the revealed notion of the divine creation of the world in and through Christ. The capacity of the created order to model God is thus a revealed, not a natural, insight."[180] As such, McGrath believes that one should not view the *analogia entis* and the *analogia fidei* in contrast.

THE PLACE OF EXPLANATION IN A SCIENTIFIC THEOLOGY

As with other issues, McGrath sees a similarity between the natural sciences and theology when it comes to their use of explanation.[181] For ST to be of greatest explanatory power, McGrath thinks that it must do three things:

1. Account for its own form and content

2. Account for the existence of alternate traditions

---

177. McGrath, *Science of God*, 196.

178. McGrath, *Scientific Theology*, vol. 3, 113.

179. Ibid., 115.

180. Ibid., 118–19.

181. Ibid., 135.

3. Offer theoretical explanations that will be seen as "appropriate and convincing to those within that tradition"[182]

In this case, ST offers an explanation that features "intrasystemic" and "extrasystemic" aspects.[183] Or, put another way, McGrath's ST offers an approach that requires both internal coherence and external correspondence.

To explain the particular content and form of Christianity, McGrath makes use of abductive reasoning, which seeks the best explanation for a particular object. Thus, to explain Christianity, McGrath looks for the acts or events that gain rise to it. With this, McGrath's view of revelation is found, suggesting that Christian doctrine might be seen as a response to the past revelatory events.[184]

So how exactly does McGrath understand revelation? Though he views the term as having a double meaning, referring to acts as well as knowledge, he follows Barth in placing a greater emphasis on the notion of act. He says:

> Revelation is first and foremost a divine act. But it is a divine act which impacts upon humanity. Barth, presumably with the shell-pocked battlefields of the recent Great War in mind, refers to the impact of revelation as "shell-holes and craters." The revelational imprint on history is like the explosion of an artillery shell, leaving a crater which may be investigated long after the immense power of the detonation has passed. Yet it is the detonation, rather than the resulting crater, which is to be considered as "revelation" in the proper sense of the word. It refers to a divine action, not a permanent state—but an action which leaves an imprint on history, at various levels.[185]

From this, Myers rightly observes that McGrath sees revelation as a past event.[186] Thus, the real question is not "what is revelation?" but "what was revelation?"[187] In McGrath's view, when properly understood, revelation is a past event that leaves a multi-layered impression on history. Adonis Vidu notes that, according to McGrath, the theologian "has no direct

182. McGrath, *Science of God*, 208.

183. McGrath, *Scientific Theology*, vol. 3, 137.

184. Ibid., 136.

185. McGrath, *Science of God*, 209–10.

186. Myers, "McGrath's Scientific Theology," 17.

187. McGrath, *Scientific Theology*, vol. 3, 150–51.

access to revelation (which by the way is said to be contained in various strata of reality), just like the evolutionary biologist has no direct access to the Big Bang or whatever. The only way of access is via the traces of that origin, through the effects which are still visible today."[188]

Understood this way, McGrath's belief is that revelation leaves a multi-layered impression on history and culture, which can, in some sense, also be spoken of as revelation.[189] Though he thinks that others could be listed, McGrath identifies eight such levels, which include texts, patterns of worship, ideas, communities, institutional structures, images, distinctive vocabulary, and religious experience.[190] For McGrath, one might account for this multi-layered reality by way of revelation. That is, by abduction, one might suggest that these levels are best explained by the past event of revelation. He notes:

> We must affirm that revelation is something that has happened, and that the biblical witness concerns both the nature of such events, and their interpretation. On this definition, revelation is not something we currently experience; rather, we now encounter its aftermath, its indentation on the historical process. As Barth rightly stresses, the reality of God cannot be statically and objectively described.[191]

Following Barth, McGrath says:

> [W]e do not *presently* have access to the totality of whatever "revelation" might be. We know it primarily by its effects—by the impact it has had upon history—such as Scripture, various ecclesiastical institutions, and the liturgy, which point to something decisive having happened, and mediate its perceived significance to us . . . If theological analysis is to be based upon presently available experience, the conclusion must be drawn that revelatory events, precisely because they are past events, are not directly accessible to us; what is directly accessible to us takes the form of its aftermath.[192]

McGrath argues that this understanding of revelation offers a helpful explanation of how the Christian tradition arose.

188. Vidu, "Alister E. McGrath," 273.

189. McGrath, *Scientific Theology*, vol. 3, 146.

190. Ibid., 147–48.

191. Ibid., 151.

192. Ibid., 153.

As he explains, in order for a tradition to have any explanatory power, it must be able to explain its own existence as well as other traditions'. McGrath reminds the reader of his earlier discussion on natural theology and says it explains the "trans-traditional quest for truth, beauty and goodness."[193] In other words, McGrath thinks that natural theology gives the Christian this ability of explanation. In his approach, natural theology is "tradition-specific, yet possesses a universal applicability, thus offering an explanation of other traditions, while at the same time reinforcing the plausibility of its own tradition."[194] Moreover, McGrath also shows how the Christian doctrine of creation offers the best explanation of the natural world. He notes how a "Christian doctrine of creation offers an explanatory window into both the ordering of the natural world and the capacity of the human mind to discern and represent this ordering."[195] Noting his agreement with Richard Swinburne's work *The Existence of God*, McGrath avoids a god-of-the-gaps approach and contends that "more recent theistic writers have stressed the importance of belief in God in explaining the 'big picture'—that is to say, the overall patterns of ordering which are discerned within the universe."[196]

McGrath also considers the important issues of heresy and orthodoxy. His major concern is to describe how these terms should be understood and what role they play in ST. For him, discussion of these matters leads one to think about how doctrines develop throughout history. To explain the nature of doctrinal development, McGrath borrows the analogy of Otto Neurath's ship at sea.[197] He says, "The entire theological enterprise, as medieval writers never tire of reminding us, is undertaken *in via*; it is not something which can be constructed *de novo* or *ab initio* in some hypothetical dry dock, in that the historical trajectory of the Christian tradition is such that a return to origins is impossible . . . The business of theological explanation must take place while the journey is under way."[198] In other words, theology, like all other disciplines, does not start from scratch, but rather interacts with

193. Ibid., 195.

194. McGrath, *Science of God*, 222.

195. Ibid., 222.

196. McGrath, *Scientific Theology*, vol. 3, 195.

197. See Neurath, *Empiricism*.

198. McGrath, *Scientific Theology*, vol. 3, 218.

existing ideas.[199] As Colyer notes, doctrinal development entails three important aspects which, extending the metaphor, include *"unpacking*, the process of learning to live with the confines of the ship by exploring its structures; *reconstruction*, the activity, like that of the Reformation, of rebuilding parts of the ship damaged by adverse conditions; and *incorporating driftwood*, the process of borrowing intellectual or cultural resources 'floating in the water of history' to strengthen or reconstruct part of the ship."[200]

As doctrinal development takes place, one would expect certain ideas to be viewed as appropriate while others will be seen as inappropriate. Historically, the church has used the terms *orthodoxy* and *heresy*, respectively, to refer to such ideas. But what exactly are heresy and orthodoxy, and is it profitable to maintain these categories? As McGrath notes, both purely historical and theoretical understandings of the term *heresy* have encountered difficulties that make it a somewhat slippery term.[201] Likewise, because some viewed the earliest teaching of the church as most authentic while others felt the more recently developed doctrinal statements should be preferred, the issue of orthodoxy has also been widely debated. Nevertheless, like doctrine itself, McGrath sees it as inevitable that these terms will continue to have a significant role to play. Promising to publish a book-length exploration of the nature of both heresy and orthodoxy,[202] McGrath does not give a clear definition of how these terms are to be understood. Nevertheless, he makes it clear that these terms should not be abandoned.

The Place of Metaphysics in A Scientific Theology

In the last chapter of volume 3, McGrath considers the place that metaphysics occupies in ST. He includes within his consideration of metaphysics "such questions as why the world exists, and what place humanity has within it."[203] Noting the influence of A. J. Ayer, he begins by reminding the reader that metaphysics was largely rejected in the twentieth century. He says, "The classic affirmations of theology were declared to be non-sense, because they aspired to affirm truths about God without being able to specify how these might be verified, or under what

---

199. McGrath, *Science of God*, 228.

200. Colyer, "Scientific Theology, vol. 3," 238–39.

201. McGrath, *Scientific Theology*, vol. 3, 221–28.

202. To date he has published the first of these volumes. See McGrath, *Heresy*.

203. McGrath, *Science of God*, 235.

circumstances they might be shown to be true."[204] Although McGrath mentions the influence of David Hume and Auguste Comte,[205] he notes that the stronger critique of metaphysics came from thinkers like Ernst Mach, and Otto Neurath and Rudolf Carnap of the Vienna Circle, who felt that "terms in statements or propositions had to be directly related to what we experience. Every proposition must therefore be capable of being stated in a manner which relates directly to the real world of experience."[206] As Colin Brown explains, the Vienna Circle (also known as the Logical Positivists) "claimed that statements were meaningful and genuine if they could be verified in a manner comparable to the way in which scientific hypotheses are tested by public experiment."[207]

Nevertheless, McGrath thinks that this anti-metaphysical point of view cannot be sustained. While commenting on Ayer, he notes how this view often "entails the highly problematic *a priori* denial of the *a posteriori* possibility of metaphysics."[208] In other words, "Ayer proposes to declare the entire metaphysical enterprise to be invalid in advance of any such engagement, on the basis of a methodologically confused reading of the traditions and tasks of the natural sciences."[209] Thus, McGrath argues that the criticisms put forth by the Vienna Circle are largely unpersuasive and premature, and at best cause theologians to modify their claims.[210]

The Vienna Circle was not the only group to reject metaphysics. It has also been opposed by those within the postmodern camp.[211] For postmodernists like Jacques Derrida and Michel Foucault, McGrath says, there is "a link between metaphysics and a plethora of social, political and economic evils. In part, this is linked with the vigorous espousal of metaphysical interests by Martin Heidegger, whose Nazi political sympathies were regarded with intense distaste by his critics."[212]

---

204. McGrath, *Scientific Theology*, vol. 3, 237.

205. Ibid., 252–53.

206. McGrath, *Science of God*, 235.

207. Brown, *Philosophy & the Christian Faith*, 170.

208. McGrath, *Scientific Theology*, vol. 3, 239.

209. Ibid.

210. Ibid., 239.

211. McGrath, *Scientific Theology*, vol. 3, 260. McGrath notes a number of important postmoderns who rejected metaphysics. See Derrida, "White Mythology"; Rorty, *Consequences of Pragmatism;* Foucault, *Ethics: Subjectivity and Truth*.

212. McGrath, *Scientific Theology*, vol. 3, 261.

McGrath, however, observes two problems with the postmodern rejection of metaphysics. First, he thinks the postmodern outlook is challenged by the success of the natural sciences.[213] Second, the postmodern rejection is inconsistent in nature. He says, for example, that Foucault's belief that repression is wrong "appears to be determined by what is, in effect, an objective moral value—namely, that freedom is to be preferred to repression."[214] Because of this, McGrath believes that metaphysics cannot be abandoned, since metaphysical "assumptions are actually implicit within the ideologies of those who oppose the notion."[215]

This, however, is not all that McGrath has to say about the importance of metaphysical discussion. He also suggests that the use of metaphysics is important for theological reasons. For him, any "theology" that seeks to speak about God himself instead of merely addressing certain sociological, cultural, and religious issues, is already committed to making metaphysical claims.[216] The task, then, is to determine what role metaphysics will play in ST. On this McGrath is quite clear. Within his ST, metaphysics "is understood to arise *a posteriori*—in other words, as a result of an engagement with reality. Far from being the *precondition* of any such investigation, metaphysics is its *outcome*."[217] While some would think this an inappropriate way to approach metaphysics, he suggests that it is the only way to do it responsibly. As he has made clear in volume 3, all theories or doctrines must be formulated in response to a thorough engagement with reality itself.[218]

SUMMARY

Before this chapter concludes, a summary will be helpful. In volume 1, McGrath introduces ST to the reader and proposes that nature should be seen as creation. This means that there is an ontological relation between the creator and creation. For the theologian, this means that something of God can be known from creation. For the scientist, creation explains what the scientist can only assume, that there is order and structure in

---

213. McGrath, *Science of God*, 239.

214. McGrath, *Scientific Theology*, vol. 3, 266.

215. Ibid., 266.

216. Ibid., 290.

217. McGrath, *Science of God*, 240–41.

218. McGrath, *Scientific Theology*, vol. 3, 293.

the universe that can be examined and explained at least partially. With that in mind, McGrath reintroduces natural theology as "the enterprise of seeing nature as creation, which both presupposes and reinforces fundamental Christian theological affirmations."[219] Here, McGrath recasts natural theology as a legitimate aspect of Christian theology that operates from within the Christian tradition. Thus, McGrath uses natural theology as a confirmation of the faith, as opposed to something that offers proof.

In volume 2, while distinguishing his view from classical foundationalism, post-liberal coherentism, and postmodern anti-realism, McGrath defends a realist position. In reliance upon Roy Bhaskar, he adopts a critical realist approach to knowledge, which is of great importance to ST. After considering the way in which natural theology is helpful in explaining other traditions, McGrath outlines the basic features of ST.

In volume 3, McGrath examines important issues relating to the representation of reality and defends the theological enterprise against Christian and non-Christian objections by showing how the development of theory is an inevitable outcome of theology and natural science. After considering the way past revelatory events offer an explanation of the Christian tradition, McGrath closes by outlining the way metaphysics functions in ST.

Having presented a review of McGrath's ST in this chapter, chapters 3 and 4 will offer a critique of the project. On the whole, this book argues that McGrath's theological method does much to commend itself to evangelicals. That does not mean, however, that there are no points of concern. Chapter 3 will focus on some of the ambiguities within McGrath's ST, while chapter 4 will present the strengths of McGrath's theological method.

---

219. McGrath, *Science of God*, 113.

3

Ambiguities Associated
with McGrath's Scientific Theology

Tʜɪs ᴄʜᴀᴘᴛᴇʀ ꜰᴏᴄᴜsᴇs ᴏɴ some apparent ambiguities related to several theological concepts associated with Alister E. McGrath's scientific theology (ST). The ambiguities, which result from a lack of detailed
attention given to each certain issue within the discussion of ST, include
the doctrine of revelation, methodological naturalism, the role of experience and history in theology, the Christocentric nature of ST, and the
status of universals. In the case of natural theology, however, ambiguities arise from McGrath's lack of clarification regarding the differences
between natural theology and natural revelation. These ambiguities appear in *A Scientific Theology* and *The Science of God*, as well as in other
works that deal with issues relating to science and theology.[1] The present
concern is that, although the apparent ambiguities do not defeat ST, they
may unfortunately give some pause in embracing ST as an evangelical
position. This chapter argues that these issues are not detrimental to his
ST since upon examination they are found either to be unproblematic or
inessential to his ST. At most, these issues might call for further clarification or development, but not for rejection of McGrath's ST. Thus, this
chapter defends McGrath's ST against some possible objections. Since
very little has been written in response to McGrath's ST as of yet, the
concerns raised in this chapter do not necessarily represent the views to
date of other evangelicals regarding his ST. Instead, this chapter points
to areas where opposition to his ST might be anticipated and attempts to
show that such objections do not defeat ST.

---

1. See McGrath, *Dawkins Delusion*, and McGrath *Dawkin's God*.

CLARIFICATIONS RELATING TO CHRISTIAN REVELATION

In *A Scientific Theology* and *The Science of God*, McGrath presents a particular understanding of the concept of divine revelation. Following Alasdair MacIntyre's call for a tradition to give an account of itself,[2] McGrath argues that the Christian tradition does this by reference to revelation. He says, "A scientific theology sets itself the agenda of determining what called the Christian tradition into being, and how this can and should continue to sculpture its intellectual contours. The only adequate explanation, as will become clear, is that of a series of original revelational events, which give rise to a 'deposit of faith' which is itself revelational."[3] In other words, by examining the effects of past revelational events, theologians are able to explain the Christian tradition itself. As McGrath unpacks his understanding of revelation, a number of ambiguities surface that call for clarification or further development. These ambiguities relate to general similarities between McGrath and Karl Barth's view of revelation, the Bible's status as revelation, and the issue of divine inspiration.

General Similarities Between McGrath and Barth on Revelation

McGrath clearly acknowledges the similarities of his view of revelation to Barth's when he says:

> Revelation is first and foremost a divine act. Barth . . . refers to the impact of revelation as "shell-holes and craters." The revelational imprint on history is like the explosion of an artillery shell, leaving a crater which may be investigated long after the immense power of the detonation has passed. Yet it is the detonation, rather than the resulting crater, which is to be considered as "revelation" in the proper sense of the word. It refers to a divine action, not a permanent state—but an action which leaves an imprint on history, at various levels.[4]

The similarities between McGrath and Barth are also seen in volume 3 of *A Scientific Theology*. While speaking about the process of revelation, McGrath argues that "revelation is not something we currently experience; rather, we now encounter its aftermath, its indentation on the

---

2. McGrath, *Science of God*, 208. Also see McGrath, *Scientific Theology*, vol. 2, 75.

3. McGrath, *Science of God*, 210.

4. Ibid., 209–10.

historical process. As Barth rightly stresses, the reality of God cannot be statically and objectively described. Revelation itself must be conceived as 'a revealing and not a state of being revealed.'"[5] He goes on to say, "The basic idea I want to develop maintains Barth's emphasis upon God's freedom in revelation, and especially that revelation is an act of God rather than a permanent state of 'revealedness.' A revelational act gives rise to revelational interpretations of these acts, which we find recorded in Scripture."[6]

With these statements, McGrath notes the similarities between his view of revelation and Barth's. Throughout *A Scientific Theology* and *The Science of God*, however, he does not clarify or distinguish his view from Barth's in any discernable fashion. McGrath affirms certain aspects of Barth's view without making it clear where the difference, if any, might lie. Thus, what stands out most regarding McGrath's view of revelation are the similarities between himself and Barth. Because of this, McGrath seems to open himself to criticism from evangelicals who are uncomfortable with Barth. Norman Geisler, for one, expresses concerns with Barth's view. He says, "As he turned to the Bible, the Reformers, and Søren Kierkegaard, Barth moved from liberalism in the direction of orthodoxy, embracing Trinitarianism, the Virgin Birth, and Christ's deity and the bodily resurrection. Unfortunately, however, he did not return to an orthodox view of Scripture . . . neo-orthodoxy insists that the Bible is a fallible human witness to the Word of God (Christ) that only *becomes* the Word of God to us in an existential encounter with the Christ it conveys."[7]

Barth himself expresses this when he says, "The prophets and apostles as such, even in their office, even in their function as witnesses, even in the act of writing down their witness, were real, historical men as we are, and therefore sinful in their action, and capable and actually guilty of error in their spoken and written word."[8] While he definitely believes the Bible can be in error with regard to historical facts and details, he also believes that the real "vulnerability of the Bible, i.e., its capacity for

---

5. McGrath, *Scientific Theology*, vol. 3, 151. Here McGrath is quoting in agreement from Barth.

6. McGrath, *Science of God*, 210.

7. Geisler, *Systematic Theology*, 372.

8. Barth, *Church Dogmatics*, vol. 1, 529.

error, also extends to its religious or theological content."[9] From this, it is clear that Barth denies the inerrancy of Scripture. As Steven Stahl notes, Barth "refuses to make Holy Scripture what it cannot become . . . and still be truly what it is—a word written by men. Barth will have nothing to do with a Bible conceived of as an infallible biblical word of man."[10] Or as Gabriel Fackre puts it, for Barth the words of Scripture are "human words, subject to error in all about which they speak, theology and ethics as well as science and history."[11] Thus, as Norman Geisler plainly states, "Whatever else may be said for it, the neo-orthodox view of the Bible is not biblical—it is contrary to what the Bible claims for itself."[12]

Thus, if McGrath's works on ST are read in isolation, it appears that McGrath aligns himself with Barth on all matters pertaining to the doctrine of revelation. This is unfortunate since Barth denies the inerrancy of Scripture. Fortunately, however, by examining McGrath's additional works, one can identify some differences between McGrath and Barth on this issue. For example, where Barth would deny the inerrancy of Scripture, McGrath, who hesitates to use the word inerrancy due to its association with the Enlightenment, says:

> In common with all evangelicals, I affirm the total trustworthiness and reliability of Scripture in all that it teaches. I believe that words penned by James I. Packer, affirming this unique authority of Scripture back in 1962, remain as relevant as they have ever been: "Infallible" means "not liable to be mistaken, or to mislead"; "inerrant" means "free from all falsehood." Both words express negatively the positive idea that the Bible is entirely reliable and trustworthy in all that it asserts. To profess faith in the infallibility and inerrancy of Scripture is therefore to express the intention of believing all that it is found to teach, on the grounds that it is true . . . The conservative evangelical differs from his liberal brother, not by committing himself to interpret the Bible in a different way, but by committing himself in advance to believe whatever the Bible turns out to be saying.[13]

Therefore, while McGrath's other works reveal some differences from Barth on certain aspects of the doctrine of revelation, he has not made

9. Ibid., 509.

10. Stahl, "Concept of Revelation," 123.

11. Fackre, *Doctrine of Revelation*, 131.

12. Geisler, *Systematic Theology*, 383.

13. McGrath, "Rejoinder."

this clear within his works on ST. Because of this, a word of clarification would be helpful for those who wish to embrace his ST but are also uncomfortable with Barth's neo-orthodox views on revelation.

The Bible's Status as Revelation

Another area of ambiguity relating to McGrath's treatment of revelation—within his works on ST—comes from the question of whether or not the Bible itself *is* revelation. On the surface, McGrath seems to say no. He says:

> The essential point here is that we do not presently have access to the totality of whatever "revelation" might be. We know it primarily by its effects—by the impact it has had upon history—such as Scripture, various ecclesiastical institutions, and the liturgy, which point to something decisive having happened, and mediate its perceived significance to us . . . If theological analysis is to be based upon presently available experience, the conclusion must be drawn that revelatory events, precisely because they are past events, are not directly accessible to us; what is directly accessible to us takes the form of its aftermath.[14]

Because he primarily understands revelation to be God's self-disclosure of himself through events and actions, McGrath seems reluctant to speak of the Bible itself as revelation. In fact, he even goes as far as saying that it is not revelation in the proper sense of the word.[15]

Taken by themselves, these statements would suggest that McGrath denies the Bible as revelation. If so, then McGrath's position can once again be likened to Barth's. The Bible, according to Barth, is not to be understood as revelation. Rather, it is a witness to revelation. While speaking about the contents of the Old and New Testaments, Barth says, "The Old Testament like the New Testament is the witness to revelation, which is decidedly to be regarded as a free, utterly once-for-all, concrete action of God."[16] As Avery Dulles notes, "The Bible and the preaching of the Church bear witness to divine revelation but are not themselves revelation. In Barth's well-known terminology, Bible and proclamation as such are not the word of God, but they can become God's word and

---

14. McGrath, *Scientific Theology*, vol. 3, 152–53.

15. McGrath, *Science of God*, 209.

16. Barth, *Church Dogmatics*, vol. 1, 80.

his revelation if and insofar as Jesus Christ, the revealed Word of God, is pleased to speak to us through these chosen witnesses."[17]

One might read McGrath as following Barth in denying the Bible as God's revelation. Nevertheless, on closer examination, this view cannot be sustained. McGrath contends that "we must begin our analysis by noting the double meaning of the term 'revelation' within Christian dogmatics, embracing the notions of both revelatory *acts* and *knowledge* . . . The New Testament clearly presupposes that revelation has taken place, and that what has been entrusted to the community of faith represents a 'deposit' . . . which results from this revelation, and which may in itself legitimately be regarded as revelatory."[18] Then, while speaking about the eight different strata left by the original revelatory events, he says, "On a critical realist reading of the development of Christianity, a number of different levels of social construction may be identified . . . *which may be described as 'revelation' in the developed sense of the term*, which were brought into existence, or given a new depth of meaning, as a result of the original revelatory events which lie behind them, and which are handed on and transmitted through history."[19] Here McGrath seems to recognize that evangelicals use the word *revelation* to refer to the Bible, and appears to be comfortable doing the same. This is confirmed in *A Passion for Truth*, where McGrath suggests "revelation concerns the *oracles* of God, the *acts* of God, and the *person and presence of God*."[20] Therefore, unlike Barth, one can find places where McGrath is willing to refer to the Bible as revealed knowledge of God.

Thus, while it may appear that McGrath denies the Bible as God's revelation with his emphasis on revelation as an event, a closer examination shows that this is not the case. In truth, he affirms revelation as the event or action of God revealing himself to mankind while at the same time acknowledging that the Bible is understood to be revelation in the more developed sense of the word. Thus, McGrath's statement that "we do not presently have access to the totality of whatever 'revelation' might

17. Dulles, *Models of Revelation*, 87.

18. McGrath, *Scientific Theology*, vol. 3, 144.

19. Ibid., 146. Emphasis is mine. These eight levels include (1) texts—Bible, (2) patterns of worship, (3) ideas, (4) communities, (5) institutional structures, (6) images, (7) distinctive vocabulary, and (8) religious experience.

20. McGrath, *Passion for Truth*, 107.

be"[21] is not as problematic as it first appears. McGrath is not denying the Bible as revelation. Rather, he is simply showing how this doctrine can be used to explain the Christian tradition itself. Nevertheless, McGrath's ST could be strengthened by giving further clarification on this issue within the course of *A Scientific Theology* and *The Science of God*.

McGrath on the Inspiration of Scripture

Before the biblical concerns can be set aside, one further concern relating to the issue of inspiration needs to be addressed. Historically speaking, evangelicals affirm the doctrine of inspiration. As Dulles explains, evangelicals argue that the "Bible as a whole and in all its parts is so inspired that, in the original manuscripts, it is entirely free from error and is God's written word."[22] David Dockery and David Nelson describe an evangelical view of inspiration saying:

> First, Scripture is verbally inspired. That is, all the words (*graphe*, i.e., "writings") of the Bible are inspired. Second, the Scriptures are completely inspired. That is, all (*pas*) the words are inspired. Third, the Scriptures are divinely inspired. That is, God inspired all the words of Scripture (i.e., the words are *theopneustos*). Taken together, these truths form the concept of plenary-verbal inspiration. That is, all the words of the Bible are inspired by God. Fourth, we affirm that not only the text of the Bible, but the human authors were inspired by the Holy Spirit. That is, while they are truly human words, the words of the Scriptures, inspired by God, are truly the words of the divine author. Again, Scripture is the Word of God written in the words of man.[23]

An affirmation similar to this is found in *The Chicago Statement on Biblical Inerrancy*, which states, "We affirm that the whole of Scripture and all its parts, down to the very words of the original, were given by divine inspiration. We deny that the inspiration of Scripture can rightly be affirmed of the whole without the parts, or of some parts but not the whole."[24] Likewise, Carl F. H. Henry defines inspiration as "a supernatural influence upon divinely chosen prophets and apostles whereby the Spirit of God assures the truth and trustworthiness of their oral and

---

21. McGrath, *Scientific Theology*, vol. 3, 152.

22. Dulles, *Models of Revelation*, 38.

23. Dockery and Nelson, "Special Revelation," 134.

24. "Chicago Statement," 211–19.

written proclamation. Historic evangelical Christianity considers the Bible as the essential textbook because, in view of this quality, it inscripturates divinely revealed truth in verbal form."[25]

From what has already been said regarding McGrath's view of revelation, one should understand McGrath as affirming an evangelical view of inspiration as well. Nevertheless, throughout *A Scientific Theology* and *The Science of God*, McGrath is mostly silent on this issue. Yet, in his more recent work entitled, *The Order of Things: Explorations in Scientific Theology*, McGrath suggests that the "Bible is the creation of the church, intended to preserve both the foundational narratives of the Christian faith and their correct interpretation. It cannot be regarded as a text that fell from heaven."[26] While it is certainly true that the Bible did not fall from heaven, it is difficult to see that evangelicals will be comfortable with the statement that "the Bible is a creation of the church" since it seems to undermine the inspiration of Scripture and does not account for the Old Testament. The problem here is that McGrath makes this statement without any explanation as to what he means or why he says it. McGrath may simply be referring to the church's role in defining the canon, but this is not at all clear from the context of the statement. Thus, it would be helpful for McGrath to clarify this statement to avoid suspicion by fellow evangelicals.

Overall, there are some areas relating to McGrath's views on the doctrine of revelation that call for clarification or further development. Yet, the examination of these issues suggests that they are not as problematic as they first appear. Thus, the concerns do not warrant the rejection of his ST.

Clarifications Relating to Methodological Naturalism

In addition to the ambiguities relating to McGrath's view of revelation, there appears to be a methodological ambiguity that comes from McGrath's acceptance of theistic evolution.[27] By accepting theistic evolution, one wonders if McGrath may be tacitly accepting methodological naturalism (MN) as well. Since McGrath has not openly affirmed MN, however, one must be cautious in ascribing it to him. Nevertheless, if McGrath does

25. Henry, *God, Revelation and Authority*, 129.

26. McGrath, *Order of Things*, 217.

27. See McGrath, *Scientific Theology*, vol. 3, 273.

accept MN, evangelicals who are uncomfortable with this approach to science and theology will likely be uncomfortable with his ST. Thus, it is worth exploring this issue to see if it can be determined that McGrath affirms MN, and if he does, is this affirmation essential to his ST?

MN should be distinguished from metaphysical naturalism. Metaphysical naturalism suggests that natural or material entities are all that exist. In this view, there are no non-physical or non-material aspects of reality. In methodological naturalism, however, one may affirm the existence of non-material entities, but still require that science proceed on purely natural grounds. As J. P. Moreland notes, one of the major features of MN is its attempt to "explain contingent natural phenomena strictly in terms of other contingent natural phenomena . . . explanations refer only to natural objects and events and not to the personal choices and actions of human or divine agents."[28]

Interestingly, Garrett J. DeWeese and J. P. Moreland observe how those who affirm theistic evolution "usually hold that science presupposes methodological naturalism."[29] In their view, MN and theistic evolution seem to go together. Therefore, by accepting theistic evolution, one wonders if McGrath also accepts MN. Suspicion of McGrath on this point is increased by considering his reason for rejecting creationism and intelligent design (ID). In his mind, accepting any form of creationism or ID requires one to hold a god-of-the-gaps approach to the relationship between theology and science.[30] This, as Del Ratzsch notes, is one of the major reasons that a person typically embraces MN.[31]

While explaining his reason for rejecting ID in *The Dawkins Delusion*, McGrath says it "argues for an 'Intelligent Designer' based on gaps in scientific explanation, such as the 'irreducible complexity' of the world. It is not an approach which I accept, either on scientific or theological grounds. In my view, those who adopt this approach make Christianity deeply—and needlessly—vulnerable to scientific progress."[32] Thus, as one opposed to a god-of-the-gaps approach to science and theology, McGrath rejects ID and embraces theistic evolution. Though not conclusive, this raises the question as to whether or not McGrath has

---

28. Moreland, "Theistic Science," 46.

29. DeWeese and Moreland, *Philosophy Made*, 140.

30. McGrath and McGrath, *Dawkins Delusion*, 10–12.

31. Ratzsch, *Science & Limits*, 122.

32. McGrath and McGrath, *Dawkins Delusion*, 12.

tacitly accepted MN. If so, evangelicals who are opposed to MN may view his ST with suspicion.[33]

Thus, McGrath's rejection of ID and acceptance of theistic evolution raises the question of whether or not he affirms MN. Nevertheless, one must remember that McGrath has not explicitly stated that he accepts MN as the appropriate model for scientific investigation. At most, one could simply say that an acceptance of MN is implied in his acceptance of theistic evolution. Second, the fact that McGrath is insistent on viewing nature as creation indicates a commitment to incorporate theological considerations into the explanation of reality. For example, as chapters 2 and 4 explain, McGrath uses the Christian doctrine of creation as an ontological and epistemological basis for the scientific enterprise.[34]

In the end, it does not appear that McGrath requires MN in his ST, even though there are some philosophers who observe a connection between theistic evolution and MN.[35] Even if McGrath does accept MN, however, the fact that he does not explicitly affirm it in his writings on ST demonstrates that it is non-essential to his project. Thus, evangelicals who are opposed to MN can embrace McGrath's ST without hesitation. At most, McGrath's acceptance of theistic evolution and rejection of ID call for clarification on the issue of MN. It does not, however, mean that his ST should be rejected by opponents of MN.

CLARIFICATIONS RELATING TO NATURAL THEOLOGY

Leaving the constructive aspects of McGrath's natural theology for chapter 4, this section explores the ambiguities that arise from his reintroduction of natural theology into Christian theology. This section will address issues in need of clarification:

1. Does McGrath's natural theology have any appeal to nonbelievers?

2. Does McGrath see any distinction between natural theology and natural revelation?

3. Does McGrath see any value in the arguments for God's existence?

---

33. Examples of evangelicals who find MN to be problematic include Reynolds, "Getting God Pass"; Plantinga, "Methodological Naturalism," 143–54; DeWeese and Moreland, *Philosophy*, 140. See also Moreland, "Theistic Science," and "Science, Miracles, Agency Theory," 127.

34. McGrath, *Scientific Theology*, vol. 1, 222.

35. See Moreland, DeWeese, and Ratzsch above.

Issue 1 arises, not from a lack of clarification in McGrath's ST, but from William Abraham's criticisms of McGrath's approach to natural theology. Since Abraham is only one of the few evangelicals to criticize McGrath's ST, this is an important issue for this chapter to consider.

The Appeal of McGrath's Natural Theology for the Nonbeliever

William Abraham suggests that McGrath's use and development of natural theology is inadequate since it does not give the non-believer any reason to believe that nature is God's creation in the first place. That is, according to Abraham, McGrath's approach to natural theology works fine for the believer, but there is nothing about it that would cause the non-believer to accept it. He says:

> The conclusion he drives home is that it is possible to have a genuine natural theology so long as we relocate natural theology within revealed theology. Over against natural theology as an autonomous, independent exercise, we can bring new life back into it by reconstructing it as an appeal to the order of creation that confirms what God made known in special divine revelation through Jesus Christ. Thereby we can overcome Karl Barth's veto on natural theology, vindicate T. F. Torrance's extension of Barth's epistemological vision, and open up a fresh engagement with the natural sciences."[36]

He later adds that the major problem with McGrath's approach to natural theology is

> that it has no way of securing its initial commitment to the divine revelation from which it derives its theory of universal rationality . . . Now we can well grant that theologians are at liberty to work from within this circle of faith. However, they surely need to provide some account as to why we should enter this circle of faith in the first place. These are massively substantial proposals that cannot simply be built into the operation at the outset. Yet this is precisely what Torrance and McGrath do.[37]

In short, Abraham thinks that McGrath's approach to natural theology provides no reason for those outside the Christian tradition to accept it. Thus, Abraham has been resistant to accept McGrath's approach to natural theology for this reason.

36. Abraham, "Revelation and Natural Theology," 266–67.
37. Ibid., 272.

Is Abraham's assessment of McGrath's position valid? McGrath does not think so. For one thing, McGrath thinks that Abraham's approach requires a universally accepted rationality held by all people. He says, "Where Abraham and I differ is that I hold that rationality is mediated and constituted by traditions. In taking this position, I have been influenced both by the general collapse of the Enlightenment project, by a reading of modern Western philosophy which stresses its failure to achieve its own goals."[38] Moreover, McGrath suggests that Abraham's criticisms are premature since they were written prior to the completion of volumes 2 and 3 of *A Scientific Theology* in which McGrath explains the way his approach does appeal to those outside the Christian tradition. He says:

> In a nutshell, my approach is particularist with universal extensions; in other words, I hold that the Christian tradition is determined and defined by a set of particularities, but that it nevertheless possesses universal explanatory potential and salvific efficacy. A Christian natural theology, speaking from within the Christian tradition and from a Christian—not universal—perspective offers a specific vantage point from which the intellectual landscape may be charted and explained. Though tradition specific, it has aspirations to universality precisely because the story that it relates offers an ultimate and coherent organizing logic that accounts for its own existence, as well as that of its rivals. In short: natural theology offers and accounts for a transtraditional rationality, which is grounded in the particularities of the Christian tradition alone.[39]

As McGrath indicates, Abraham's objection is answered in volume 2, where McGrath shows how a natural theology that operates from within the Christian tradition can be used to explain mathematics in addition to the quest for beauty and goodness.[40] In volume 3, McGrath also argues that his version of natural theology can also be used to explain other religious traditions. He says, "The kind of natural theology which a scientific theology seeks to justify and commend offers an account of the trans-traditional truth, beauty and goodness which does not require the interposition of an additional tradition . . . in order to offer an expla-

---

38. McGrath, "Contributors," 358.

39. Ibid., 359–60.

40. McGrath, *Scientific Theology*, vol. 2, 78–96.

nation of some of the most fundamental impulses of the human mind. A Christian natural theology is a tradition-specific construal with universal applicability, thus both offering an explanation of other traditions, while at the same time reinforcing its own plausibility."[41] Elsewhere he suggests that his approach to natural theology "offers a comprehensive means by which theology may address the world, and engage in productive dialogue concerning the legitimation and consequences of belief systems."[42] Because of this, McGrath's natural theology has an explanatory power that transcends the Christian tradition. This in turn gives it the ability to appeal to those outside the Christian tradition. Therefore, Abraham's critique of McGrath appears to be premature and unfounded.

Distinctions between Natural Theology and Natural Revelation

Within *A Scientific Theology* and *The Science of God*, McGrath does not make any distinction between natural theology and natural revelation. In fact, he tends to describe natural theology in language typically applied to natural revelation. For example, McGrath sees natural theology as the practice of seeing the world in such a way that one can find support for the preexisting belief in God. He defines natural theology "as the enterprise of seeing nature as creation, which both presupposes and reinforces fundamental Christian theological affirmations."[43] Elsewhere he says, "The traditional view, with which I can find no convincing reason to disagree, is to affirm that there is an intrinsic capacity within the created order to disclose God. Here, nature-as-creation is understood to have an ontologically grounded capacity to reflect God as its maker and originator."[44] Thus, for McGrath, "Natural theology is not intended to prove the existence of God, but presupposes that existence; it then asks, 'What should we expect the natural world to be like if it has indeed been created by such a God?' The search for order in nature is therefore intended not to demonstrate that God exists, but to reinforce the plausibility of an already existing belief."[45] This understanding of natural theology, as chapter 4 will show, has some positive and helpful aspects. Nevertheless, what is lacking in McGrath's definition is any distinction between natural theology and natural revelation.

41. McGrath, *Scientific Theology*, vol. 3, 195.

42. McGrath, *Scientific Theology*, vol. 1, 303.

43. McGrath, *Science of God*, 113.

44. McGrath, *Scientific Theology*, vol. 1, 297.

45. McGrath, *Science of God*, 81.

While McGrath may simply see natural theology and natural revelation as one and the same, William Lane Craig makes a clear distinction. He says, "I think it is clear that the arguments of natural theology are not identical with general revelation; general revelation is the traits of the author reflected in his product, the fingerprints of the potter in the clay, so to speak, whereas the arguments of natural theology are the human products of men's rational reflection upon general revelation."[46] The difference here is that, in the mind of Craig, natural revelation deals with what can been known of God through creation, while natural theology deals with the application of that knowledge in the formulation of arguments for God's existence. Either way, those who distinguish between natural revelation and natural theology will see this as an ambiguity in need of clarification.[47]

McGrath and the Arguments for God's Existence

A final ambiguity in McGrath's natural theology arises from the previous one. Even if McGrath makes no distinction between natural revelation and natural theology, it would be helpful to know if he sees value in any of the arguments for God's existence. Since he does not answer this question within his writings on ST, philosophers interested in doing apologetics may see McGrath's natural theology as being of no significant value.

Throughout *A Scientific Theology*, McGrath has much to say about natural theology in general, but very little of this discussion centers on the arguments for the existence of God. It seems that McGrath considers such arguments to be a product of modern versions of natural theology that attempted to arrive at certain theological conclusions without reference to the Bible. He argues, "Historically, it is clear that patristic writers did not see natural theology as offering proofs of God's existence. The existence of God was taken for granted."[48] Like the patristic writers, McGrath wants to avoid using natural theology as a proof for God's existence. He suggests that "natural theology gains its plausibility and derives its intellectual foundations from within the Christian tradition . . . It is not a tradition-independent or autonomous intellectual discipline, in that its legitimation rests upon a Christian doctrine of creation—

46. Craig, "Classical Apologetics," 39.

47. Ibid., 39; Erickson, *Christian Theology*, 194–96; and Spykman, *Reformational Theology*, 168–70.

48. McGrath, *Scientific Theology*, vol. 1, 266.

including the related concepts of the contingent ordering of the created world, and the epistemic and spiritual capacities of human nature."[49] Thus, James Keating thinks that McGrath returns to a premodern approach to natural theology. He says, "In premodern theologies, consideration of how nature provides some access to God took place within a theological framework determined by Christian revelation. In contrast, the modern conception of natural theology bears the marks of its origins in the Enlightenment desire to create a theology free of the church and beholden to universal reason alone."[50]

Nevertheless, it is not clear that the arguments for God's existence must be employed in this modernistic fashion. That is, it seems that one can start within the Christian tradition—as McGrath clearly wants to do—and use the arguments for God's existence as a confirmation of an already existing belief in God. This is the approach suggested by the late Ronald Nash who, for epistemological reasons, wanted to avoid a foundationalist approach to religious belief. He says, "Suppose, in other words, that instead of seeking coercive proofs for conclusions that all right-minded and open-minded persons would accept, we view our task as the more modest one of seeing if the Christian worldview does what we should expect any worldview to do."[51]

As chapter 4 argues, there is much about McGrath's approach to natural theology that is commendable for evangelicals. Here, however, a number of questions have been raised that, if clarified, would make his treatment of natural theology even clearer. In particular, it would be helpful for McGrath to clarify whether he sees a difference between natural revelation and natural theology and whether or not he sees any value in the arguments for God's existence. Nevertheless, these questions do not require one to discard his approach to natural theology, much less his larger project of ST.

ADDITIONAL ISSUES IN NEED
OF CLARIFICATION OR DEVELOPMENT

Before this chapter closes, it is worth mentioning a few more areas where some clarification would be helpful. First, in reading *A Scientific*

---

49. McGrath, *Scientific Theology*, vol. 2, 74.

50. Keating, "Natural Sciences," 132.

51. Nash, *Faith & Reason*, 96.

Theology, one wonders how McGrath keeps nature, history, and experience from playing a larger role than the Bible in informing Christian theology. This issue arises in McGrath's theological application of Roy Bhaskar's notion of a stratified reality.[52] He says, "A somewhat overdue theological 'return to history' was signaled with the publication of the collection of essays, edited by Wolfhart Pannenberg, entitled *Revelation as History.* Fundamental to Pannenberg's argument is the idea that God's self-revelation is indirect, rather than direct; and that this indirect revelation takes place within the publicly accessible history."[53] Then, while speaking about the value of experience, McGrath suggests, "Some seem to believe that a theology may be grounded in experience simply as a means of progressing beyond experience, and reaching out to new and more relevant theological pastures. Yet the key to engagement with any aspect of reality is not to leave it behind, abandoning it in favour of some more attractive goal. Rather, it is to be incorporated into the vision of reality that theology offers; it is to be transformed, not discarded."[54] In short, when applying the notion of stratification to theology, McGrath appears to elevate things like experience and history to the same level as the Bible. This becomes even clearer when he says "Christian revelation holds that God's revelation is to be located in nature, history, in personal experience, in the life of the church, and especially in Scripture."[55]

The concern here is not that McGrath allows history and experience to inform theology. Rather, it seems that he may be allowing experience and history to play too large a role in the development of theology by elevating them to the level of revelation. According to Elmer Colyer, this is one of the crucial aspects of McGrath's ST that is underdeveloped.[56] Theologians may use the life of the church, history, and experience as interpretive tools, but this is different from viewing them as actual sources of divine revelation. To do the latter seems to place them on equal footing with the Bible itself, and opens the door for them to play an inordinately large role in informing Christian theology. Thus, further development or clarification by McGrath on this point would be of value.

52. McGrath, *Scientific Theology,* vol. 2, 239.

53. Ibid., 242.

54. Ibid., 243.

55. Ibid., 227.

56. Colyer, "Scientific Theology, vol. 2," 494.

A second issue in need of clarification stems from McGrath's proposal of ST as being Christocentric in nature. He notes:

> To engage with, or operate faithfully within, the Christian tradition thus demands a recognition of the central role of Christ in Christian life, thought and devotion. It may be attractive to treat Christianity simply as a variant of theism; this however fails to do justice to its Trinitarian morphology, which in turn represents its incarnational foundations. A scientific theology, by seeking to do justice to Christianity *as it actually is*—rather than some reconstructed variant—will thus have to take the centrality of Christ with the uttermost seriousness.[57]

On the surface, this certainly appears to be harmless and even faithful to the Christian tradition. Some evangelicals, however, could see this as a cause for concern. Colyer says, "I suspect that this will generate some concern among conservative evangelicals, for it distances McGrath from those evangelical rationalists whose focus is more on propositionalist *Scriptocentrism*."[58] By choosing to be Christocentric, as opposed to bibliocentric, one may open the door for the abandonment of orthodox Christianity. This could happen if one substitutes the Christ of the Bible and history with the Christ of faith. McGrath notes this concern in his earlier work *A Passion for Truth* while speaking about others who have taken a Christocentric approach. He says, "It is very difficult to read the writings of, for example, the noted German liberal Protestant theologian Adolf von Harnack (1851–1930) without gaining the impression that the Jesus whom he regards as significant is ultimately a construction of his own making, representing an objectification of his own values and feelings."[59] Thus, as McGrath rightly notes, a Christocentric approach can be undesirable if the Christ in view is anything other than the biblical figure.

In fairness to McGrath, he acknowledges and attempts to resolve this concern in *A Passion for Truth*. He says, "Evangelicalism argues that authority is inherent in the person of Christ, and insists that it is of paramount importance to remain as faithful as possible to the New Testament portrayal of Christ, no matter how complex and nuanced this may prove to be."[60] He later adds, "Scripture centers on and enfolds Christ, who can

57. McGrath, *Scientific Theology*, vol. 2, 301.

58. Colyer, "Scientific Theology, vol. 2," 495.

59. McGrath, *Passion for Truth*, 29.

60. Ibid., 30.

be known definitively only through its medium. Scripture, when rightly interpreted, leads to Christ; Christ can be known properly only through Scripture."[61] Thus, this concern should not be a major issue for evangelicals. It would, however, be helpful for McGrath to make this position clearer in his works on ST.

A final area in need of clarification and development deals with the relationship between universals and particulars. In volumes 1 and 2, McGrath makes a clear connection between particulars (creation) and that which transcends and gives existence to the particulars (God). He says, for example, "Creation exists because God exists; the reality of creation both mirrors and models the reality of God . . . The reality of God and the derived and contingent reality of the creation can thus be seen as distinct, yet clearly related, strata of reality."[62] Earlier, McGrath suggests this connection while pointing to the Christological dimensions of creation. He argues:

> The Christological dimensions of the doctrine of creation are such that the divine rationality—whether this is conceptualized as logos or as ratio—must be thought of as being embedded in creation and embodied in Christ. The same divine rationality or wisdom which the natural sciences discern within the created order is to be identified within the logos incarnate, Jesus Christ. Creation and Christ ultimately bear witness to the same God, and the same divine rationality.[63]

Thus, in McGrath's ST, Christ is the one who caused creation and is also reflected in it. But this does not mean that he goes as far as affirming the existence of universals.[64] In fact, epistemologically speaking, McGrath places a high priority on particulars and seems to view the concept of universals with suspicion. He says:

> At their most authentic, and hence also at their best, both the natural sciences and Christian theology are characterized by a living empirical curiosity about particulars—particulars which may well lead on to the founding of a universal view of reality, or may equally lead to its foundering through a failure to account for them in sufficient detail or number. As we shall see presently,

---

61. Ibid., 54.

62. McGrath, *Scientific Theology*, vol. 2, 228.

63. McGrath, *Scientific Theology*, vol. 1, 24–25.

64. Moreland and Craig, *Philosophical Foundations*, 147.

> to abandon reverential attention for particularities . . . is to value
> provisional derived universalities over and above what brought
> them into being in the first place, and must ultimately determine
> their credibility and utility. A healthy suspicion of universals is
> thus the natural epistemological attitude of a scientific theology,
> which insists upon redeeming particulars, rather than submerg-
> ing and losing them in an allegedly universal theory.[65]

He later adds that "the particulars always take epistemological prece-
dence over the universal, precisely because the validity of the allegedly
'universal' is to be regarded as provisional, rather than final."[66]

Given what McGrath has to say about the ontological connection
between God and creation, it is hard to imagine that McGrath would
deny the existence of universals altogether. If he should, however, the
basis for knowledge and morality would be undermined substantially.
But this does not seem to be what McGrath has done. In fact, volume 1
is primarily concerned with showing how creation (particulars) is ontologically dependent on God. In truth, he is placing the emphasis on
particulars epistemologically while keeping them ontologically dependent on universals. That is, creation (particulars) derives its existence
from God and is thus ontologically dependant upon him. At the same
time, man gains knowledge of the metaphysical realm by way of particulars and therefore cannot pretend to have full and perfect knowledge
of universals. Thus, epistemologically speaking, McGrath places greatest
emphasis on the particulars. He has raised some important issues concerning the way knowledge is gained from particulars, but the issue of
universals would benefit from further development in his ST.

CONCLUSION

This chapter focuses on some of the areas of ambiguity within McGrath's
ST. Though each of the issues is important epistemologically and theologically, it appears that they should not prevent evangelicals from
adopting McGrath's critical realist approach to theological method.
At most, the areas of concern discussed in this chapter call for further
clarification or development, but do not serve as defeaters for his ST. The
book now turns to consider the constructive aspects of his project.

---

65. McGrath, *Scientific Theology*, vol. 3, 31.
66. Ibid., 41.

4

A Positive Assessment
of McGrath's Scientific Theology

THIS CHAPTER FOCUSES ON the constructive aspects of Alister E. McGrath's scientific theology (ST). The discussion centers around three major issues that are essential to McGrath's ST, including Roy Bhaskar's critical realism, the Christian Doctrine of creation, and the function of natural theology. It will be argued here that McGrath's work on these points makes a valuable contribution toward an evangelical theological method.

MCGRATH'S APPLICATION OF BHASKAR'S CRITICAL REALISM

At the very center of McGrath's ST is an endorsement and application of Roy Bhaskar's critical realism (CR). Like other critical realists, Bhaskar observes the need to deal with the objective and subjective aspects of human knowledge. By positing a transitive as well as an intransitive dimension of knowledge, Bhaskar thinks this can be accomplished. He notes, "Any adequate philosophy of science must be capable of sustaining and reconciling both aspects of science; that is, of showing how science which is a transitive process, dependent upon antecedent knowledge and the efficient activity of men, has intransitive objects which depend upon neither. That is, it must be capable of sustaining both the social character of science and the independence from science of the objects of scientific thought."[1] Elsewhere he says:

---

1. Bhaskar, *Realist Theory*, 24. Bhaskar refers to the transitive aspects of science as those that arise from previous knowledge while the intransitive deals with that which exists independently of human observation.

> If the objects of our knowledge exist and act independently of the knowledge of which they are the objects, it is equally the case that such knowledge as we actually possess always consists in historically specific social forms. Thus to think our way clearly in the philosophy of science we need to constitute a *transitive* dimension or philosophical sociology to complement the intransitive dimension or philosophical ontology already established. A moment's reflection will show that, unless one does so, any attempt to establish the irreducibility of knowable being to thought must end in failure.[2]

Thus, Bhaskar thinks that human knowledge is derived from objective entities as well as socially determined factors. Such a view is typically referred to as a critical realist position.

John Polkinghorne notes that CR is "a realist position because it claims the attainment of increasingly verisimilitudinous knowledge of the nature of the physical world. It is a critical realist position because that knowledge is not directly obtained by looking at what is going on, but it requires a subtle and creative interaction between interpretation and experiment. This acknowledgement of somewhat oblique discernment gives science a degree of kinship with other forms of human enquiry."[3] Elsewhere, he suggests:

> Critical realists] believe that it is possible to attain best explanations of experience that correspond to a verisimilitudinous account of what is going on. They acknowledge that there are constraints of cultural perspective and expectation to be taken into account in assessing this search for understanding, but they believe these constraints can be allowed for and that they do not determine the outcome of the inquiry. The latter arises from conformity with the way things are.[4]

As noted earlier, in chapter 2, McGrath says, "The term 'critical realism' has come to be used within theological circles to designate a style of realism which is sensitive to the historically situated and personally involved character of theological knowledge, while resolutely declining to let go of the ideals of truth, objectivity and rationality."[5] To help distin-

---

2. Bhaskar, *Possibility of Naturalism*, 11.

3. Polkinghorne, *Science & Theology*, 17.

4. Polkinghorne, *Scientists as Theologians*, 4.

5. McGrath, *Scientific Theology*, vol. 2, 195.

guish CR from a modern or postmodern epistemology, McGrath makes the following distinctions:

1. Naïve realism: Reality impacts directly upon the human mind, without any reflection on the part of the human knower. The resulting knowledge is directly determined by an objective reality within the world.

2. Critical realism: Reality is apprehended by the human mind which attempts to express and accommodate that reality as best it can with the tools at its disposal—such as mathematical formulae or mental models.

3. Postmodern anti-realism: The human mind freely constructs its ideas without any reference to an alleged external world.[6]

Thus, as McGrath explains it, CR is realism that recognizes "the active involvement of the knower in the process of knowing."[7]

Throughout *A Scientific Theology* and *The Science of God*, McGrath makes it clear that he is influenced specifically by Roy Bhaskar's version of CR. He says, "Bhaskar's work was hailed as marking a 'Copernican Revolution' in the study of the natural sciences precisely because it transcended an increasingly sterile conflict concerning the achievements of the natural sciences, as well as illuminating the classic conflict between empiricists and rationalists."[8] As McGrath explains, "The attractiveness of Bhaskar's critical realism lies partly in its advantages in dealing with the classic issues of the philosophy of science in the light of the increasing recognition of the socially-conditioned character of scientific practice, and partly in its clear potential as a means of engaging with intellectual disciplines beyond the natural sciences."[9]

McGrath also believes that Bhaskar's approach is valuable since it recognizes that different levels of reality require different methods of investigation. In Bhaskar's view, "Only the concept of ontological depth can reveal the actual historical stratification of the sciences as anything other than an accident. For this can now be seen as grounded in the multi-tiered stratification of reality, and the consequent logic-of-discov-

6. McGrath, *Science of God*, 141.
7. McGrath, *Scientific Theology*, vol. 2, 196.
8. Ibid., 209.
9. Ibid., 213.

ery *that* stratification imposes on science."[10] He then says, "Now for the transcendental realist the stratification this form of explanation imposes upon our knowledge reflects a real stratification in the world. Without the concept of real strata apart from our knowledge of strata we could not make sense of what the scientist, striving to move from knowledge of one stratum to knowledge of the next, is trying to do."[11]

As McGrath then explains, "Bhaskar explicitly recognizes the importance of ontology in the philosophy of science. Any theory of knowledge, he argues, ultimately presupposes and rests upon an ontological commitment concerning the objects of that knowledge, whether this is explicitly acknowledged or not."[12] According to McGrath, instead of forcing all modes of inquiry to use the same methodology, "Bhaskar argues that each science develops methodologies appropriate to their ontologies—that is to say that the proper working method of any given science is determined by the character of its objects of investigation, and cannot be determined *a priori* on the basis of some implicit foundationalism. Methodology is consequent upon ontology, and is hence to be determined *a posteriori*."[13] Bhaskar underscores this by saying:

> A general pattern of scientific activity emerges from this. When a stratum of reality has been adequately described the next step consists in the discovery of the mechanisms responsible for behavior at that level. The key move in this involves the postulation of hypothetical entities and mechanisms, whose reality can then be ascertained. Such entities need not be smaller in size, though in physics and chemistry this has normally proved to be the case.[14]

Thus, according to McGrath, ST is most helped by the following conclusions from Bhaskar's CR:

1. A scientific theology may legitimately be regarded as a response to an existing reality whose existence is independent of the actuality or possibility of human observation.

2. Each intellectual discipline must adopt a methodology appropriate to, and determined by, the ontology of its specific object. Its methodology is thus determined *a posteriori* rather than *a priori*.[15]

---

10. Bhaskar, *Possibility of Naturalism*, 13.

11. Bhaskar, *Realist Theory*, 170.

12. McGrath, *Scientific Theology*, vol. 2, 210–11.

13. Ibid., 12.

14. Bhaskar, *Realist Theory*, 169.

15. McGrath, *Science of God*, 151.

With Bhaskar's notion of CR in hand, McGrath contends that ST is marked by four essential characteristics. He says ST

1. takes the form of a coherent response to an existing reality;

2. is an *a posteriori* discipline;

3. takes account of the unique character of its objects;

4. offers an explanation of reality.[16]

Thus, McGrath is heavily influenced by Roy's Bhaskar's CR. In this, he thinks that evangelicals can avoid the pitfalls of modernity and postmodernity. In the next section, McGrath's use of CR is examined to show how it is advantageous to a modern and postmodern perspective.

Assessment of McGrath's Use of Critical Realism

Throughout *A Scientific Theology* and *The Science of God*, McGrath argues that a critical realist perspective is superior to a modern or postmodern perspective. He says, "Against postmodernism, critical realism affirms that there is a reality, which may be known, and which we are under a moral and intellectual obligation to investigate and represent as best as we can. Against certain types of modernism, critical realism affirms that the human knower is involved in the process of knowing, thus raising immediately the possibility of the use of 'constructions'—such as analogies, models, and more specifically social constructs—as suitably adapted means for representing what is encountered."[17] Although Nancey Murphy believes that CR is not the answer to the difficulties raised by modernity and postmodernity,[18] others such as Arthur Peacocke suggest that CR is "the most appropriate and adequate philosophy concerning religious language and theological propositions."[19] In the following pages, an assessment of McGrath's use of CR is given, which highlights the benefits that come from his approach. It is argued that his approach is beneficial for evangelicals, since it avoids the dangers of modernity and postmodernity by steering a middle way between the two. McGrath's ST does this by:

16. McGrath, *Scientific Theology*, vol. 2, 246.

17. McGrath, *Science of God*, 142.

18. See Murphy, *Theology*, 198. Also see "Relating Theology and Science," 7.

19. Peacocke, *Theology for a Scientific Age*, 14.

1. Affirming realism and the possibility of knowledge

2. Affirming a correspondence theory of truth

3. Moving beyond classical foundationalism

4. Acknowledging the mediated nature of knowledge

5. Establishing a unified theory of knowledge

6. Avoiding reductionism

7. Giving a balanced perspective on the issue of certainty

ST Affirms Realism and the Possibility of Knowledge

As mentioned in chapter 2, McGrath clearly distinguishes his critical realist understanding of reality from a postmodern anti-realist view that leads to skepticism or relativism. McGrath explains how postmodernism contends that "the alleged 'objectivity' of knowledge has been called into question, and displaced by an increasing emphasis upon the social construction of reality. Postmodern writers have argued that our intellectual worlds are free constructs of the autonomous individual, who is unrestricted in that process of construction by external limitations or pressures."[20] In McGrath's view, however, there is a real objective world that exists independently of individual minds and that can be known. He says, "Realism remains the most satisfying and resilient account of the outcome of the human engagement with the natural world, despite the rhetoric of scorn directed against it by postmodern thinkers and others. The natural sciences are widely judged to have successfully seen off postmodern criticisms of their fundamental assumptions."[21] As Benjamin Myers explains, McGrath "critiques postmodern anti-realism, noting that postmodern thinkers have typically failed to reckon seriously with the explanatory successes of the natural sciences."[22] Likewise, Elmer Colyer says, "McGrath points to the profound explanatory success of natural science and its approach, which is realist without being foundationalist and constructivist without being relativistic. By so doing, McGrath establishes that there are critical realist alternatives to the either/or modern/postmodern epistemological debate."[23]

20. McGrath, *Science of God*, 106.

21. McGrath, *Scientific Theology*, vol. 2, 197.

22. Myers, "McGrath's Scientific Theology," 11.

23. Colyer, "Scientific Theology, vol. 2," 493.

While talking about the epistemological commitments of the natural sciences, McGrath says, "Despite all the qualifications that must be entered against our broad statement that theory must be grounded in or consistent with experimental observations, the general principle holds: scientific theories must be grounded in the real world. They are accountable to the reality they purport to represent. Ontological finality thus rests with nature itself."[24] He then says, "The natural sciences and mathematics are the two most awkward stumbling-blocks to the advancement of the postmodern agenda. The natural sciences offer no support for the relativism of the postmodern project."[25]

But this is not all. McGrath also thinks that a realist perspective is preferred for theology as well. He says, "In the case of Christian theology, it is possible to argue for an *extrasystemic* accountability to a set of realities which are held to be 'foundational' to the Christian tradition (meaning that they underlie its distinctive claims), without falling into the discredited and outmoded Enlightenment belief that they are 'foundational' in the sense of being purely rational axioms, independent of the contingencies of history and culture."[26] Thus, as John Roche concludes, McGrath's "critically realist theology would wish to affirm the reality of all of these elements independently of our attempts to describe them, and that these rich realities control our descriptions."[27] Unlike his postmodern counterparts, McGrath clearly affirms a realist perspective of reality.

By adopting a realist perspective, McGrath places himself in the company of a significant number of evangelicals who defend this position. Noting that a realist perspective is clearly the dominant position of natural scientists, Alan Padgett, for example, also thinks that this is the preferred position in religion as well. He says, "I believe there are good arguments for realism even in religion. The first is that this is the viewpoint of almost all religious believers. The Ultimate Reality that they worship and live for must be real in order for it to be worshiped and for prayer to make sense."[28] Albert Mohler seems to agree when he says, "Our claim is not to preach one truth among many, about one savior among many, through one gospel among many. We do not believe that

24. McGrath, *Scientific Theology*, vol. 2, 16.

25. McGrath, *Science of God*, 107.

26. Ibid., 101.

27. Roche, "Scientific Theology Project," 54.

28. Padgett, *Science and Study*, 36.

the Christian gospel is a socially constructed truth, but the truth that sets sinners free. It is objectively, historically, and universally true."[29] Mohler goes on to suggest that the "anti-realism of postmodern theology is faced with severe limitations, and is thus unsustainable. Some correspondence understanding of truth is inherent to every important truth claim. Once again, we could not operate in everyday life without a basic dependence upon a correspondence theory of truth."[30]

Others reject postmodern anti-realism because it does not make sense of human experience. Kees van Kooten Niekerk explains:

> Sensations (at least of the exemplified type) confront me with a world which I have good reasons to believe is a real, external world, and which exists independently of me. At the same time, however, they cannot be precise reflections of that world. This appears from the fact that I can have different sensations of the same thing in different situations. My table looks different from different angles. Its color changes with the light.[31]

David Clark seems to agree, claiming that most people "assume that various sorts of entities, beings, properties, or relations actually exist outside a speaker's mind. Most people, in other words, are metaphysical realists."[32] Perhaps this is why a realist position has been the dominant position of the western world from the classical period forward. As Mortimer Adler puts it, "In the history of Western thought . . . a profound understanding of truth has prevailed from the time of Plato and Aristotle to the present. This understanding rests upon a single supposition; namely, that there exists, quite independent of the human mind, a reality which the human mind thinks about and tries to know."[33]

Before moving on, one further point is worth noting. Some evangelicals are also uncomfortable with anti-realism because it seems to lead toward skepticism or relativism. Esther Meek, for example, says "the central thrust of what we call postmodernism would have us reject the ideas of truth and reality. That is why I suggest that postmodernism calls us to skepticism."[34] And, as she makes clear, skepticism is not an acceptable position. She notes:

29. Mohler, "Truth and Culture," 59.

30. Ibid., 68.

31. van Kooten Niekerk, "Critical Realist Perspective," 55–56.

32. Clark, *To Know and Love God*, 353.

33. Adler, *Truth In Religion*, 116.

34. Meek, *Longing to Know*, 34.

For knowing nothing at all, you and I seem to know quite a lot. Or at least we seem to live like it—that is, when it isn't more personally advantageous to be skeptics. Vast portions of our lives and jobs and society are devoted to information, learning, and discovery. What's more, we continually make advances from unknowing to knowing, whether in the classroom or the science lab or in the ordinary affairs of life.[35]

Later on, she adds: "It is not responsible to deny objective truth and reality in knowing; it is irresponsible. It is not responsible to make the human knower or community of knowers the arbiters of a private truth and reality; it is irresponsible."[36] Mohler agrees, saying he is "convinced that postmodernism is an irresponsible, cowardly abrogation of the duties that constitute a disciple's calling to be a Christian intellectual and teacher."[37]

For those evangelicals who are uncomfortable with postmodernism because of its anti-realist commitments, McGrath's ST offers a viable alternative since it is "unquestionably committed to a realist perspective."[38] Though McGrath is careful to distinguish himself from the naïve realism of the Enlightenment, he has clearly affirmed his belief in an objective reality that can be known.

ST Affirms a Correspondence Theory of Truth

McGrath's ST is also advantageous to a postmodern perspective since it affirms a correspondence theory of truth. Throughout *A Scientific Theology* and *The Science of God*, McGrath clarifies that scientific theories and religious doctrines are only valid if they correspond to the reality they seek to explain. According to McGrath:

[Theories] are determined and controlled by the external reality to which they are a response. Yet theories are not passive responses to reality; they are constructed by human minds, and therefore bear at least something of a socially located imprint. We must therefore give thought to the process by which theories are generated, developed and received within the scientific and theological communities from a critical realist perspective.[39]

35. Ibid., 31
36. Ibid., 148.
37. Mohler, "Truth and Culture," 91.
38. McGrath, *Scientific Theology*, vol. 2, 199.
39. McGrath, *Scientific Theology*, vol. 3, xiv.

Thus, McGrath contends that his ST "is impelled, by its vision of reality, to attempt to offer an account of the totality of all things, believing that the Christian tradition both encourages such an enterprise in the first place, and in the second, makes the necessary resources available through its understanding of the economy of salvation, particularly its doctrine of creation."[40] Put another way, McGrath says, "A scientific theology holds that theories, whether scientific or theological, are not free creations of the human mind, but are constructed in response to an encounter with an existing reality. Theory is responsible, in that it is accountable to the community of faith for the manner in which it depicts its corporate vision of reality—a vision which it did not create in the first place, and to which it represents a considered and faithful response."[41]

Since McGrath argues for the necessity of theories (whether scientific or theological) to represent things the way they actually are, it is hard to see how he could be labeled as anything but a proponent of a correspondence theory of truth. A theory simply cannot represent the world as it is without a degree of correspondence. To be sure, however, one should note that McGrath believes his ST offers "a view of the world, including God, which is both internally consistent and which is grounded in the structures of the real world. It aims to achieve extra-systemic correspondence with intra-systemic coherence, regarding both these criteria as of fundamental importance."[42] Here McGrath affirms the correspondence and coherency criteria for determining truth. In other words, for McGrath something may be considered true only if it corresponds to the way things actually are in the world and is consistent with everything else one knows to be true. Because of this, one should take McGrath as affirming a correspondence theory of truth while at the same time affirming the importance of coherence in assessing truth claims. Therefore, one should not mistake McGrath's rejection of foundationalism as a denial of the correspondence theory of truth. He clearly states that to "abandon foundationalism is not to abandon a correspondence theory of truth, and thus become reliant solely upon a coherentist account of truth."[43]

---

40. Ibid., 194.

41. Ibid., xi.

42. McGrath, *Scientific Theology*, vol. 2, 56.

43. Ibid., 38.

This is an important point since Douglas Groothuis has taken McGrath's concerns relating to modernity (expressed in earlier works) as a rejection of correspondence. In *A Passion for Truth*, for example, McGrath expresses concern over the high emphasis placed on propositional revelation by evangelicals during the modern period. There he said, "Any view of revelation which regards God's self-disclosure as the mere transmission of facts concerning God is seriously deficient, and risks making God an analogue of a corporate executive who disperses memoranda to underlings. Revelation is God's self-disclosure and self-involvement in history and supremely God's decision to become incarnate in Jesus Christ, so that whoever has seen Jesus Christ has seen the Father."[44] He went on to say: "It is a Travesty of the biblical idea of 'truth' to equate it with the Enlightenment notion of conceptual or propositional correspondence, or the derived view of evangelicalism as the proclamation of the propositional correctness of Christian doctrine."[45] Because of statements like these, Douglas Groothuis has suggested that McGrath "joins postmodernists in dismissing the correspondence view of truth."[46]

Nevertheless, Groothuis's assessment is probably not accurate. To begin with, in *A Passion for Truth*, McGrath does not appear to be rejecting correspondence *per se*, but Enlightenment versions of correspondence, which require a one-to-one correspondence between the object and the proposition. This kind of correspondence assumes a complete objectivity on the part of the knower that is difficult to maintain. As Hiebert explains, "Critical realism does not claim pure objectivity for human knowledge . . . knowledge in critical realism is the correspondence between our mental maps and the real world; it is objective reality subjectively known and appropriated in human lives."[47]

Second, McGrath's greatest concern appears to be an overemphasis on propositional revelation that "regards God's self-disclosure as the *mere* transmission of facts concerning God."[48] In other words, McGrath does not want to see revelation as the disclosure of facts *only*, but instead prefers an understanding of revelation that includes God's involvement in history. This understanding does not deny correspondence or the

---

44. McGrath, *Passion for Truth*, 107.

45. Ibid., 177.

46. Groothuis, *Truth Decay*, 130.

47. Hiebert, *Missiological Implications*, 74.

48. McGrath, *Passion for Truth*, 107. Emphasis mine.

propositional nature of revelation, it simply expands it. After all, in *A Passion for Truth*, McGrath goes on to say, "Revelation concerns the *oracles* of God, the *acts* of God, and the *person and presence of God*."[49] Furthermore, as his more recent works on ST have shown, McGrath clearly affirms a correspondence theory of truth for both science and theology. Thus, unlike postmodern theologies, McGrath's ST affirms a correspondence theory of truth.

McGrath is certainly not alone in taking this position. Clark argues that the correspondence theory of truth is a common sense position, which is necessary for rational thought and investigation. He suggests:

> Since virtually all people, including those who have never stud-ied epistemology, typically assume something like this notion of truth, it is a *pretheoretic* intuition regarding truth . . . This is pre-theoretic in that it is not an idea that *results from* complex theory building about the nature of truth but a belief that people *bring* to their theorizing about truth. It is a basic assumption, rooted in experience. It is something people philosophize *with*, not some-thing they philosophize *to*.[50]

Adler seems to agree. He contends that a realist conception of real-ity leads one to think "truth consists in our thinking that that which is, is; and that which is not, is not. Our thinking is in error or false when we think that which is, is not; or that which is not, is."[51] The famous physical-ist philosopher John Searle makes the same point. He affirms the corre-spondence theory of truth as the default position, meaning that these are views "we hold prereflectively so that any departure from them requires a conscious effort and a convincing argument."[52] He then adds, "In our ordinary everyday lives, these views are so much taken for granted that I think it is misleading to describe them as 'views'—or hypotheses or opinions—at all . . . These taken-for-granted presuppositions are part of what I call the background of our thought and language."[53]

Thus, the vast majority of thinkers within the history of western thought have affirmed a correspondence theory of truth. Groothuis con-tends that from Aristotle forward, the western world has accepted the notion that a "belief or statement is true only if it matches with, reflects,

49. Ibid.

50. Clark, *To Know and Love God*, 354.

51. Adler, *Truth In Religion*, 116.

52. Searle, *Mind, Language and Society*, 9.

53. Ibid., 10.

or corresponds to the reality to which it refers. For a statement to be true it must be factual. Facts determine the truth or falsity of a belief or a statement. This is the nature and meaning of truth."[54] Millard Erickson agrees, saying, "For much of its history, philosophy and theology held to a correspondence view of truth, that is, the view that truth is the agreement of language or ideas to reality. For this, postmodernism has substituted either a coherence or a pragmatic theory."[55] So, then, when evangelicals deviate from a correspondence theory of truth, they deviate from what seems to be the historic position of the western world.

Groothuis raises one additional point regarding the importance of the correspondence theory of truth. In his view, the correspondence theory of truth seems to be necessary since coherency, by itself, is insufficient in determining the validity of truth claims. This, of course does not mean that the criteria of coherence is irrelevant. As he explains, if a "worldview contains core beliefs that contradict each other, that worldview must be false."[56] He argues:

> The logical consistency of the biblical worldview is a necessary condition of its truth, but it is not a sufficient condition. For any worldview to be true, its essential tenets must be consistent with one another logically, in accordance with the laws of noncontradiction and excluded middle. Yet some have tried to make logical consistency the definition of truth itself and have rejected correspondence with reality as the definition of truth.[57]

Nevertheless, he believes this is insufficient by itself since is it possible for belief systems to be internally consistent without representing the world the way that it actually is. He says:

> Coherence theories of truth argue that what makes a statement or belief true is its coherence or consistency with one's other beliefs. If my "web of belief" is large and internally consistent—that is, if none of my beliefs contradict each other—my beliefs are true. A belief is false if it fails to cohere with the rest of my beliefs. In other words, truth is simply defined as logical coherence. The main problem with this view is that a set of beliefs held by fallible human beings may be coherent, but false.[58]

54. Groothuis, "Truth Defined," 65.

55. Erickson, "Theological Fog," 328–29.

56. Groothuis, "Truth Defined," 74.

57. Groothuis, *Truth Decay*, 97.

58. Groothuis, "Truth Defined," 73.

He then says:

> A set of beliefs may be internally coherent and not match reality.
> A set of beliefs may produce some good outcomes (at least in this
> life) and fail to connect with reality in important ways. A culture
> may construct beliefs that grant it meaning and significance—
> e.g., the idea that if one perishes in an Islamic jihad one goes
> directly to paradise—yet those beliefs may be false in light of
> the facts. We are, then, left with the reality of the truth—truth
> that is recalcitrant and resistant to any coercion. Christians, of
> all people, must swear allegiance to the notion that truth is what
> corresponds to reality—and we must do so unswervingly what-
> ever the postmodern winds of doctrine may be blowing in our
> faces. Whenever postconservative evangelicals depart from the
> correspondence view of truth—which is both biblical and logi-
> cal—and thus sink into the postmodernist swamps of subjectiv-
> ism, pragmatism, or constructivism, they should be lovingly but
> firmly resisted. Nothing less than the integrity of our Christian
> witness is at stake.[59]

Thus, according to Groothuis, a correspondence theory of truth is man-
dated by the fact that a belief system may be internally consistent but fail
in its representation of the real world.

From the concerns mentioned above, McGrath's ST "aims to
achieve extra-systemic correspondence with intra-systemic coherence"
in the development of theory (scientific or theological).[60] Because of
this, his approach seems to meet the concerns of evangelicals who feel
the need to maintain a correspondence theory of truth while at the same
time acknowledging the role of coherence in assessing different beliefs.
Thus, McGrath's treatment of correspondence and coherence in his ST is
consistent with what other evangelicals have affirmed in their works.

ST Moves Beyond Classical Foundationalism

Thus far, this chapter has focused on two different ways that McGrath's
ST is favorable over a modern or postmodern perspective. In this section, however, it will be argued that McGrath's ST also is commendable
to evangelicals in that it avoids the problems associated with classical
foundationalism. John Fienberg offers a concise description when he
suggests that "classical foundationalism (which has been a predominant

---

59. Ibid., 79.

60. McGrath, *Scientific Theology*, vol. 2, 56.

theory of knowledge within the modern era) claims that a belief has sufficient support if it is supported by evidences and arguments that are ultimately supported by (inferred from) beliefs that are properly basic. A properly basic belief is a belief that is either self-evident (like "all bachelors are unmarried men"), evident to the senses, or incorrigible (like the *cogito*)."[61] As chapter 2 noted, throughout *A Scientific Theology* and *The Science of God*, McGrath clearly distances himself from this epistemological system. For example, he says, "As has often been pointed out, foundationalism has now been rejected by virtually every major epistemologist and philosopher of science of the last half of the century, from the later writings of Ludwig Wittgenstein through Karl Popper, W. F. Sellars and W. V. O. Quine. The belief that foundationalism is philosophically indefensible is the closest thing to a philosophical consensus there has been for a very long time."[62]

At the heart of McGrath's rejection of foundationalism is the concern to protect Christianity's unique perspective of reality. Instead of yielding to the Enlightenment's requirement to build one's belief system on basic beliefs that are objective and certain—thus submitting Christianity to a supposed universal rationality—McGrath believes theologians are justified in beginning with the Christian tradition itself. Noting the influence of Alasdair MacIntyre, he says, "MacIntyre's greatest achievement, from the perspective of a scientific theology, is to rehabilitate the notion that Christianity possesses a distinct yet rational understanding of reality—a coupling which the Enlightenment regarded as impossible. Christianity is once more free to reassert its distinctiveness, instead of submitting itself to the Enlightenment insistence on a universal human reason which determined all things, seeing divergence from its judgments as 'irrationality.'"[63]

Examples of how McGrath does this himself can be seen in at least two places: his use of the doctrine of creation and his use of natural theology. Regarding creation, McGrath denies that there is one objectively correct way of viewing nature and suggests that, because of this, theologians are free to speak of nature as God's creation. He says:

---

61. Feinberg, *No One Like Him*, 87.

62. McGrath, *Science of God*, 99.

63. Ibid., 111.

"Nature" is thus not a neutral entity, having the status of an "observation statement"; it involves seeing the world in a particular way—and the way in which it is seen shapes the resulting concept of "nature." Far from being a "given," the idea of "nature" is shaped by the prior assumptions of the observer. One does not "observe" nature; one constructs it. And once the importance of socially mediated ideas, theories and values is conceded, it is impossible to avoid the conclusion that the concept of nature is, at least in part, a social construction. If the concept of nature is socially mediated—to whatever extent—it cannot serve as an allegedly neutral, objective or uninterpreted foundation of a theory or theology. Nature is already an interpreted category.[64]

Elsewhere he suggests that "the Christian theologian is not under any obligation to accept a normative definition of nature originating from outside the Christian tradition. Instead, Christian theology may deploy and explore its own distinctive understanding of what others call nature, but which the Christian tradition prefers to name 'creation.'"[65] As Colyer explains, for McGrath the "doctrine of creation (rooted in Scripture and as developed within creedal Christian orthodoxy) provides the 'spectacles' through which we can interpret nature as God's creation *ex nihilo*, called into being and given an order or rationality sustained by and reflective of God's own uncreated rationality."[66] Thus, with the doctrine of creation, McGrath begins from within the Christian tradition, not from outside, and considers what this unique perspective may add to the dialogue between science and theology.

The same thing can be said regarding McGrath's use of natural theology. Instead of submitting natural theology to Enlightenment foundationalism, where it must first prove the existence of God before theism is deemed acceptable, McGrath uses natural theology from within the Christian tradition by making it dependent on its own revealed theology.[67] Following T. F. Torrance, McGrath "argues that natural theology must be reconceived as an account of nature, undertaken from within the sphere of a revealed knowledge of God. To undertake natural theology, some revealed notions of God are required—above all, a doctrine

64. McGrath, *Scientific Theology*, vol. 1, 113.

65. McGrath, *Science of God*, 45.

66. Colyer, "Scientific Theology, vol. 1," 228.

67. Namely, the Bible and all articles of faith within Christianity itself.

of creation."[68] As with creation, McGrath locates natural theology within the Christian tradition, not outside. In this, McGrath shows that his ST develops and functions without classical foundationalism.

Like McGrath, Stephen T. Davis and W. Jay Wood also acknowledge the ever-decreasing popularity of classical foundationalism. Davis, for example, says that it is "an epistemological theory with a long history that seemed so obviously true to so many people that it was not even recognized as a theory, or at least not one that needed defending, until fairly recently. This could hardly be less true today—one can scarcely pick up a book or article in epistemology, theology, or even popular intellectual culture, without encountering confident declarations of the death of foundationalism."[69] Likewise, Wood claims that almost "every element of Cartesian foundationalist theory, those central as well as those peripheral, has been the target of criticisms whose numbers are legion these days."[70]

But why, exactly, is classical foundationalism now seen to be so dissatisfying for epistemologists? Wood explains:

> Critics have posed what they deem to be devastating objections against human knowledge's being grounded in beliefs that are epistemically basic as described by the strong foundationalist. Why, critics ask, should we think that only beliefs that are self-evident or incorrigible or evident to the senses are properly basic? True, any belief meeting one or more of these standards is an ideal candidate for proper basicality, but is it necessary that a basic belief meet these standards? . . . Consider one's beliefs in the reliability of one's senses or memory or consciousness; none of these beliefs [are] either self-evident or incorrigible or evident to the senses, yet they are held as properly basic by virtually everyone.[71]

Expressing similar concerns with narrow foundationalism, Ronald Nash says:

> True memories fail the test of rationality since they are themselves neither basic beliefs nor based on properly basic beliefs. But surely, any theory that casts doubt on the rationality of not

68. McGrath, *Science of God*, 86–87.

69. Davis, *God, Reason & Proofs*, 78.

70. Wood, *Epistemology*, 88.

71. Ibid., 88–89.

> only memory-beliefs but also all kinds of other beliefs, such as our belief in the external world or other minds, is deficient. Our knowledge of true memories or other persons or the continuing existence of the external world is not inferential, that is, based on more basic beliefs. But it most assuredly is knowledge.[72]

In the end then, classical foundationalism appears to be overly restrictive in what it allows to qualify as knowledge.

But this is not all. Classical foundationalism is also problematic in light of the fact that it cannot justify its most fundamental claim. Wood, for example, questions the claim that *only* beliefs that are self-evident, evident to the senses, and incorrigible qualify as being properly basic. He asks, "Is this belief *itself* self-evident or incorrigible or evident to the senses? No. Is it logically rooted in basic beliefs that meet these conditions? Again, the answer seems to be no. Strong foundationalism's acceptance of the criteria for proper basicality thus runs afoul of its own standards."[73]

Nash also notes the difficulty of establishing the narrow foundationalist's criteria. He says:

> It is clear that the narrow foundationalist himself accepts a belief (i.e., his theory) as properly basic even though it fails to satisfy his own criteria of proper basicality. Since the narrow foundationalist fails to provide any arguments, reasons, or evidence for his thesis and since it fails his own tests for proper basicality, it follows that his acceptance of his thesis violates his own epistemic duties. Since being rational means fulfilling one's epistemic duties, it follows that the narrow foundationalist is behaving irrationally when he advances his thesis.[74]

According to these sources, it does not appear that narrow/classical foundationalism is able to justify the claim that all affirmations must be based on beliefs that are themselves properly basic.

In short, like McGrath, a number of evangelicals suggest that classical foundationalism simply cannot be sustained. One constructive aspect of McGrath's ST is that it moves beyond the questionable epistemological system of classical foundationalism by adopting a critical realist perspective.

72. Nash, *Faith & Reason*, 86.

73. Wood, *Epistemology*, 89.

74. Nash, *Faith & Reason*, 86.

ST Acknowledges a Mediated Aspect of Knowledge

Earlier in this chapter, McGrath's realist perspective was explored to show how his ST is favorable in comparison to postmodern anti-realism. By adopting a realist perspective, McGrath affirms objective reality and the ability of mankind to gain genuine knowledge of that reality. With this, McGrath successfully avoids some of the problems with postmodern thought. Throughout *A Scientific Theology* and *The Science of God*, however, McGrath is careful to note that he adopts a specific version of realism known as critical realism. Having shown the advantages of a critical realist perspective to a postmodern perspective in the first two sections of this chapter, it will now be argued that McGrath's CR is preferable to the naïve realism of the Enlightenment since it acknowledges a mediated aspect of knowledge.

Whereas the modernist assumed that one could have complete and total objectivity in his perception of reality, the postmodernist denied this idea.[75] Postmodernists reject this idea and emphasize the social and historical factors that shape a given truth claim. By embracing CR, McGrath navigates between the extremes of modernity and postmodernity, affirming both the objective and subjective aspects of human knowledge. McGrath's thoughts on objective reality were dealt with in earlier sections; it is now time to consider what he says regarding the issue of subjectivity.

McGrath presents a balanced understanding of truth when he says, "Truth is not an objective reality in its own right, nor is it the subjective creation of the individual; rather, truth lies in the relationship between text and interpreter."[76] From a theological perspective, he says, "Theology does not just address history, nor does it just address nature—it addresses *and is addressed* by these and other strata of reality, and has the responsibility of coordinating these different levels of being, and showing how they are coherent with its overall vision of reality."[77] Put another way, he affirms that "reality or realities can be known, however approximately, and that statements which are made concerning it cannot be regarded totally or simply as subjective assertions concerning personal attitudes or feelings. It is possible to gain at least some degree of epistemic access to a reality

75. Groothuis, "Truth Defined," 60.

76. McGrath, *Scientific Theology*, vol. 2, 196.

77. Ibid., 239.

which exists 'objectively,' while at the same time conceding that the manner in which this is apprehended or conceptualized may, to some extent, be conditioned by cultural, social and personal factors."[78] McGrath offers the use of CR in his ST as being "sensitive to the historically situated and personally involved character of theological knowledge, while resolutely declining to let go of the ideals of truth, objectivity and rationality."[79]

There are a significant number of evangelicals today willing to acknowledge, along with McGrath, that there are subjective factors in human knowledge. Wondering whether or not a person has direct access to reality, Davis says, "In one important sense, surely not. There is no way to by-pass our own conceptual equipment in order to compare our ideas with reality as such. Doing the comparing would obviously involve using our conceptual equipment."[80] As Erickson notes, "While it is one thing to say that we have absolute truth, it is another thing to say that we know and understand it absolutely . . . There is a full recognition that in the knowing process we are affected by the conditioning that postmodernism has described so vividly. We have no absolute assurance that our sensations exactly represent the objects that we are perceiving."[81] Even Groothuis, a staunch defender of absolute truth, admits that the objectivity of God's truth does not "diminish the reality of the church as an interactive and interdependent community of believers. Postmodernism has tended to stress communal norms and practices over the existence of objective truth, but biblically there should be no conflict between the two."[82] He later adds, "God's truth is not provincial, parochial or partial; it is universal in scope and application. Yet it also allows for unique cultural expression and the creative individuality of people made in the divine image and redeemed through the Lamb. The truth does not flatten us out into faceless conformity, but liberates each of us to be who we ought to be under the Lordship of Christ."[83] Daniel Taylor agrees, saying, "We belong to communities of belief which help shape, whether we are conscious of it or not, our views of the world and our actions in it. We

78. McGrath, *Scientific Theology*, vol. 1, 75.

79. McGrath, *Scientific Theology*, vol. 2, 195.

80. Davis, *God, Reason & Proofs*, 92.

81. Erickson, *Truth or Consequences*, 260.

82. Groothuis, *Truth Decay*, 68.

83. Ibid., 73.

both draw from these communities and contribute to them, the reflective and the unreflective alike. They help determine what we are."[84]

Meek, Padgett and Hiebert also acknowledge some degree of mediation and subjectivity in human knowledge. As Meek notes, people have become "increasingly aware of how presumptuous it was to think that everybody's mind works the way Descartes's (or ours) does. Plus, we gradually had to admit that every knower's interests and culture and outlook significantly shape what he or she is knowing . . . How can there be certain, infallible, objective knowledge when what we claim is true seems to be determined by subjective factors such as our cultural upbringing or our personal ambitions?"[85] Padgett contends that all "our knowing arises from our location, from our point of view and cultural context. Even the natural sciences are located in culture, language, and history. None of us have a God's-eye view, a 'view from nowhere.' Any approach that hopes to grasp the object of our studies will need a host of contrasting, alternative points of view on that object."[86] Hiebert, on the other hand, notes that any given theology or interpretation of Scripture is "influenced by our sense percepts and the ways our minds work, by the language we use and our hermeneutical processes, by our personal interests, by the culture and community in which we participate, and by the historical context in which we live. We may 'see through a glass darkly,' not because of the limits of divine revelation but because of the limits of our human knowledge."[87]

Because of this, Padgett believes that a "new kind of objectivity is called for—not a supposedly neutral or value-free science, which is impossible . . . but an objectivity that takes the particularity of things seriously."[88] According to some scholars, CR offers the kind of approach that Padgett has in mind. As Hiebert notes, "Critical realists argue that community investigation is an essential part of the hermeneutical process of searching for truth, and that far from undermining the process, it is a powerful corrective against the subjective biases of individual scholars."[89] Polkinghorne agrees, claiming that "it is a critical realism

---

84. Taylor, *Myth of Certainty*, 21.

85. Meek, *Longing to Know*, 31.

86. Padgett, *Science and Study*, 24.

87. Hiebert, *Missiological Implications*, 99.

88. Padgett, *Science and Study*, 27.

89. Hiebert, *Missiological Implications*, 94.

that the scientist-theologians defend. No naïve objectivity is involved in either discipline."[90] J. Wentzel van Huyssteen's comments are also especially helpful:

> [CR] not only highlights the role of metaphorical reference in scientific theory formation, while at the same time honoring the provisionality and sociohistorical nature of all knowledge, but it also enables us to retain the ideals of truth, objectivity, rationality, and intellectual progress in a radically reconstructed way. Certainly the strength of the critical realist position lies in its insistence that both the objects of science and the objects of religious belief often lie beyond the range of literal description . . . In their respective quests for intelligibility, the scientific and theological enterprises share alike the groping and tentative tools of humankind: words, ideas, and images that have been handed down and which we refashion and reinterpret for our context in light of contemporary experience.[91]

Because of CR, then, van Huyssteen believes "we are obliged neither to commit to some form of universal rationality nor to plunge into a sea of relativism where many rationalities proliferate."[92]

Like many other evangelicals then, McGrath acknowledges a mediated aspect of human knowledge. By doing so, McGrath, and other evangelicals, will be able to by-pass the naïve realism of the Enlightenment that assumed an absolute perspective of reality. At the same time, however, by taking a critical realist approach, McGrath's ST is able to affirm the "ideals of truth, objectivity and rationality."[93] In McGrath's ST, the theologian is not so naïve to think that his perspective perfectly represents the nature of reality. On the other hand, he does not assume that nothing of reality can be known or affirmed.

Thus, McGrath's ST presents a humble epistemological position that evangelicals should be comfortable embracing. This is an important contribution to evangelical theology since it takes the important aspects of modernity and postmodernity without yielding to the extremes of either approach.

---

90. Polkinghorne, *Scientists as Theologians*, 14.

91. van Huyssteen, *Shaping of Rationality*, 218.

92. van Huyssteen, *Alone in the World?*, 3.

93. McGrath, *Scientific Theology*, vol. 2, 195.

ST Establishes a Unified Theory of Knowledge

As chapter 1 pointed out, one consequence of the modern period was a bifurcation between the humanities and the natural sciences. As Edward O. Wilson explains, the "free flight bequeathed by the Enlightenment, which disengaged the humanities during the Romantic era, had by the middle of the twentieth century all but erased hope for the unification of knowledge with the aid of science. The two cultures described by C. P. Snow in his 1959 Rede Lecture, the literary and the scientific, were no longer on speaking terms."[94] This division is problematic since, as chapter 1 argued, it marginalizes religious knowledge and ultimately leads to reductionism, which undermines many of the areas of inquiry that are critically important to humanity.[95] McGrath himself acknowledges this as one of the major problems of modernity. He says, "Perhaps the greatest rift to open up in recent centuries has been between the natural sciences and the humanities."[96] McGrath considers this an unacceptable situation and suggests that one of the central themes throughout his ST is that it establishes a unified theory of knowledge (UTK). He says:

> That vision of God destroys any restrictive categorizations which insist that certain domains of knowledge are to be deemed religious, and others secular. A scientific theology, grounded in a unitary conception of reality, insists that the engagement with every aspect of the world offers the potential to deepen an appreciation of its creator, according to its own distinctive nature and the capacity of a fallen human mind to discern it. A scientific theology gladly and joyfully embraces the totality of reality, while never losing sight of the fact that the theological grid which allows it to affirm and engage the world in this manner is grounded in the specifics of the Christian revelation, and mediated through the Christian tradition.[97]

He later adds, "A scientific theology is motivated by the quest for a unified explanation of reality . . . the reality that requires to be explained is complex, multilayered and often opaque. We do not experience that reality as neatly divided into separate compartments, some of which may be designated as 'physical,' others 'biological,' and others as 'religious.'

---

94. Wilson, *Consilience*, 42.

95. Such as theology, philosophy, ethics, art, literature, etc.

96. McGrath, *Scientific Theology*, vol. 1, 28.

97. McGrath, *Scientific Theology*, vol. 3, 4.

Rather, we experience reality in its wholeness and interconnectedness before we develop particular disciplines and techniques to study different aspects of it."[98]

McGrath's desire to establish a UTK is further evidence of Bhaskar's influence on ST. By introducing the notion of a stratified reality, Bhaskar affirms a unified reality and rejects reductionism and the division between the natural and social sciences. He says, "To posit an essential unity of scientific method is to posit an account which conceives the sciences as unified in the form that scientific knowledge takes, the reasoning by which it is produced and the concepts in terms of which its production can be most adequately theorized or reconstructed."[99] Thus, like Bhaskar, McGrath affirms a UTK and argues against the problematic epistemological division of science and theology.

Bhaskar and McGrath are certainly not alone in their desire to correct the modern bifurcation of western epistemology. In fact, a considerable number of scholars are currently arguing that recovering a UTK is essential for the western world. For example, though there are important differences between him and McGrath, Wilson says, "The greatest enterprise of the mind has always been and always will be the attempted linkage of the sciences and humanities. The ongoing fragmentation of knowledge and resulting chaos in philosophy are not reflections of the real world but artifacts of scholarship."[100]

Polkinghorne and others also contend that a UTK is essential given the nature of reality. In his view, this bifurcation is not acceptable since there is only one reality. He says, "Those who adopt this position must then go on to ask what is the relationship between the contents of knowledge proffered by natural science on the one hand and theology on the other. If it is the one world of existing reality that both are investigating, then the stories they tell of it must be reconcilable with each other."[101] Ted Peters agrees, saying, "Since the Enlightenment we have pretty much assumed that they represent separate domains of human knowing. We have erected a high wall of separation between church and laboratory. Yet this is most unfortunate, because we all assume there is but one reality. So sooner or later we will become dissatisfied with consigning our

98. Ibid., 133.

99. Bhaskar, *Possibility of Naturalism*, 18.

100. Wilson, *Consilience*, 6.

101. Polkinghorne, *Scientists as Theologians*, 4.

differences to separate ghettos of learning."[102] Likewise, Padgett argues for a UTK. He says, "If there exists a real world, independent of human experience, then our worldview should be aimed at understanding that world as fully as possible. For this fuller understanding we need all the disciplines of the university, including the human sciences and theology. We will expect greater coherence in our worldview because we believe that at bottom there is one reality, which is whole and connected."[103] He then adds, "If theism is true, then there is one God, one world, and one complete system of truth (God's own knowledge)."[104]

Adler also contends for a UTK and ties it to the law of noncontradiction. He says, "In the realm of all truths consisting of propositions that can be affirmed or denied, incompatible truths cannot coexist. All the diverse parts of knowledge, including religious knowledge or knowledge by faith, must coherently form one and only one integral whole."[105] Therefore, he argues:

> [This is] merely an extension, but nonetheless a very important extension, of the principle of noncontradiction. To affirm the unity of truth is to deny that there can be two separate and irreconcilable truths which, while contradicting of one another and thought to be irreconcilably so, avoid the principle of noncontradiction by claiming to belong to logic-tight compartments. Thus, for example, one approach to the conflicts between religion and philosophy, or between science and either philosophy or religion, is to claim that these are such separate spheres of thought or inquiry, employing such different methods or having such different means of access to the truth, that the principle of noncontradiction does not apply. One thing can be true in religious belief and quite another, though contradictory of it, can be true in scientific or philosophical thought.[106]

Groothuis argues similarly, claiming that "truth is one, as God is one. All truths cohere with one another as expressions of God's harmonious objective reality—of his being, his knowledge and his creation. Something cannot be true in religion and false in science (or vice versa), or true in philosophy but false in theology (or vice versa). There is only one world,

102. Peters, *Cosmos as Creation,* 13.

103. Padgett, *Science and Study,* 30.

104. Ibid., 31.

105. Adler, *Truth In Religion,* 32.

106. Ibid., 118.

God's world; it is a universe, not a multi-verse."[107] Thus, the modern bi-furcation of reality is rejected by some philosophers since it seems to imply that there are two realities (as suggested by modernity's epistemo-logical split). This is not, however, the only reason that it is rejected.

Peters has also noted some theological concerns. If theologians continue to work without a UTK, he believes that theology itself will continue to be marginalized. He says, "The liberal two-language theory separating science and theology is a modern one . . . Both science and theology could speak of things divine. Both natural revelation and special revelation pointed us in one direction: toward God. The two-language theory, in contrast, points us in two different directions: either toward God or toward the world."[108]

Thus, while the split between science and theology may appear to offer peace to both sides, this peace comes at the expense of communica-tion between science and theology, which would otherwise serve as an enhancement to each discipline. Because of this, Peters argues that this peace is of no value:

> It gains peace through separation, by establishing a demilitarized zone that prevents communication. In the event that a scientist might desire to speak about divine matters or that a theologian might desire to speak about the actual world created by God, the two would have to speak past one another on the assumption that shared understanding is impossible. Why begin with such an assumption? The method of hypothetical consonance makes just the opposite assumption, namely, there is but one reality and sooner or later scientists and theologians should be able to find some areas of shared understanding.[109]

He then says, "The real problem with the two-language theory is that it forbids cross-disciplinary conversation . . . We could not explore the possibility that the language of one might serve to illumine the other. We could not develop the assumption that both are speaking about the same reality. Conversation would come to a dead end, even if it did get started."[110]

---

107. Groothuis, *Truth Decay*, 79.

108. Peters, "Science and Theology," 18.

109. Peters, Preface, 18.

110. Ibid., 17.

Like Peters, Peacocke believes that theologians have a vested interest in working toward a UTK and keeping an open dialogue with the natural sciences. That is, unless theologians are willing to participate in an interdisciplinary dialogue with the natural sciences, theology will not be taken seriously. He suggests that an isolated theology will be intellectually and culturally inferior:

> [It operates] in a cultural ghetto quite cut off from most of those in Western cultures who have good grounds for thinking that science describes what is going on in the processes of the world at all levels. The turbulent history of the relation of science and theology bears witness to the impossibility of theology seeking a peaceful haven, protected from the science of its times, if it is going to be believable. Indeed, theology has been most creative and long-lasting when it has responded most positively to the challenges of its times, as when the Cappadocian Fathers used Greek philosophy to express the categories of Christian theology and when St. Thomas Aquinas faced up to and triumphantly utilized the then overwhelming intellectual resources of Aristotelianism to reshape that same theology into a form that endured for centuries.[111]

He later notes, "One of the principal causes of the weakness of the churches' mission to western humanity must be their failure to find a convincing way of expressing their beliefs, that is, of having a theology which is capable of coping with the contemporary cultural and intellectual situation and of out-thinking it."[112] Thus, these philosophers and theologians believe that theology may be enhanced by an on-going interdisciplinary dialogue with the natural sciences.

Del Ratzsch suggests that theologians are not the only ones who would benefit from a dialogue between science and theology. In his mind, the natural sciences may also benefit from this approach since, by themselves, they are limited to the empirical realm of reality. He says, "If any part of reality lies outside the boundaries imposed on science by its methods, that part of reality will be beyond the competence of science; and if knowledge is artificially restricted to scientific knowledge, we will thus be sheltering ourselves and our beliefs from the relevant portions

---

111. Peacocke, *Theology*, 6–7.
112. Ibid., 10.

of reality."[113] In other words, being limited to the investigation of the empirical realm, the natural sciences are not able to address some of the more important aspects of human life, such as value, meaning, purpose, truth, and morality. Hugh Ross also makes this point. He says, the "division of truth into separate domains, objective (fact-based) and subjective (feeling-based), with science on the objective side and religious notions on the subjective side, may seem an easy way out of the conflicts. However, philosophical reality makes such a separation untenable. The very concept of truth comes from the spiritual domain. Christianity upholds the values and ethics crucial to the scientific endeavor, including support for the laws of logic."[114]

Meek believes that reaffirming the oneness of reality is of considerable importance for the future of human thought. In fact, if the western world hopes to overcome its current epistemological crisis, she suggests that "our only hope lies in reuniting these domains. It is our only hope not simply for the sake of justifying claims to know God. It is also our only hope for having any knowledge at all. The well-entrenched misperception about the nature of knowledge, one that divorces 'proper' knowledge from its inarticulable roots, has in fact led to the widespread skepticism and relativism of our time. Both sides of the presumed dichotomy . . . face death by absurdity apart from this reconciliation."[115] Likewise, Padgett believes that "both theology and science are needed in the task of developing a worldview that will meet the needs of twenty-first-century women and men."[116] He then says, "Theological, philosophical, and scientific evidence are all relevant to answering important worldview questions, and any attempt to hermetically seal-off these disciplines will lead to incoherence. Neither reality nor human reason can be so neatly sliced into pieces."[117] Polkinghorne sees the necessity of this as well, arguing that "religion must listen to what science has to tell it about the nature and history of the physical world, and that religion can offer science a deeper and more comprehensive account of reality within which the latter's search for understanding can find an intellectually comfortable home."[118]

113. Ratzsch, *Science & Limits*, 92.

114. Ross, *Creation as Science*, 37.

115. Meek, *Longing to Know*, 44.

116. Padgett, *Science and Study*, 1.

117. Ibid., 20.

118. Polkinghorne, *Scientists as Theologians*, 6.

McGrath's attempt to establish a UTK, by the acceptance of CR as the methodology of his ST, is something that should be applauded by evangelicals. As this survey has shown, a significant number of philosophers see this as being necessary for the future of both theology and science. McGrath acknowledges this need and uses CR to accomplish the task. Thus, McGrath's ST provides a viable epistemology for attaining a UTK.

Before moving forward, it is necessary to consider one further question. Having shown that McGrath's ST is concerned with developing a UTK and that a growing number of philosophers and theologians recognize the need for a UTK, it will be necessary to understand how CR is helpful in making a UTK possible. Once again, Bhaskar's distinct form of CR is very important to this question. By arguing for a stratified view of reality, his approach allows each discipline to function according to its own proper methods of investigation and inquiry. As a result, his version of CR allows for a UTK without submitting to reductionism. This issue is significant enough to warrant a section all its own. Before considering this, however, a few other observations must be made.

Hiebert explains that CR helps make a UTK possible because it offers a perspective of reality to both theology and science that affirms the objective nature of reality while acknowledging its subjective comprehension. He says:

> We recognize that there can be no true integration between a science based on one epistemology and a theology based on another. A science based on realism and a theology based on idealism simply talk past each other. Second, we would reject the old view that science is based on acts and theology is based on faith. This view is so deeply ingrained in Western thought that even Christians and theologians make the distinction. Critical realists argue that science is not a distinct way of knowing, nor is it logically prior to the other forms of inquiry or superior to them as a way of knowing. In other words, theology and science are not different ways of knowing. Both seek to make sense of the world and of our experiences . . . Both begin with belief in their underlying premises and draw on historical experiences to help them understand the order and meaning in reality. Both assume a real world characterized by an order that is continuous over time. Both assume the ability of human reason to understand the world, at least in part.[119]

---

119. Hiebert, *Missiological Implications*, 103–4.

Likewise, van Kooten Niekerk makes the same observation. He suggests that science and theology are both "justified in claiming that their statements and propositions tell something about a mind-independent reality, since it is not impossible to attain knowledge of that reality."[120]

Another way that CR facilitates an interdisciplinary approach to knowledge is that it shows how theology and science both share a common mode of representing reality. Once again, van Huyssteen offers a helpful explanation of this aspect of CR. He says:

> Critical realism has developed into one of the most important positions in the current philosophy of science debate. It not only highlights the role of metaphorical reference in scientific theory formation, while at the same time honoring the provisionality and sociohistorical nature of all knowledge, but it also enables us to retain the ideals of truth, objectivity, rationality, and intellectual progress in a radically reconstructed way. Certainly the strength of the critical realist position lies in its insistence that both the objects of science and the objects of religious belief often lie beyond the range of literal description . . . In their respective quests for intelligibility, the scientific and theological enterprises share alike the groping and tentative tools of humankind: words, ideas, and images that have been handed down and which we refashion and reinterpret for our context in light of contemporary experience.[121]

Hiebert agrees and suggests:

> Critical realism affirms that human knowledge does represent reality, but by "represent" it does not mean the formal or literal one-to-one correspondence of photographs. Rather, it sees knowledge as models, maps, or blueprints of reality. These may be "true," but in a certain way. The nature of representation and truth in critical realism can be seen by analyzing the relationship between a map and the reality it maps. In the first place, the correspondence between map and reality is symbolic and analogical. A map is not a photograph of reality. It is a model, a mental diagram or schema, an analogical representation that conveys limited but accurate information about reality.[122]

---

120. van Kooten Niekerk, "Critical Realist Perspective," 78.

121. van Huyssteen, *Shaping of Rationality*, 218.

122. Hiebert, *Missiological Implications*, 76–77.

According to van Huyssteen and Hiebert, then, CR helps establish a UTK since it identifies the common mode of representation in both disciplines.

Thus, CR seems to offer a viable epistemological methodology for integrating theology and science in a UTK. CR makes a UTK possible since it allows theology and science to affirm objective reality while at the same time allowing for subjective comprehension. Moreover, it helps theologians and scientists recognize the nature of representation in their respective doctrines and theories. Therefore, McGrath's ST offers a considerable advantage to a modern or postmodern methodology in that it establishes a UTK that should be embraced by evangelicals.

ST AVOIDS REDUCTIONISM

Another constructive aspect of McGrath's ST is that it moves toward a UTK without conceding to reductionism. To better understand just what this means, one could compare McGrath's approach to Edward O. Wilson's, which moves toward a UTK, but does so at the expense of religion, philosophy, and a number of other important dimensions of reality. McGrath says, "Harvard biologist Edward O. Wilson, one of the founders of sociobiology, argues that social behaviour is to be explained by the principles of biology, biology by the principles of chemistry, and chemistry by the principles of physics. Eventually all higher disciplines will be reduced to nothing but the laws of chemistry and physics."[123] Wilson himself says, "The unification agenda does not sit well with a few professional philosophers. The subject I address they consider their own, to be expressed in their language, their framework of formal thought. They will draw this indictment: conflation, simplism, ontological reductionism, scientism, and other sins made official by the hissing suffix. To which I plead guilty, guilty, guilty."[124] He later adds, "We are approaching a new age of synthesis, when the testing of Consilience is the greatest of all intellectual challenges. Philosophy, the contemplation of the unknown, is a shrinking dominion. We have the common goal of turning as much philosophy as possible into science."[125] Thus, Wilson's approach would be unacceptable for theologians and philosophers since it eliminates their respective disciplines and denies the existence of non-physical entities.

123. McGrath, *Scientific Theology*, vol. 2, 216.

124. Wilson, *Consilience*, 9.

125. Ibid., 10.

McGrath, for one, is clearly opposed to Wilson's approach. Like Wilson, he develops an approach that contends for a UTK. Unlike Wilson, however, he does so without conceding to reductionism. As McGrath makes clear, his ST is "stridently opposed to any form of reductionism—the rather crude and wooden approach which seems to collapse everything into one allegedly fundamental level."[126] This, as noted earlier, is perhaps the area where McGrath's CR is most informed by Bhaskar's works. Contrary to reductionism or scientism, Bhaskar argues "for a qualified anti-positivist naturalism, based on an essentially realist view of science. Such a naturalism holds that it is possible to give an account of science under which the proper and more or less specific methods of both the natural and social sciences can fall. But it does not deny that there are significant differences in these methods, grounded in real differences in their subject-matters and in the relationships in which their sciences stand to them."[127]

As McGrath notes, Bhasker's critical realism "insists that the world must be regarded as differentiated and stratified. Each individual science deals with a different stratum of this reality, which in turn obliges it to develop and use methods of investigation adapted and appropriate to this stratum. Stratum *B* might be grounded in, and emerge from, Stratum *A*. Yet despite this relation of origin, the same methods of investigation cannot be used in dealing with these two different strata. These methods must be established *a posteriori*, through an engagement with each of these strata of reality."[128] Adopting Bhaskar's stratification, McGrath contends that "different strata must be handled in different manners, reflecting their individual identity, any notion of an absolute distinction of method must be abandoned in terms of a spectrum of methodologies, each adapted to the nature of the level of reality under study."[129] He further explains this when he says:

> There is then no generalized scientific methodology which can be applied without variance and uncritically to all sciences. While certain general principles may be argued to lie behind the specific approaches found in any given natural science, the point is that the nature of the field to be investigated shapes the approach to be ad-

126. McGrath, *Science of God*, 147.

127. Bhaskar, *Possibility of Naturalism*, 3.

128. McGrath, *Science of God*, 146.

129. McGrath, *Scientific Theology*, vol. 3, 82.

opted. In that each science deals with a different object, it is under an obligation to respond to that object according to its distinctive nature. The methods which are appropriate to the study of one object cannot be abstracted and applied uncritically and universally. Each science develops procedures which it deems or discovers to be appropriate to the nature of its own particular object in which it has solved its own inductive problem of how to arrive at a general conclusion from a limited set of particular observations.[130]

In McGrath's ST, the unity of reality is affirmed, which makes it possible to develop a UTK. That being the case, particular assumptions—realism, correspondence, etc.—about reality may be shared by all disciplines. On the other hand, there are many different dimensions of reality, which, given their particular natures, require diverse methods of investigation. As McGrath argues, "The critical realist perspective which informs a scientific theology insists upon the recognition of a plurality of levels within reality, each demanding its own distinct mode of investigation and representation. Ontology determines epistemology."[131] As Colyer notes, McGrath contends that Bhaskar's stratification "undermines all forms of reductionism in which higher levels of reality are viewed as purely explicable in terms of lower levels."[132]

By accepting a stratified view of reality, McGrath avoids reductionism of other naturalists like Wilson. Other evangelicals have taken a similar approach in affirming the oneness of reality while at the same time acknowledging that it is multi-dimensional or multi-layered. David Clark, for example, says, "Both of these fields of study are legitimate. They may even investigate and explain the same realities. But the disciplines amount to different perspectives that necessarily explain different aspects or dimensions of the same things. That is, each discipline is valid, but no discipline is ever able to capture all dimensions of the reality . . . Scientific and theological descriptions represent different realms of discourse. They view the same reality in terms of different perspectives, and each is limited to its own dimension of the whole."[133] He says:

130. McGrath, *Scientific Theology*, vol. 2, 283.

131. McGrath, *Scientific Theology*, vol. 3, 82.

132. Colyer, "Scientific Theology, vol. 2," 494.

133. Clark, *To Know and Love God*, 273.

A significant problem is that the various academic disciplines have become institutionally separated from each other in their own intellectual ghettos. Seeing this as a problem does not mean, of course, that we see the distinctions between the disciplines as entirely invalid. But it does demand that we acknowledge that academic disciplines are, to a degree, social constructs. They reflect what is real. They are facets of the diamond of a unified and holistic understanding of truth. They are meaningful and helpful in clarifying the different frames of reference through which we can view reality . . . And so we need strategies for expressing, both theoretically and practically, the fundamental unity of the disciplines. We need to seek out, in the end, an organic fusion of disciplinary horizons.[134]

For Clark, then, it is both possible and necessary to affirm the oneness of reality while at the same time allowing for the individual disciplines to maintain their distinct modes and methods of inquiry. This is because the nature of reality determines what and how something of reality can be known.

Likewise, Padgett says the "dialogue between theology and the special sciences is best understood as taking place between different levels of explanation . . . My philosophical approach is post-Enlightenment, or 'postmodern,' which among other things implies a holistic approach to our understanding of reality."[135] Since each discipline responds to a different level or dimension of reality, Padgett believes that each is able to maintain its distinct mode and methodology of investigation. He says, "The special sciences and theology, even though they have their own domains as disciplines, can rationally influence each other, in special situations, without giving up their own important distinctive and methods."[136]

Polkinghorne takes a similar view. He says those "who seek to speak of God are attempting to refer to the One who is the creative ground of all that is. They must, therefore, take into account all that we have learned about the variety of the world. This requires engagement with the full range of human disciplines—from natural science to anthropology and sociology, to aesthetics and ethics—that seek to explore the

134. Ibid., 178.

135. Padgett, *Science and Study*, 9.

136. Ibid., x–xi.

many-layered reality of our experience."[137] Polkinghorne clearly affirms the unity of reality and sees the necessity of having a UTK, but also acknowledges that science and theology each have their own "particular subject matter and [their] own resulting conceptual system[s], which have to be respected and which cannot just be transferred across to the other."[138] Because of this, Polkinghorne believes that "we need a willingness to recognize the many-layered character of that experience, so that the same event can be interpreted as a part of physical process, as an occasion for moral decision, as the carrier of beauty, and as an encounter with the divine presence. A crass physical reductionism will exclude by decree not only religion, but also the truly humane."[139]

Adler offers some additional insight. Like the others, he affirms the unity of reality and knowledge while at the same time allowing for the particular distinctions in each discipline. He says, "To say that there is one whole of truth all the parts of which must coherently and consistently fit together does not preclude the parts from being different from one another in a variety ways—with respect to the objects with which they are concerned, with respect to the methods by which inquiry is conducted, and with respect to the sources or bases of the truth being sought."[140] He then goes on to say, "No matter how diverse may be the objects, methods, and sources involved in the different parts of truth, they all remain, nevertheless, parts of one whole, and as such coherently and consistently fit together."[141]

By embracing Bhaskar's notion of stratification, then, McGrath is able to develop a unified approach to knowledge through CR that does not result in Wilson's problematic reductionism. Whereas Wilson's unity comes by eliminating the important areas of human inquiry—such as theology, philosophy, and ethics—McGrath's ST allows for all the important disciplines to function according to their own methods and modes of investigation. Thus, McGrath's ST makes a valuable contribution to the dialogue between science and theology and the development of an evangelical, theological, epistemological method that affirms a UTK without falling into reductionism.

137. Polkinghorne, *Scientists as Theologians*, 1.
138. Ibid., 7.
139. Ibid., 11.
140. Adler, *Truth In Religion*, 123.
141. Ibid., 123.

ST and the Issue of Epistemological Certainty

One final advantage of McGrath's use of CR in ST comes from his treatment of the sensitive, though important, issue of epistemological certainty. In a recent work entitled *Doubting*, McGrath makes the following observation:

> The beliefs that are really important in life concern such things as whether there is a God and what he is like, or the mystery of human nature and destiny. These—and a whole host of other important beliefs—have two basic features. In the first place, they are *relevant* to life. They matter, in that they affect the way we think, live, hope and act. In the second place, by their very nature they make claims that *cannot be proved* (or disproved) with total certainty. At best we may hope to know them as probably true. There will always be an element of doubt in any statement that goes beyond the world of logic and self-evident propositions. Christianity is not unique in this respect: an atheist or Marxist is confronted with precisely the same dilemma.[142]

This issue comes up in the final volume of *A Scientific Theology* when McGrath addresses the issue of closure in science and theology. Noting the difficulty of gaining certainty/closure for many of the theological and scientific claims one makes, McGrath thinks it is best not to demand certainty of beliefs, theories, and claims of knowledge. At the same time, however, it seems irresponsible to suggest or imply that this leads to skepticism or relativism. He argues that, in theology, "the process of wrestling with a mystery thus remains open, not closed. What one generation inherits from another is not so much definitive answers as a shared commitment to the process of wrestling . . . Traditionally, Christian doctrine has been well aware of its limits, and has sought to avoid excessively confident affirmations in the face of mystery. Yet at the same time, Christian theology has never seen itself as totally reduced to silence in the face of divine mysteries."[143]

With this in mind, McGrath's ST offers a balanced approach to this sensitive issue. As chapter 2 pointed out, McGrath notes how theories never give a perfect and complete representation of reality and that, because of this, a given interpretation of reality may never be regarded as final. "[In] what way," he wonders, "and at what point can the right

142. McGrath, *Doubting*, 24–25.
143. McGrath, *Scientific Theology*, vol. 3, 49.

interpretation of a set of particulars be regarded as being settled? How can a specific theory be regarded as having secured 'closure' of an issue, when the particularities it claims to represent are more open-ended than this closure suggests?"[144] Here, McGrath observes the need for continued dialogue and theological formulation within Christian theology. At the same time, however, McGrath does not want to side with postmodern thinkers, such as Hillary Lawson, who might see doctrines as "at the very best 'temporary resting places,' determined by the specifics of history and culture," and which "cannot be regarded as a permanent or universal 'safe and final truth.'"[145]

McGrath's solution to the problem is to show how there are different degrees of closure and assurance that one may have, depending on the nature of the object under consideration. Firmly insisting that "ontology determines epistemology,"[146] McGrath notes that "the degree of theoretical closure that may be secured for any aspect of reality is determined by its intrinsic nature. We are thus obliged to think in terms of a range of possibilities of closure, depending on which stratum of reality is being encountered and represented in this manner."[147] That is, "the extent of closure is determined by the subject matter. The nature of the object determines the extent of closure possible, according to its own distinctive nature."[148] Thus, McGrath rightly acknowledges that human beings are limited in their ability to understand and represent reality and that, because of this, there are few things in life about which one can have absolute certainty. At the same time, however, McGrath clearly rejects religious or scientific skepticism. He says:

> Let's be quite clear: Nobody can prove Christianity with total certainty. But that's not really a problem. The big questions concern the reliability of its historical foundations, its internal consistency, its rationality, its power to convert and its relevance to human existence. As C. S. Lewis stressed in *Mere Christianity*, Christianity has exceptionally fine credentials on all counts. Look into them. You can totally commit yourself to the gospel in full confidence, as a powerful, credible and profoundly satisfy-

144. Ibid., 43.

145. Ibid., 46.

146. Ibid., 82.

147. McGrath, *Science of God*, 187.

148. Ibid.

> ing answer to the mystery of human existence. Faith is basically the resolve to live our lives on the assumption that certain things are true and trustworthy, in the confident assurance that they are true and trustworthy, and that one day we will know with absolute certainty that they are true and trustworthy.[149]

In short, though McGrath thinks one cannot have absolute certainty or complete closure on theological matters, as well as many scientific matters, he does believe that Christian theology has excellent intellectual credentials that offer considerable assurance and confidence for the believer. Thus, Christian theology is not counted inferior to scientific knowledge when it does not achieve absolute epistemological certainty.

Like McGrath, a growing number of philosophers and theologians feel it necessary to abandon the modern quest for epistemological certainty. As Davis explains, the "search for absolutely certain statements from which one can (through an absolutely reliable method) warrant statements that were uncertain has indeed thus far proved to be a will-o'-the-wisp. The prospects for Cartesian foundationalism or Lockean foundationalism do not look particularly promising."[150] The reason for this, as noted earlier in the chapter, is that one simply does not have a God's-eye-view of reality from which he may view things. Thus, it is always possible that one's view of reality is clouded by things that prevent him from achieving an absolute certain understanding of it. Moreover, as Taylor points out, man is fallen, which further prevents him from gaining perfect knowledge. He says that as fallen creatures "our knowledge of any absolute is not only partial, it is distorted. Even if by some stretch of the imagination we could extrapolate the infinite from the finite, arguing that partial knowledge of an absolute demonstrates the existence of the whole, we confront the claim of Christian orthodoxy itself that all our perceptions are at least partially flawed as well as limited."[151]

There are other reasons why philosophers deny the possibility of achieving absolute certainty. Meek, for example, thinks that the quest for certainty should be abandoned because it seems to deny much of what man claims to know. She writes, "The ideal of certainty in knowledge is this: I must accept as true only those claims of which I am rationally certain, having no shadow of doubt. The search for such certainty, we

---

149. McGrath, *Doubting*, 27.

150. Davis, *God, Reason & Proofs*, 93.

151. Taylor, *Myth of Certainty*, 92.

have found in the centuries of our Western tradition, has led the stalwart to part with even the dearest of the commitments to which we might be naturally inclined."[152] She then adds, "Driven to attain an ideal of certainty, thinkers have over the centuries tightened the parameters of 'proper' knowledge so restrictively that what was left was at best truisms, or so minimalistic and private that all the mess of reality has been squeezed out of them."[153] If certainty is what is required for one to claim knowledge on a given issue, then Meek thinks there is very little that will qualify as knowledge. She says, "If we limit 'knowledge' to statements that meet this standard of certainty, we end up having to say that we know precious little. Even if we could attain certain and infallible knowledge, that 'knowledge' would be so sterile and disconnected from both the knower and the known reality as to be useless."[154] As already noted in this section, McGrath shares Meek's concern.

Adler and Wood share the same. In Wood's view, "The strict demands for unimpeachable certainty leave one with so small a set of basic beliefs that they can't possibly bear the heavy weight of all that we believe. A moment's reflection shows that the thousands of beliefs we hold about matters aesthetic, moral, religious, political, economic, historical, scientific, philosophical and so on can't all be derived from the very small set of basic beliefs insisted on by strong foundationalists."[155] Likewise, Adler says, "There is little in all the fields of our natural knowledge, based upon empirical research and rational reflection, that we know with certitude— little that is beyond the shadow of a doubt."[156] Like Meek, Adler, and Wood, McGrath thinks that if certainty is necessary to claim knowledge, then most important things in life will be excluded from the realm of knowledge. Thus, requiring certainty as a criterion for knowledge seems to be a dangerous move. [157]

Meek and Taylor point to an additional concern. In their view, the quest for certainty may have a counterproductive result. For those who seek to prove every detail of their beliefs and knowledge, the final outcome may be skepticism, not certainty. Meek, for instance, notes, "If

152. Meek, *Longing to Know*, 32.

153. Ibid., 33.

154. Ibid.

155. Wood, *Epistemology*, 94–95.

156. Adler, *Truth in Religion*, 31.

157. McGrath, *Doubting*, 23–24.

knowledge is as philosophers have thought for centuries, if our efforts to know have certainty as their uncompromising ideal, then skepticism seems the inevitable alternative."[158] Like Meek, Taylor acknowledges this concern, but shows how it may be of special concern for the church. He says, "Unfortunately, much of the church has also sold out to the myth of certainty. One kind of Christian apologetic claims certainty based on faith, another on a combination of faith and a rationalistic analysis of evidence. Their ultimate goal is the same: an unquestionable, undoubtable foundation on which to base all subsequent claims."[159] Taylor goes on to say:

> In order to promote this feeling of certainty, conservative Christendom erects an elaborate system of apologetics, group psychology (each feeds off the certainty the other supposedly has), and, often, legalism. Even the reflective person often succumbs to the false either-or of institutional belief: "Either you have the certainty about God and His will that we do, or you are possibly not even a believer at all." As a result, many either try to "believe harder," seeking the tranquil unquestioning that seems the ideal, or, out of a sense of confused integrity, sever themselves from the church whose standard they cannot meet.[160]

He further explains how the quest for certainty is counterproductive to Christianity when he says, "A naïve conception of absolutes offers a truth packaged in an illusion accompanied by a danger. The truth, which I affirm by faith in response to evidence, is that the essential Christian claims are actually so. The illusion is that I can be certain that they are so. The danger is that my eventual discovery that certainty is an illusion (one that never should have been offered in the first place) may lead me, mistakenly, to disavow the truth it enveloped."[161]

Thus, a number of evangelicals agree with McGrath that it is best not to require certainty as a criterion for knowledge. At the same time, however, like McGrath, they are also careful to note that the lack of certainty in knowledge does not lead to agnosticism, skepticism, or relativism. As Hiebert says, "Because critical realists realize that their theories are models and not photographs of reality, they are less rigidly

---

158. Meek, *Longing to Know*, 27.

159. Taylor, *Myth of Certainty*, 78–79.

160. Ibid., 79.

161. Ibid., 91.

dogmatic and are more open to examining the claims of other theories in the light of the data . . . This does not mean that critical realists do not believe in their theories deeply. They are committed to truth and want to make certain that their theories represent it. But they realize that their knowledge is human and therefore finite and limited."[162] He says, "Although no model provides a complete picture of reality, and although it simplifies or omits nonessential information so that the human mind can grasp certain essentials, it must be accurate on those essentials if it is to serve as a true and useful map."[163] Or, he puts it another way, saying, "Approximate knowledge may not be complete or exact, but that does not make it relative or arbitrary. We may measure the table and say that it is six feet long. A careful measurement shows it to be 6.17 feet long, and more exact study shows it is 6.1735 feet long. Each of these statements is true at a certain level of exactness. They all tell us something about the actual length of the board. Approximations are tied to a reality—to a fixed given, the better the approximation, the closer it is to reality."[164]

Similarly, Polkinghorne offers a balanced view of the situation. He says, "The Cartesian and Enlightenment programme of the search for clear and certain ideas as the basis for unshakeable knowledge has simply proved to be a failure. It would have been nice if it could have succeeded, but we have discovered painfully that it has not. I am sufficiently postmodern to recognize that this is the case."[165] Nevertheless, he does not believe that this acknowledgement leads to total skepticism. He says:

> This acknowledgement, however, does not lead me to intellectual despair, for my second observation is that our minds are so constituted, and we live in a world itself so constituted, that intellectual daring in the pursuit of a strategy of cautious circularity proves capable of yielding reliable knowledge. I say that not because the world had to be that way, but because, as a matter of contingent fact, it has proved to be so. The defense of critical realism depends upon an appeal to historical experience rather than to metaphysical necessity. We do appear able to gain knowledge of what is the case.[166]

162. Hiebert, *Missiological Implications*, 95–96.

163. Ibid., 99.

164. Ibid., 92.

165. Polkinghorne, *Scientists as Theologians*, 16.

166. Ibid.

Since the rise of modernity, the issue of certainty has been an issue of major importance.[167] In more recent times, however, it has become increasingly popular for philosophers to question or deny the possibility of achieving absolute certainty. At the same time, they feel obligated to note that the denial of certainty should not result in skepticism or relativism. One of McGrath's valuable contributions is that he offers a balanced way of dealing with this important issue, with which he removes the stifling demands of the Enlightenment to gain epistemological certainty, and does so without falling into relativism. In McGrath's theological method, the theologian strives for assurance or confidence, but does not require the unreasonable demand for certainty.

The Value of McGrath's Use of CR in ST

As this chapter has shown thus far, McGrath's use of CR in ST brings some genuine advantages to evangelical epistemology, in that it offers a way of doing theology which uses the natural sciences as a dialogue partner and does not succumb to the epistemological problems of modernity or postmodernity. This is seen by the way ST

1. Affirms realism and the possibility of gaining knowledge of reality

2. Affirms a correspondence theory of truth

3. Avoids classical foundationalism

4. Acknowledges the mediated nature of knowledge

5. Moves toward a UTK

6. Avoids reductionism

7. Offers a balanced approach to the issue of certainty

Because of these things, McGrath's use of CR is beneficial to evangelical theology. The chapter now turns to consider the benefits of McGrath's use of the doctrine of creation and his use of natural theology.

MCGRATH'S USE OF THE DOCTRINE OF CREATION

Like CR, the doctrine of creation is absolutely central to McGrath's ST and is the major topic of volume 1 of McGrath's trilogy. As chapter 2 noted, McGrath's treatment of this issue begins with an exploration of

---

167. Morris and Petcher, *Science & Grace*, 25.

the more general concept of nature, and concludes that there is no one universally accepted understanding to which this term *nature* refers. McGrath says, "A close examination of writings on nature over the last two thousand years reveals a disturbing and immensely significant fact. Far from being an autonomous and self-sufficient notion, nature turns out to be an interpreted concept. There is no single 'correct' notion of nature, but a multiplicity of competing notions."[168] That is, "There is no self-evidently correct definition of nature which has been accepted at all times, in all places, and by all people—or anything even approaching such a consensus."[169] McGrath demonstrates this by showing that, in the twentieth century alone, nature was understood as a mindless force, an open-air gymnasium, a wild kingdom, and a supply depot.[170] Elsewhere, he notes how the concept has been understood as a stage by Shakespeare and the poets, and as a book by Pierre Viret and Francis Bacon.[171] Given the various ways that nature has been understood, McGrath thinks that it is a "serious candidate for the most socially conditioned of all human concepts . . . The concept of nature is constructed by various groupings, largely to serve their own ends and lend intellectual legitimation to their enterprises."[172]

Because of this, McGrath believes that the theologian is justified in positing a view of nature as God's creation. As James Keating explains, "If the natural sciences are seen as offering interpretations of nature, and not the single fundament upon which all must build, nothing prevents Christians from asserting their particular interpretation of nature as God's creation and entering into dialogue with the sciences on an equal footing."[173] Or, put another way, McGrath argues that the "Christian theologian is not under any obligation to accept a normative definition of nature originating from outside the Christian tradition. Instead, Christian theology may deploy and explore its own distinctive understanding of what others call nature, but which the Christian tradition prefers to name 'creation.'"[174] Again, he says, since "there is no au-

168. McGrath, *Science of God*, 36.

169. Ibid., 36–37.

170. Ibid., 38.

171. See McGrath, *Scientific Theology*, vol. 1, 103 for his discussion on these views.

172. McGrath, *Scientific Theology*, vol. 1, 88.

173. Keating, "Natural Sciences," 129–30.

174. McGrath, *Science of God*, 45.

tonomous character to creation, which forces humanity to see it in one way, to the exclusion of all others, then Christianity is free to reassert its distinctive understanding of nature . . . There is, after all, a distinctive Christian way of looking at nature—as creation."[175]

McGrath's use of creation entails not just the acceptance of this term in referring to nature, but the acceptance of the Christian doctrine of creation itself. Thus, McGrath's use of *creation* to refer to nature is markedly different from Wilson's approach, which also has recently elected to use the term creation to refer to nature. As a naturalist, however, Wilson rejects the biblical understanding of nature although he employs the term creation when speaking of it. While addressing a Southern Baptist pastor, he describes their different understandings of creation. He says, "For you, the glory of an unseen divinity; for me, the glory of the universe revealed at last. For you, the belief in God made flesh to save mankind; for me, the belief in Promethean fire seized to set me free. You have found your final truth; I am still searching."[176] Unlike Wilson, McGrath's proposal encapsulates the biblical teaching on creation. That is, McGrath sees nature as the creation of God who created *ex nihilo* and reveals himself, at least partially, through creation. Thus, McGrath accepts the doctrine of creation in reference to nature, not just the term, and believes creation should be the term of choice when speaking about nature for the Christian.

Assessment of McGrath's Use of Creation

What, then, should one make of McGrath's proposal to speak of nature only as creation? In this next section, an assessment of McGrath's proposal is given, which notes three different ways his use of the Christian doctrine of creation makes a valuable contribution to the dialogue between science and theology and the development of a theological method. Because of this, it will be argued that McGrath's use of the Christian doctrine of creation in his ST adds an additional benefit for evangelical theology.

175. Ibid., 44.
176. Wilson, *Creation*, 4.

THE THEOLOGICAL BENEFITS OF THE DOCTRINE OF CREATION

It may seem incidental to say that there are theological benefits in McGrath's ST that come from his acceptance of the doctrine of creation. But McGrath thinks that this doctrine can be quite helpful for theological tasks, as it allows insights gained from creation to play a part in the development of theology. McGrath explains this more fully when he says:

> The Christian understanding of creation leads directly to the conclusion that there is a correspondence—the degree of which requires clarification—between the works of God and the being of God. Creation and redemption are not merely interconnected within the economy of salvation; they can each be argued to embody the character of God. For the Christian, the creation is not divine, but bears the hallmarks of divine crafting. The fundamental assumption of a responsible natural theology, to which we shall return later in this project, is that we are authorized by Scripture to seek a partial disclosure of the glory of God through the works of God in creation. God is rendered in and through the creation.[177]

For McGrath, then, creation is a source of divine revelation that will be helpful in the quest for knowledge in general and in Christian theology more specifically. As Colyer explains, "McGrath finds a fundamental congruence between divine rationality on the one hand and the rationality found within the creation, including humanity itself, on the other."[178]

Because of this, McGrath believes that the natural sciences can serve as a handmaiden to theology, not simply because they share common assumptions and methodologies, but also because they may be helpful in confirming or disconfirming a given doctrine where some aspect of the physical world is under consideration. He says, "The natural sciences seem to offer to contemporary Christian theology the same intellectual opportunities that earlier generations discerned within Aristotelianism or Cartesianism—the possibility of a dialogue partner with genuine insights to offer, which might be accommodated and exploited within the theological enterprise."[179] He goes on to say, "In one sense, the natural sciences can be seen as offering a stimulus to Christian theology, to

---

177. McGrath, *Scientific Theology*, vol. 1, 193.

178. Colyer, "Scientific Theology, vol. 1," 228.

179. McGrath, *Scientific Theology*, vol. 1, 18–19.

consider whether it has, in fact, achieved a correct interpretation of its foundational resources on points of importance . . . Augustine pointed out that certain passages were genuinely open to diverse interpretations, without calling into question any fundamental doctrines of the church. It was therefore important to allow further scientific research to assist in the determination of which was the most appropriate mode of interpretation for a given passage."[180] Putting it another way, he says, "The natural sciences thus offer an important resource to Christian theology, in that they invite the church continually to reconsider its present interpretations of Scripture, in order to ensure that the settled scientific assumptions of earlier generations—now known or suspected to be incorrect—have not inadvertently been incorporated into the teachings of the church. The importance of this role of the natural sciences is recognized by many theologians, including the influential evangelical writer Benjamin B. Warfield."[181]

McGrath thinks that theologians must take the theories of the natural sciences into consideration when questions pertaining to creation are under consideration. At the same time, however, McGrath is careful to note that the natural sciences do not function in a magisterial fashion. This is what he means when he describes his ST as being "governed at all points by Holy Scripture," and "offer[ing] a faithful and coherent account of what it finds there, using additional intellectual resources in a ministerial, rather than magisterial, manner."[182] Clark takes a similar view as McGrath in showing how science can be a helpful interpretive tool, so long as it is not allowed to displace the Bible. He says:

> We place a particular scientific idea or theory into conversation with a particular theological tradition, model, or doctrine. That is, we bring *interpretations of Scripture*—theology—into conversation with *interpretations of nature*—science. So, we do not allow science to supersede the Bible itself. We allow it to override *interpretations* of the Bible. No particular scientific theory, model, or idea possesses authority over Scripture, but there could be a scenario where a scientific claim trumps the deliverances of theology. The better way to think of this is to say that for evangelical theology, both theology (interpretations of special revelation) and science (interpretations of general revelation) come

180. Ibid., 61.
181. Ibid., 64.
182. Ibid., 44.

under the authority of Scripture itself. This means that we can place science and theology into dialogue without giving science veto power, as it were, over Scripture, and thus undermining the authority of the Bible.[183]

Like McGrath, Clark thinks "scientific discoveries could function evidentially to confirm or disconfirm certain theological claims."[184] Thus, McGrath and others suggest that natural science can serve as a hermeneutical tool for Christian theology.

THE SCIENTIFIC BENEFITS OF THE DOCTRINE OF CREATION

According to McGrath, the natural sciences may also benefit from the Christian doctrine of creation. Though scientists typically avoid the incorporation of any theological or supernatural affirmations into their theories, McGrath thinks there are certain scientific assumptions and presuppositions given intellectual support and justification with the doctrine of creation. For example, natural scientists accept that the universe is rational and that this rationality can be discovered and explained by human beings, but can offer no satisfying reason why this is the case.[185]

This situation has been described by a number of philosophers. As Polkinghorne notes, for example, "We are so familiar with the fact that we can understand the world that most of the time we take it for granted. It is what makes science possible. Yet it could have been otherwise. The universe might have been a disorderly chaos rather than an orderly cosmos. Or it might have had a rationality which was inaccessible to us."[186] Likewise, van Kooten Niekerk says that in the "investigation of the natural world [science] finds itself confronted with phenomena, which it must take for granted as science, but which at the same time raise questions of meaning that transcend science. I think of questions like 'Why is there a universe at all?' 'Why is the universe of this particular kind?' and 'How is it possible that it has brought forth conscious human beings that are able to know the world and themselves?'"[187] Peacocke makes a similar point when he says, "We cannot help pressing 'why?' questions to their intelligible limits. Science directs such questions to the nexus of events

183. Clark, *To Know and Love God*, 288.

184. Ibid., 285.

185. McGrath, *Science of God*, 59–71.

186. Polkinghorne, *Science and Creation*, 29.

187. van Kooten Niekerk, "Critical Realist Perspective," 79–80.

in the natural world: it seeks to provide answers to the question 'why?' by depicting the realities of the natural world in metaphorical language. But there are other broader 'why?' questions than those directed to what is in and going on in the natural world. Why is there a universe at all?' 'Why should it be of this particular kind?' 'Why is it open to rational inquiry?' 'Why is it beautiful?' 'Why does it generate a creature that can discern values?'"[188]

Other philosophers and theologians make similar observations. Vern Poythress, for example, says, "Now, the work of science depends constantly on the fact that there are regularities in the world. Without the regularities, there would ultimately be nothing to study. Scientists depend not only on regularities with which they are already familiar, such as the regular behavior of measuring apparatus, but also on the postulate that still more regularities are to be found in the areas that they will investigate."[189] Similarly, Clark, says that science must "assume metaphysical principles such as that an external world exists and that this world is orderly, stable, and properly interpreted numerically . . . Science also presupposes the laws of logic, the reliability of human cognitive capacities, and the adequacy of language. And science depends on epistemic values that are not themselves provable by science."[190] Thus, natural science finds itself assuming a rationality and regularity that it cannot explain.

Padgett notes some additional difficulties for the natural sciences in answering questions relating to meaning and value. He says, "The natural and social sciences are limited. They are unable to answer our deepest needs for meaning, values, and purpose, needs which are theological or philosophical in nature. So science is important but not all-important. Science cannot save us. It is itself based upon important assumptions and values that it cannot justify in its own terms but must assume from other disciplines. There are fundamental presuppositions in science which the disciplines own but cannot ground."[191] Ratzsch also notes how science alone cannot deal with all of the issues important to human beings. He says, "A method of investigation deliberately restricted to the naturalistic (or the purely material or mechanistic) will not be competent to deal

188. Peacocke, *Theology*, 87.

189. Poythress, *Redeeming Science*, 15.

190. Clark, *To Know and Love God*, 268–69.

191. Padgett, *Science and Study*, 20.

with most of the fundamental questions of morality and value, psychology, theology and religion, philosophy and some other areas as well."[192] Thus, as these philosophers and theologians suggest, science by itself is not able to deal adequately with important questions pertaining to intelligibility, rationality, morality, meaning, and value.

McGrath thinks that the Christian doctrine of creation is helpful to the natural sciences on these points since it offers an explanation of such issues. That is, the Christian doctrine of creation offers an explanation of what science can only assume or has no answer. As Roche observes:

> Creation *ex nihilo*, for example, allows the scientist committed to this doctrine to expect that divine rationality would somehow be reflected in the structure and workings of nature, but also to approach nature with the expectation that he does not have to look beyond the world of nature to find the proper object of his science. In an extended study of the doctrine of creation in Scripture, McGrath points out that, against any idea that the natural order is chaotic, irrational or inherently evil, the early Christian tradition affirmed that the natural order possesses an inherent goodness, rationality and orderliness, which derives directly from its creation by God.[193]

McGrath himself says, "One of the most significant parallels between the natural sciences and Christian theology is a fundamental conviction that the world is characterized by regularity and intelligibility . . . So important is this notion that it could be argued that the natural sciences are founded on the perception of explicable regularity to the world, which is capable of being represented mathematically. In other words, there is something about the world—and the nature of the human mind— which allows patterns within nature to be discerned and represented."[194] He later adds, "What the natural sciences are forced to assume—in that it cannot be formally demonstrated without falling into some form of circularity of argument or demonstration, the Christian understanding of 'wisdom' allows to be affirmed on the basis of divine revelation, and correlated with the existence of a transcendent creator God, responsible both for the ordering of the world and the human ability to grasp and

192. Ratzsch, *Science & Limits*, 96.

193. Roche, "Scientific Theology Project", 74.

194. McGrath, *Scientific Theology*, vol. 1, 218.

discern it."[195] While explaining the importance of McGrath's doctrine of creation, Roche says, "The doctrine of creation, seen as the creation of an order and coherence that reflects God and points to God, justifies the study of nature. Even more important historically for science, perhaps, is that the doctrine of creation, and the concomitant doctrine of the continual and consistent exercise of God's sustaining will, underpins a belief in the uniformity of nature, and in the existence and persistence of the 'laws of nature.'"[196] Within the course of his ST, then, McGrath uses the doctrine of creation to show how it offers an explanation of the regularity and rationality of nature, which natural science depends on for its explanation, but cannot explain on its own.

McGrath takes this a step further when he uses the doctrine of creation to explain concepts such as truth, beauty, goodness, and morality. He says, "As we have seen in our exploration of the Christian reflection on the implications of creation . . . there is a congruence between divine notions of truth, beauty and goodness and proper human notions of the same through the creaturely status of humanity."[197] He then says, "A Christian doctrine of creation affirms a congruence between the moral ordering of creation—including humanity as the height of that creation—and the mind of God."[198] Thus, he thinks that the Christian doctrine of creation can be of great value to natural science. This is because, by itself, natural science is unable to explain the regularities and rationality of nature, as well as philosophical concepts such as truth, goodness, and beauty. According to McGrath, then, the doctrine of creation can be of great value to natural science.

McGrath is not alone with this line of thinking, as several philosophers and theologians seem to agree with McGrath on this issue. For example, Polkinghorne says, "If the world is the creation of the rational God, and if we are creatures made in the divine image, then it is entirely understandable that there is an order in the universe that is deeply accessible to our minds. Putting the same point in a different way, one could say that science discerns a world which in its rational beauty and rational transparency is shot through with signs of mind, and the theist

195. Ibid., 222.

196. Roche, "Scientific Theology Project", 42–43.

197. McGrath, *Scientific Theology*, vol. 1, 216–17.

198. Ibid., 217.

can understand this because it is indeed the Mind of God that is partially disclosed in this way."[199] Clark agrees, saying:

> The meta-scientific assumptions necessary to science are themselves embedded in a worldview that identifies both the universe and also the observers who populate it as products of an intelligent creator. In Christian theology, over against pagan thought, the physical universe possesses an inner integrity that scientists can unravel. Nature is good, and it is worthwhile expending effort to understand it . . . So the idea that science can go it alone, that science can build its own platform on which to stand as it gives us knowledge of the world, is patently false. This does not by itself justify theology as a rational discipline or give theology a status that supersedes science.[200]

Finally, Padgett thinks there "are several theological conclusions that are important to the disciplines of the sciences: that God is the creator of the world and both rational and good, for example. This has been an important theological datum in the history of Western science. Other conclusions include that we can trust our senses, as well as the general view found throughout science that the world is understandable by human reasoning and experience. Science itself is good because knowledge is good, when it is used properly and in the service of God."[201]

Thus, one significant aspect of McGrath's ST is that it shows the value of the doctrine of creation for the natural sciences. In particular, when it comes to the rationality of the cosmos, the doctrine of creation explains what the natural sciences can only assume. Thus, McGrath shows how the doctrine of creation is of value, not just to the theologian, but to the scientist as well.

The Christian Doctrine of Creation and a UTK

Before moving to McGrath's use and development of natural theology, it is worth noting how McGrath's use of the doctrine of creation is helpful in developing a UTK. During the section dealing with his use of CR, this chapter argued that McGrath, by adopting CR, offers the *epistemological* basis for moving toward a UTK. With his use of the Christian doctrine of creation, however, it could also be argued that McGrath offers the

---

199. Polkinghorne, *Science & Theology*, 73.

200. Clark, *To Know and Love God*, 269.

201. Padgett, *Science and the Study*, 20.

ontological basis for developing a UTK. Evidence of this can be found in all three volumes of *A Scientific Theology* as well as in *The Science of God*. In volume 1, for example, McGrath says, "The Christian doctrine of creation demands a unitary approach to knowledge, while being responsive to diversity within that creation. If God made the world, which therefore has the status of being 'creation' as well as 'nature,' it is to be expected that something of the character of God might be disclosed through that creation."[202] Here, one should note that McGrath thinks the nature of creation itself demands a unitary approach to knowledge. At the same time, however, as with his use of CR, he is also careful to avoid reductionism in that he acknowledges the diversity of creation. Earlier in volume 1, he notes how ST argues, "largely on the basis of a detailed analysis of a Christian doctrine of creation, that there are good reasons, grounded in the structure of the world as the creation of God, for developing an approach to theology which recognizes and welcomes convergences. There is . . . both an ontological foundation and imperative for dialogue between the disciplines."[203] He then says, "A positive working relationship between Christian theology and the natural sciences is demanded by the Christian understanding of the nature of reality itself—an understanding which is grounded in the doctrine of creation."[204]

This argument is continued in volume 2, where McGrath further explains how the Christian doctrine of creation requires a unitary approach to knowledge. There, he says:

> One of the most important themes of a scientific theology is its vision of the unity of reality. Reality is to be apprehended in various ways and at different levels, with various disciplines offering themselves as the more appropriately qualified to explore certain aspects of that reality than others. The Christian doctrine of creation insists that the dual affirmation of the created status of the natural order and of the human mind leads to the recognition that there is an ontological imperative for the epistemological enterprise—that is, that the nature of reality is such that the question of how it is to be known is imposed upon us. The Christian vision of reality is such that knowledge of creator and creation, redeemer and redeemed, are interlocked. Perhaps different methods of investigation are appropriate for different purposes; yet the

202. McGrath, *Scientific Theology*, vol. 1, 21.

203. Ibid., 6.

204. Ibid., 21.

fundamental Christian vision is that of a creator, redeemer and creation which are all possessed of the same intrinsic rationality through the act of creation itself.[205]

There are two things to notice here. First, McGrath contends that the doctrine of creation encourages a unified vision of reality. Second, McGrath notes the different levels of reality, which require different methods and modes of investigation. Thus, like CR, McGrath's use of creation allows for a UTK without falling into the trap of reductionism.

In volume 3, McGrath says, "The Christian tradition posits a unitary reality, holding that the entire creation has the potential to bear witness to its creator . . . The Christian doctrine of creation provides a fundamental motivation to the investigation and appreciation of nature, in terms of both providing an intellectual framework which allows nature to be seen as a coherent witness to God, and enkindling an intellectual curiosity, a love of truth."[206] Elsewhere, in *The Science of God*, he says, "The basic argument of the 'scientific theology' project is that a positive working relationship between Christian theology and the natural sciences is demanded by the Christian understanding of reality itself. At this point, we encounter a theme of major importance to the project: the critical role of a Christian doctrine of creation. If the world is indeed the creation of God, then there is an ontological ground for a theological engagement with the natural sciences."[207]

Clark and Padgett have also noted how the doctrine of creation allows for the unification of the various disciplines. Clark, for example, makes a similar point when he says, "For evangelical theology, the ontological ground of unity in theology arises out of the One whom we know, not out of us who do the knowing. The self-revelation of this One is our path to unity."[208] Likewise Padgett notes how, as a realist, he is "committed to the unity of reality and therefore to the fruitfulness of seeking harmony among many voices and perspectives . . . The conviction that they must be in harmony is grounded in the fact, long advocated by Christian tradition, that God is the Creator of the universe and

205. McGrath, *Scientific Theology*, vol. 2, 247–48.

206. McGrath, *Scientific Theology*, vol. 3, 3–4.

207. McGrath, *Science of God*, 21.

208. Clark, *To Know and Love God*, 182.

the author of revelation. There is one God (or religious Reality) and one world, which we are all struggling to discover more fully."[209]

In addition to his use of CR, then, it seems that McGrath's use of creation is helpful in moving toward a UTK without conceding to reductionism. Unity is demanded by the fact that creation is understood to bear the marks of its creator. Thus, theologians and scientists investigate the same object and receive some of the same information. At the same time, the doctrine of creation does not demand that all aspects of creation be reduced to one mode of investigation. There is diversity in creation, which requires diversity in methodology. Thus, the need for a UTK as described earlier in the chapter is met by McGrath's use of the Christian doctrine of creation.

The Value of McGrath's Use of the Doctrine of Creation

The Christian doctrine of creation is essential to McGrath's ST. Like his use of CR, McGrath's use of this doctrine marks an additional benefit for evangelical philosophers and theologians. McGrath notes the theological benefit of this doctrine in that it shows how creation reveals, at least partially, God to mankind. Because of this, the natural sciences can be a helpful dialogue partner for theology, since they can be used to prevent theologians from coming to an incorrect understanding of nature, as well as the Bible. Scientifically speaking, with the doctrine of creation, McGrath shows how the natural sciences also have a vested interest in taking theology seriously. Where the natural sciences are not able to offer an explanation of some of their central assumptions, as well as certain philosophical concepts, such as truth, beauty, and goodness, theology offers such an explanation and reinforces natural sciences' assumptions. Moreover, McGrath shows how the doctrine of creation demands a unified approach to knowledge without yielding to reductionism. With the doctrine of creation in hand, McGrath's ST is constructive in encouraging a dialogue between science and theology and in developing an acceptable evangelical theological method.

MCGRATH'S USE OF NATURAL THEOLOGY

Like CR and the doctrine of creation, McGrath's use of natural theology is vitally important to his ST. Much of what McGrath says about,

---

209. Padgett, *Science and Study*, 20.

and does with, natural theology, however, has already been covered in chapter 2. Nevertheless, before an assessment of his approach is given, it will be helpful to offer a brief comparison of the way natural theology is typically understood and the way McGrath understands it. It seems there are at least two ways McGrath's approach differs from more recent versions of natural theology.[210]

Where more recent versions have tended to focus on specific arguments for the existence of God, such as the cosmological or teleological arguments, McGrath's approach is broader in nature and seems more akin to what today is typically referred to as natural revelation. This becomes evident in his treatment of the Reformed tradition on the subject. Here he cites John Calvin, who, according to McGrath, clearly acknowledged that "a general knowledge of God may be discerned throughout the creation—in humanity, in the natural order, and in the historical process itself."[211] McGrath then says, "It is important to stress that Calvin makes no suggestion whatsoever that this knowledge of God from the created order is peculiar to, or restricted to, Christian believers. Calvin is arguing that anyone, by intelligent and rational reflection upon the created order, should be able to arrive at the idea of God."[212] McGrath also notes the Gallic and Belgic confessions, which make similar affirmations regarding the knowledge of God that comes from creation.[213] Thus, where some make a distinction between natural theology and natural revelation,[214] McGrath does not seem to do so. According to Eugene Long, this should not be problematic, since, in his view, it is quite possible to understand natural theology in this more broad fashion. He says, "Philosophers and theologians often limit the expression natural theology in such a way that it refers primarily to the classical arguments for the existence of God. It is clear, however, that natural theology is also used in a broader and more inclusive sense to refer to all natural knowledge of God arrived at without appeal to the authority of revelation and faith as manifested in a particular community of faith."[215]

210. By "more recent versions," I am referring to the way natural theology has been used from the Enlightenment forward.

211. McGrath, *Scientific Theology*, vol. 1, 273.

212. Ibid., 274.

213. McGrath, *Science of God*, 73.

214. Craig, "Classical Apologetics," 39.

215. Long, "Introduction," 2.

The second difference with McGrath's use of natural theology is that he places it within the Christian tradition and allows it to operate as "the enterprise of seeing nature as creation, which both presupposes and reinforces fundamental Christian theological affirmations."[216] Thus, for McGrath, "natural theology gains its plausibility and derives its intellectual foundations from within the Christian tradition. Its roots lie *intra muros ecclesiae*, even if its relevance extends *extra muros ecclesiae*. It is not a tradition-independent or autonomous intellectual discipline, in that its legitimation rests upon a Christian doctrine of creation—including the related concepts of the contingent ordering of the created world, and the epistemic and spiritual capacities of human nature."[217] But, as McGrath acknowledges, this is not the way that natural theology is typically understood today. For an example, he points to William Alston who defines natural theology as "the enterprise of providing support for religious beliefs by starting from premises that neither are nor presuppose any religious beliefs."[218] Like Alston, C. Stephen Evens says natural theology is the "attempt to determine the truth of theism without assuming the standpoint of a particular religion . . . The natural theologian attempts to see what can be knowledge about God independently of any special religious authority."[219] One will notice that, in this approach, the natural theologian is not permitted to begin with any particular theistic beliefs or assumptions. He must start from outside of Christianity, not within.

By placing natural theology inside the Christian tradition, McGrath believes that his own approach is more in line with the regular practice of church history and suggests that the modern approach (as represented by Alston and Evens) is a product of the Enlightenment. He says, "By the end of the eighteenth century, an approach to natural theology had developed which saw a rational appeal to the natural order, without reference to revelation, as a means of defending the Christian faith at a time of intellectual ferment."[220] But what happened that caused such a shift in the practice of natural theology? McGrath identifies four different factors:

216. McGrath, *Science of God*, 113.
217. McGrath, *Scientific Theology*, vol. 2, 74.
218. Alston, *Perceiving God*, 289.
219. Evans, *Philosophy of Religion*, 38.
220. McGrath, *Science of God*, 76.

1. The rise of biblical criticism, which called into question the reliability or intelligibility of Scripture, and hence generated interest in the identification and exploitation of more accessible knowledge of the divine.

2. A growing impatience with and dislike of ecclesiastical authority caused more libertarian individuals to seek for sources of knowledge which were seen to be independent of ecclesiastical control. The church might have control of the Bible; nobody could control the natural order.

3. A dislike of the pomposity of organized religion and the apparent complexity of Christian doctrines caused many to seek for a simpler form of religion, free of complications and distortions. A highly idealized quest for an original religion of "nature" thus began to take place, in which nature was given priority as source of revelation and object of worship over the Christian equivalents.

4. The continuing successes of the mechanical world-view prompted many to wish to gain a deeper knowledge of God through the intricacies of creation. The invisible God could be studied through God's visible works.[221]

In McGrath's view, "these four factors led to a new interest in a specific form of natural theology which went far beyond anything known to the first sixteen centuries of Christian theological reflections."[222] Thus, as McGrath shows, by requiring natural theology to operate as the basis for theistic belief, the Enlightenment brought a marked change in the way natural theology was used.

Davis seems to agree. As he points out, where natural theology had once operated within the Christian tradition, it was now used as the basis for Christian belief itself. He says, "In short, by the time we reach the Enlightenment, it seems that theistic provers feel somehow responsible to atheists and religious skeptics; it seems that the main job that theistic provers accept for themselves is to produce arguments that would or should be convincing to those same skeptics. If skeptics cannot be convinced that God exists, the fall-back position is at least to convince them that theists are rational in asserting that God exists. But whether a given

---

221. McGrath, *Scientific Theology*, vol. 1, 244.
222. Ibid.

[theistic proof] is a successful argument will be decided by the skeptics at whom it is directed, not by believers."[223] Nash makes the same observation, suggesting that in the Enlightenment, Christian thinkers began to act as "though natural theology was a necessary first step in establishing the credibility of theism."[224] He further explains this by saying, "Whether done intentionally or not, natural theology has usually involved a major concession to the evidentialist-foundationalist model of rationality. If Christian theism is to be rational on this view, it must be supported with arguments or proofs; and those arguments must eventually be linked to beliefs that narrow foundationalists regard as properly basic."[225]

Not surprising, then, natural theology came to be seen as an attempt to argue for God's existence from nature and reason alone in isolation from the Bible, since the Bible was seen as a weak foundation for theistic belief. From the Enlightenment forward then, natural theology was required to prove God's existence before one could embrace theism.

Thus, throughout all three volumes of *A Scientific Theology* and *The Science of God*, McGrath rejects an Enlightenment approach to natural theology claiming that it is not an autonomous discipline that exists apart from the Christian tradition. Roche helps explain McGrath's concern, saying that an Enlightenment approach to natural theology "pretentiously claims to grasp the ineffable nature of God; it has led to Deism, to a view of God as a clockmaker otherwise uninvolved with the world, and has thereby functioned in the past as a halfway house to atheism. It can even seem to set itself up as a 'natural' religion, independent of any existing religious tradition."[226] Thus, McGrath thinks natural theology cannot operate in isolation from revealed theology.

Assessment of McGrath's Use of Natural Theology

Natural theology is of major importance to McGrath's ST as understood within his view of creation. It is argued here that his approach makes a valuable contribution to evangelical theology and apologetics. In particular, his approach affirms creation as a source of divine revelation, focuses on the laws of nature, abandons classical foundationalism, re-

---

223. Davis, *God, Reason & Proofs*, 79.
224. Nash, *Faith & Reason*, 94.
225. Ibid., 93–94.
226. Roche, "Scientific Theology Project," 48.

moves the requirement of certainty, has great explanatory power, and can be used as a point of contact with the nonbeliever.

McGrath's Natural Theology Affirms Creation as a Source of Revelation

From a biblical standpoint, one fruitful aspect of McGrath's approach is that it recognizes how creation reveals its creator. That is, McGrath affirms that God can be known, at least partially, in and through creation. With this, McGrath ties the categories of natural revelation and natural theology to the doctrine of creation and shows how they flow out of it. If the natural world is the creation of God, then McGrath thinks that it bears the marks of its creator and reveals something about him. He argues that "there is an intrinsic capacity within the created order to disclose God. Here, nature-as-creation is understood to have an ontologically grounded capacity to reflect God as its maker and originator."[227] Elsewhere, he notes how for natural theology the "doctrine of creation plays a major role. The ability of creation to display the creator is a direct consequence of its created status."[228] He goes on to say that the "Christian doctrine of creation offers an explanatory window into both the ordering of the natural world and the capacity of the human mind to discern and represent this ordering."[229]

In McGrath's work, one sees a close connection between creation and natural theology. Because the world has been created by God, something about him can be known from it. This affirmation is certainly consistent with what the Bible has to say on this matter. For example, in Psalms 19:1, the Bible says, "The heavens declare the glory of God; and the firmament shows His handiwork." Here the Bible clearly states that creation reveals God's glory and handiwork to man. While commenting on this verse, John Calvin says:

> When we behold the heavens, we cannot but be elevated, by the contemplation of them, to Him who is their great Creator; and the beautiful arrangement and wonderful variety which distinguish the courses and station of the heavenly bodies, together with the beauty and splendor which are manifest in them, cannot but furnish us with an evident proof of his providence. Scripture,

227. McGrath, *Scientific Theology*, vol. 1, 297.
228. McGrath, *Science of God*, 72.
229. Ibid., 222.

indeed, makes known to us the time and manner of the creation; but the heavens themselves, although God should say nothing on the subject, proclaim loudly and distinctly enough that they have been fashioned by his hands: and this of itself abundantly suffices to bear testimony to men of his glory.[230]

Here, one should note that Calvin affirms that the heavens offer "proof of his providence," and "abundantly suffice to bear testimony to men of his glory." James Barr takes a similar position on this passage from Psalms, but also suggests that it lays the foundation for natural theology. He maintains that "there are . . . units, substantial literary units, complete speeches, complete poems, even if only a few of them, which meditate mainly or even solely on natural theology; and Psalm 19 may be seen as one of these."[231] Thus, for Calvin and Barr, Psalm 19 supports the notion that the heavens provide man with some form of the knowledge of God. They do not claim that this knowledge is complete, or that it can lead to salvation. They simply affirm that creation gives man some knowledge about God, even if it is very limited.

In addition to Psalm 19, scholars also point to Romans 1:18–20 in support for general revelation and natural theology. In this passage, Paul says, "For the wrath of God is revealed from heaven against all ungodliness and unrighteousness of men, who suppress the truth in unrighteousness, because what may be known of God is manifest in them, for God has shown it to them. For since the creation of the world His invisible attributes are clearly seen, being understood by the things that are made, even His eternal power and Godhead, so that they are without excuse." There are several affirmations in this passage that should be highlighted. To begin with, Paul affirms that God has placed knowledge of himself within man. Paul says that this knowledge is "manifest in them." This idea appears to be what Calvin would call the *sensus divinitatis*.[232] Second, this passage affirms that some knowledge of God can be known through the things that are created. Third, this passage affirms that this knowledge leaves man "without excuse."

Those who oppose natural theology find these passages difficult to explain. Erickson explains how Barth, for example, argued that the "persons in view do find God in the cosmos, but they do so because

---

230. Calvin, *Calvin's Commentaries*, vol. 4, 309.

231. Barr, *Biblical Faith*, 89.

232. Calvin, *Institutes*, 1/3:1.

they already know God from his special revelation. Therefore, what has happened is that they have read into, or projected upon, the created order, what they have known of him from the revelation."[233] But this understanding of Romans appears to be a stretch. As McGrath puts it, "Barth's engagement with the biblical texts are increasingly being seen in terms of the imposition of Barth's views upon those texts, rather than a faithful attempt to expound them."[234] Erickson, who also critiques Barth's exegesis,[235] concludes by saying, "The language of this passage is clear and strong. It is hard to interpret expressions like 'what can be known about God' . . . and 'has shown' . . . as pointing to anything other than an objectively knowable truth about God."[236] Thus, the Bible seems to support the idea that genuine knowledge of God can be gained from creation, even if that knowledge is incomplete or obscured. As Calvin notes, "God is in himself invisible; but as his majesty shines forth in his works and in his creatures everywhere, men ought in these to acknowledge him, for they clearly set forth their Maker."[237] Thus, drawing from the doctrine of creation, McGrath develops a natural theology that is consistent with what the Bible has to say about creation's ability to reveal the glory of God.

McGrath's Natural Theology Focuses on the Laws of Nature

Another important aspect of McGrath's natural theology is that it focuses more on the laws of nature, as opposed to specific arguments for God's existence, such as the cosmological or teleological arguments, which have come under serious attack in recent centuries. This is not to say that McGrath totally disregards an approach to natural theology that uses such arguments.[238] It is only to say that his approach places a greater emphasis on the regularities and the laws of nature. He says, "The older habit of positing a 'God of the gaps' has now been generally discarded as useless. Rather than suggesting that God offers an explanation of what the natural sciences are currently unable to explain more recent theistic writers have

233. Erickson, *Christian Theology*, 190.

234. McGrath, *Science of God*, 83.

235. Erickson, *Christian Theology*, 190.

236. Ibid., 193.

237. Calvin, *Calvin's Commentaries*, vol. 19, 70. This comes from his commentary on Rom 1:20.

238. See McGrath, *Christian Theology*, 190.

stressed the importance of belief in God in explaining the 'big picture'—that is to say, the overall patterns of ordering which are discerned within the universe."[239] In volume 1, he says, "The perceived ordering of the world is unquestionably one of the most important themes demanding to be investigated and explained by the natural sciences. In investigating such regularities, however, the natural sciences find themselves obliged to presuppose what they investigate—namely, that such ordering is a universal, rather than spatially or chronologically local, phenomenon."[240] In McGrath's view, "Christian theology offers an account of this. The scientific tradition recognizes that the natural world has a rationality which human rationality can discern and systematize; Christian theology, however, offers an explanation of why this is the case."[241]

McGrath thinks that the beauty of these laws is displayed in what has come to be referred to as the *anthropic principle*. He says, "One single example may be cited to illustrate the capacity of theism to illuminate the world—namely, the apparent 'fine-tuning' of the universe to permit carbon-based life forms to emerge and survive. The term 'anthropic principle' is now widely used to refer to this remarkable degree of 'fine-tuning' uncovered by the natural sciences within the natural order."[242] He then adds, "A constant theme to emerge from this discussion is that the anthropic principle, whether stated in a weak or strong form, is strongly consistent with a theistic perspective. A theist (for example, a Christian) with a firm commitment to a doctrine of creation will find the 'fine-tuning' of the universe to be an anticipated and pleasant confirmation of his religious beliefs."[243]

Like McGrath, other philosophers, theologians and scientists have seen this approach as a more feasible attempt at natural theology since it focuses the argument on an issue that science cannot explain. For example, where the design argument is seen to be weak, given the alternate explanation provided by natural selection, some philosophers think that a natural theology that places the emphasis on the larger metaquestions of reality may be more promising. Polkinghorne suggests that this new approach to natural theology is "concerned not only with a revived

239. McGrath, *Scientific Theology*, vol. 3, 195.
240. McGrath, *Scientific Theology*, vol. 1, 231.
241. McGrath, *Scientific Theology*, vol. 2, 75.
242. McGrath, *Scientific Theology*, vol. 3, 196.
243. Ibid., 197–98.

natural theology but also with a *revised* natural theology."[244] In his view, this more recent approach can be seen as a revision of natural theology because it "points to law and circumstance (the assumed data of science and so not open to scientific inquiry) rather than to particular occurrences (such as the coming-to-be of life or the eye)."[245] Likewise, Richard Swinburne argues that "regularities of succession are all-pervasive. For simple laws govern almost all successions of events . . . The laws of their behaviour can be set out by relatively simple formula which men can understand and by means of which they can successfully predict the future. The orderliness of the universe to which I draw attention here is its conformity to formula, to simple, formulable, scientific laws. The orderliness of the universe in this respect is a very striking fact about it. The universe might so naturally have been chaotic, but it is not—it is very orderly."[246] He later notes how "the universe is characterized by vast, all-pervasive temporal order, the conformity of nature to formula, recorded in the scientific laws formulated by men. Now this phenomenon, like the very existence of the world, is clearly something 'too big' to be explained by science. If there is an explanation of the world's order it cannot be a scientific one, and this follows from the nature of scientific explanation."[247] Polkinghorne explains:

> The new natural theology looks to the ground of all science's explanation, the laws of nature that it has to take as the assumed and unexplained basis for all its explanation, and it asks whether there is more to be understood about these laws beyond their mere assertion. This new natural theology is in no way a rival to science within science's proper domain. It does not purport to provide answers to what are essentially scientific questions but it serves as a complement to science, going beyond the latter's self-limited realm of enquiry and addressing metaquestions, that arise from scientific experience but which transcend the bounds of scientific understanding alone.[248]

He then says, "If God has created the world, one might expect there to be some signs that this is the case. These indications need not be supposed

---

244. Ibid., 24.

245. Ibid.

246. Swinburne, *Existence of God*, 136.

247. Ibid., 138.

248. Polkinghorne, *Science & Theology*, 71.

to be plain and unambiguous, as if creatures all bore labels saying 'Made by God,' but at least one might anticipate that there would be some hints that could be construed as pointing in a divine direction."[249] Likewise, Peacocke argues that the rationality, intelligibility, and comprehensibility of the universe "cannot but render more probable than ever before inference to the existence of a supra-rational Being as Creator as the 'best explanation' of such a world's existence and character. In other words, the affirmation of the existence of God as the supremely rational Creator is strengthened and its truth rendered more, rather than less, probable by the increasing success of science in discovering the inherent, but in content ever-surprising, rationality of the cosmos."[250]

Like the others noted here, McGrath's natural theology seems to place an emphasis on the larger questions about the existence of the universe that require explanation, such as the regularities and laws of nature. By doing so, McGrath focuses the argument on issues that are of greater difficulty, if not impossible, for natural science to explain on its own. Thus, his approach to natural theology attempts to overcome many of the modern objections that are often leveled against it.

McGrath's Natural Theology Abandons a Foundationalist Approach

An additional advantage of McGrath's approach to natural theology is that it is consistent with his non-foundationalist epistemology. This is seen in at least two ways:

1. It does not serve as the foundation for Christian belief.

2. It operates within Christian tradition without looking for a universally neutral perspective. Natural theology, according to McGrath, "is not to be understood in the sense of access to knowledge of God without recourse to revelation—an idea implicit in William Alston's definition of 'natural theology' as 'the enterprise of providing support for religious beliefs by starting from premises that neither are nor presuppose any religious beliefs.'"[251] Rather, as noted earlier, he proposes that natural theology be understood as the "enterprise of

---

249. Ibid., 69.

250. Peacocke, *Theology*, 104.

251. McGrath, *Science of God*, 74. For Alston's view, see Alston, *Perceiving God*, 289.

seeing nature as creation, which both presupposes and reinforces fundamental Christian theological affirmations."[252]

McGrath's desire to avoid using natural theology as the foundation for Christian belief becomes evident when he says, "Natural theology cannot be taken as an independent ground for affirming God's existence and nature, independent of revelation, but allows a sharpened awareness of the created character of the world. The human capacity to discern that the patterning of the world is a vestige of its divine creator has been attenuated (to a contested extent) through sin, but remains a subtle, if often unacknowledged influence over human reflection. Though insightful rather than demonstrative, natural theology has important apologetic implications."[253] If natural theology could serve as the foundation for Christian belief, then it would be necessary for it to begin with a neutral and tradition-independent perspective and then to work towards religious belief. McGrath, however, thinks that this is simply impossible and unreasonable. He says, "It is essential to appreciate that this new role for natural theology arises from the collapse of any notion that there exists a tradition-independent standpoint from which each tradition may be judged. There is no neutral transcendent vantage point from which the claims of competing traditions may be evaluated."[254] He further distinguishes his approach from the Enlightenment model by saying, "The kind of natural theology which a scientific theology seeks to justify and commend offers an account of the trans-traditional quest for truth, beauty and goodness which does not require the interposition of an additional tradition, or the imposition of a supratraditional device, in order to offer an explanation of some of the most fundamental impulses of the human mind."[255]

McGrath avoids this Enlightenment approach by allowing natural theology to function from within the Christian tradition. Following T. F. Torrance, he thinks that natural theology should be thought of as "a subordinate aspect of revealed theology, legitimated by that revealed theology rather than by natural presuppositions or insights; [Torrance] further believes that Barth himself appreciated this point. The legitima-

---

252. McGrath, *Scientific Theology*, vol. 2, 73.

253. Ibid., 71.

254. McGrath, *Scientific Theology*, vol. 3, 194.

255. Ibid., 195.

tion of natural theology lies not in its own intrinsic structures, nor in an autonomous act of human self-justification, but in divine revelation itself. *Theologia revelata* both legitimates *theologia naturalis* and defines its scope."[256]

Like McGrath, John Frame also thinks that natural theology should operate from within the Christian tradition. He says, "Certainly there can be no objection to presenting natural revelation to the unbeliever. We must, however, be careful that our statements about natural revelation are in line with scriptural teaching—that we are looking at nature through the 'spectacles of Scripture.' Showing natural revelation to the unbeliever is not an invitation to him to reason neutrally or autonomously or to ignore the Scriptures. Therefore, in a sense, natural and special revelation must never be separated in an apologetic encounter."[257]

One advantage of this approach to natural theology is that it seems to be consistent with the practice of the church up until the modern period. Thus, Keating says:

> [McGrath] combines respect and resolution in confronting the claim that a strong doctrine of revelation is ultimately incompatible with the notion that nature reveals God as well. More often than not, such a negative judgment rests upon a failure to distinguish between modern and premodern approaches. In premodern theologies, consideration of how nature provides some access to God took place within a theological framework determined by Christian revelation. In contrast, the modern conception of natural theology bears the marks of its origins in the Enlightenment desire to create a theology free of the church and beholden to universal reason alone.[258]

Likewise, Stephen Davis thinks that the major thinkers of the medieval period used natural theology in a way similar to what McGrath is suggesting. While speaking about Anselm and Aquinas, he says, "The [theistic proofs] that these and other medieval thinkers offered sound like intellectual efforts that are largely internal to faith. The central aim was not to convince that Christians are rational in asserting that God exists."[259] Thus, one advantage of McGrath's natural theology is that it

---

256. McGrath, *Scientific Theology*, vol. 1, 281.

257. Frame, *Apologetics*, 25.

258. Keating, "Natural Sciences," 132.

259. Davis, *God, Reason & Proofs*, 78–79.

abandons a foundationalist approach to knowledge and seems to return something similar to the premodern practice.

McGrath's Natural Theology Removes the Requirement of Certainty

Another constructive aspect of McGrath's approach is that it removes the requirement of certainty for the practice of natural theology. In other words, natural theology no longer has to "prove" that God exists in order to be valid or valuable. Instead, it is allowed to function as a confirmation of an already existing belief. Brooke explains, "Since the Enlightenment, natural theology has often been characterized as the attempt to construct rational 'proofs' for God's existence and attributes—a project drawing on the natural sciences but vulnerable both to philosophical critiques and to changes in scientific sensibility."[260]

McGrath's rejection of this approach is evident in a number of places throughout *A Scientific Theology* and *The Science of God*. For instance, he says that pointing to the fine-tuning of the universe does not "constitute a 'proof' of the existence of God, but would be a further element in a cumulative series of considerations which is at the very least consistent with the existence of a creator God."[261] That is, the evidence he uses in his approach does not amount to an irrefutable proof for God's existence. He says few "religious thinkers would suggest that this is the case, and I am certainly not among them. What would be affirmed, however, is that they are consistent with a theistic worldview; that they can be accommodated with the greatest of ease within such a worldview; and that they reinforce the plausibility of such a worldview for those who are already committed to it."[262] Elsewhere, he says, "Such a natural theology cannot conceivably be regarded as a 'proof' of the Christian revelation . . . Instead, such a natural theology offers a resonance—a realization that what is being proclaimed makes sense of things, even if this resonance fails to even approach the status of 'proof.' There is thus a fundamental resonance—but nothing more—between nature and theology, with the latter offering a prism through which the former may be viewed and understood."[263]

---

260. Brooke, "Natural Theology," 163–64.

261. McGrath, *Scientific Theology*, vol. 3, 198.

262. Ibid.

263. McGrath, *Science of God*, 89.

Once again, in framing natural theology this way, McGrath sees himself as following in the tradition of the great thinkers of the pre-modern period. In reply to Alvin Plantinga's charge that Aquinas attempted to use natural theology in a foundational fashion, which offered certainty, McGrath says, "Aquinas does not regard natural theology as offering proofs for faith, but as offering support for faith from within the context of an existing faith."[264] Elsewhere he says, there are "excellent reasons for suggesting that Aquinas regards natural theology as a demonstration, from the standpoint of faith, of the consonance between that faith and the structures of the world. In other words, natural theology is not intended to prove the existence of God, but presupposes that existence; it then asks, 'What should we expect the natural world to be like if it has indeed been created by such a God?' The search for order in nature is therefore intended not to demonstrate that God exists, but to reinforce the plausibility of an already existing belief."[265] Historically speaking then, McGrath says it is "clear that patristic writers did not see natural theology as offering proofs of God's existence. The existence of God was taken for granted."[266]

Polkinghorne thinks this a more promising approach to natural theology. He says natural theology's "discourse is of insight rather than proof. It does not assert that God's existence can be demonstrated in a logically coercive way (any more than God's non-existence can) but that theism makes more sense of the world, and of human experience, than does atheism. Unbelievers are not fools, but it is held that they explain less than believers can."[267] Nash also thinks it best to remove the requirement of certainty from the practice of natural theology. He says, "Suppose, in other words, that instead of seeking coercive proofs for conclusions that all right-minded and open-minded persons would accept, we view our task as the more modest one of seeing if the Christian worldview does what we should expect any world-view to do."[268]

As the earlier section of this chapter on CR argued, the requirement of certainty has brought a number of epistemological problems. In the first place, it greatly limits what might be classified as knowledge since, as

---

264. McGrath, *Scientific Theology*, vol. 1, 266.

265. McGrath, *Science of God*, 81.

266. McGrath, *Scientific Theology*, vol. 1, 266.

267. Polkinghorne, *Science & Theology*, 71.

268. Nash, *Faith & Reason*, 96.

Adler points out, only those judgments "that are made beyond a shadow of a doubt are made with certitude. We make few such judgments. Most of our judgments fall within the shadow of doubt."[269] Furthermore, as Taylor points out, the quest for certainty can be counterproductive. That is, one who thinks certainty is possible and does not achieve it will likely conclude that the belief in question is intellectually inferior and disregard it altogether. Among other things, this is one of the reasons that David Hume rejects the design argument from analogy. Through the mouth of Philo, Hume writes, "Unless the cases be exactly similar, they repose no *perfect confidence* in applying their past observation to any particular phenomenon. Every alteration of circumstances occasions a doubt concerning the event; and it requires new experiments *to prove certainly* that the new circumstances are of no moment or importance."[270] Thus, by removing the requirement of certainty, McGrath allows natural theology to serve as a confirmation, not a proof, of the Christian Faith.

McGrath's Natural Theology Has Explanatory Power

An additional advantage of McGrath's approach to natural theology is its explanatory power. Simply put, McGrath uses natural theology to offer an explanation of the natural sciences as well as competing religious traditions. In his view, natural theology functions from within the Christian tradition but is useful in explaining the natural sciences and alternative belief systems. He says, "Christian natural theology is a tradition-specific construal with universal applicability, thus both offering an explanation of other traditions, while at the same time reinforcing its own plausibility."[271] As McGrath notes, "A Christian conception of natural theology posits that something of God may be known outside the Christian tradition."[272] This, according to McGrath, is helpful in explaining why people outside the Christian tradition have an awareness of God and are able to develop their own tradition. He says:

> The essential point to make here is the following. The Christian understanding of creation, mediated through the tradition, offers both intra-systemic and extra-systemic insights . . . Yet it is the extra-systemic aspects of the doctrine of creation that particularly

269. Adler, *Truth In Religion*, 16.
270. Hume, *Dialogues*, 57.
271. McGrath, *Scientific Theology*, vol. 3, 195.
272. McGrath, *Science of God*, 114.

concern us at this point, as these converge on a natural theology. The doctrine of creation of the world and humanity is an aspect of the Christian tradition which offers predictions or retrodictions which it believes to be valid outside that specific tradition. If God has indeed created the world, imposing ordering upon it in and through the act of creation; and if God indeed has created humanity in the *imago Dei*, then some innate knowledge of God is to be expected, however attenuated, at the levels of both subjective experience and reflection on the world. Thus Calvin argued for a natural knowledge of God at two levels: an internal experience of the presence of God, and an external awareness of the ordering of nature.[273]

At the same time, however, the knowledge of God derived from creation is only partial, meaning that any tradition based on this alone will be significantly limited. Nevertheless, McGrath thinks that by using natural theology in this way the Christian tradition has at least two advantages over its rivals:

1. It offers an explanation of the world that is internally coherent, and an explanation of the externally observable fact that related insights may be held, at least to some extent, outside the Christian tradition.

2. It holds that what may be known of God through nature, although in a fragmentary and potentially inconsistent manner, may be had, in full, through the Christian revelation, which is specific to the Christian tradition.

Thus John Calvin explores the relation of a natural and revealed knowledge of God through a dialogue with Cicero, representing a comparison of two great traditions—classical pagan religion and the Christian faith.[274] Starting from within the Christian tradition, McGrath uses natural theology as a way of explaining its rival traditions. With this, his ST has the appeal of possessing the explanatory power necessary for any valid belief system.

As Nash points out, "Just as a conceptual system must pass the test of reason, it must also satisfy the test of experience. We have the right to expect world-views to touch base with human experience. World-views should throw light on our experiences of the world. They should ex-

---

273. McGrath, *Scientific Theology*, vol. 2, 76.
274. McGrath, *Science of God*, 117.

plain our experiences easily and naturally."[275] In fact, he believes that "no world-view deserves respect if it ignores or is inconsistent with human experiences."[276] Likewise, James Sire suggests that one "characteristic of an adequate worldview is that it be able to comprehend the data of reality—data of all types—that which each of us gleans through our conscious experience of daily life, that which is supplied by critical analysis and scientific investigation, that which is reported to us from the experiences of others."[277] In other words, an adequate worldview will be one that is able to offer an explanation of all of reality, not just a few parts.

By way of natural theology, McGrath's ST gives the Christian tradition a way of accounting for itself as well as rival belief systems. Thus, McGrath's ST gives explanatory power to the Christian tradition and this marks one significant aspect of his project.

McGrath's Natural Theology Can Be Used as a Point of Contact

One final advantage of McGrath's use of natural theology is that it can be used as a point of contact with the nonbeliever. As he contends, ST should be thought of as a "public theology."[278] He explains this, saying, "The proposal that we wish to advance . . . is that natural theology offers a comprehensive means by which theology may address the world, and engage in productive dialogue concerning the legitimation and consequences of belief systems."[279] Because of this, McGrath sees his approach as having significant apologetic value. He says, "The question of whether there can be a legitimate natural theology is of considerable apologetic importance, through the recognition that, if God has indeed created the world and allowed this world to bear witness to its creator, the Christian evangelist will have a number of 'points of contact' for the gospel within the created order."[280] He later says, "The experience of a sense of wonder at the glories of the natural world is an important point of contact between Christianity and the natural sciences in particular,

275. Nash, *Faith & Reason*, 55.

276. Ibid.

277. Sire, *Universe Next Door*, 196.

278. McGrath, *Scientific Theology*, vol. 1, 304.

279. Ibid., 303.

280. Ibid., 299.

and the world of human experience in general."[281] Thus, in McGrath's view, since the natural world has been created by God, it reveals something about him to all men that can then be used as a point of contact with the nonbeliever.

Historically, Aquinas and Calvin both make similar points. For example, while speaking about the way creation reveals God, Aquinas says, "Every effect in some degree represents its cause, but diversely. For some effects represent only the causality of the cause . . . Other effects represent the cause as regards the similitude of its form, as fire generated represents fire generating . . . Therefore in rational creatures, possessing intellect and will, there is found the representation of the Trinity by way of image, inasmuch as there is found in them the word conceived, and the love proceeding."[282] Likewise, Calvin says, "[God] not only sowed in men's minds that seed of religion of which we have spoken but revealed himself and daily discloses himself in the whole workmanship of the universe. As a consequence, men cannot open their eyes without being compelled to see him . . . But upon his individual works he has engraved unmistakable marks of his glory, so clear and so prominent that even unlettered and stupid folk cannot plead the excuse of ignorance."[283] He goes on to say, "Even the common folk and the most untutored, who have been taught only by the aid of the eyes, cannot be unaware of the excellence of divine art, for it reveals itself in this innumerable and yet distinct and well-ordered variety of the heavenly host."[284]

Like Aquinas and Calvin, then, McGrath affirms that creation is a source of revelation. Because of this, McGrath's ST is able to use natural theology as a point of contact with the nonbeliever. As Padgett remarks, "Evangelical theologians and church leaders would do well to reflect upon McGrath's defense of natural theology. In an important final section on 'natural theology as discourse in the public arena,' McGrath rightly points out that learned non-Christians will demand some Christian response to the natural sciences and to the ever-popular scientific atheists of our day. To be true to its mission, the church must contend in public for a Christian understanding of the natural order and

---

281. McGrath, *Scientific Theology*, vol. 2, 88.

282. Aquinas, *Summa Theologica*, 1/1/45:7.

283. Calvin, *Institutes*, 1/5:1.

284. Ibid., 1/5:2.

of natural science."[285] From an apologetic standpoint, this seems to be a significant contribution of McGrath's ST to evangelicalism. He takes the Christian doctrine of creation and shows its implications for dialogue with the nonbeliever.

The Value of McGrath's Use of Natural Theology

As chapter 1 pointed out, natural theology was greatly weakened by the philosophical and scientific developments of the modern period. Today, however, scientists and theologians are beginning to reconsider its value. As Long points out, "Natural theology, which suffered significantly in the eighteenth century as a result of the criticisms of Hume and Kant, appeared to be a terminal patient by the mid-twentieth century as a result of vetoes by both philosophers and theologians. Since the 1960s, however, several developments in philosophy and theology have led to renewed interest in natural theology."[286]

With that in mind, McGrath seems to make a valuable contribution toward the reestablishment of natural theology by the Christian tradition. In his approach, creation is acknowledged to be a valuable source of divine revelation. This is not only consistent with what the Bible has to say about creation, but is also commendable, since it gives the theologian a point of contact with the nonbeliever. By focusing his natural theology on the laws of nature as opposed to specific arguments for God's existence, like the cosmological or teleological arguments, McGrath's approach focuses on issues that require theological explanation and are not subject to the traditional objections to natural theology. In addition to this, McGrath's natural theology is not foundationalist in nature. For him, natural theology does not serve as the basis for Christian belief. Instead, the Christian begins with an already existing belief in God and uses natural theology as a confirmation of that belief. Because of this, in McGrath's approach, natural theology is not required to prove God's existence with absolute certainty in order to be of value. Moreover, his use of natural theology gives Christian theology the explanatory power necessary in giving an account of reality.

285. Padgett, "Scientific Theology, vol. 1," 110.

286. Long, Introduction, vii.

CONCLUSION

Three of the most important aspects of McGrath's ST are his use of Bhaskar's CR, the doctrine of creation, and his recasting of natural theology. As this chapter has shown, McGrath makes a constructive contribution to evangelical theology by using all three. By using CR, McGrath is able to affirm the valuable lessons of modernity and postmodernity without falling prey to their weaknesses and dangers. Moreover, McGrath's application of Bhaskar's notion of a stratified reality allows McGrath to establish a UTK without falling into a form of reductionism. By making the Christian doctrine of creation central to his ST, he shows that there is an ontological imperative for dialogue between science and theology and that both disciplines will benefit from this dialogue. Finally, with natural theology, McGrath recasts the project in such a way that the objections often raised against it are no longer valid. This gives natural theology the advantage of functioning as a confirmation of theistic belief, not as its basis.

All things considered, then, McGrath's ST offers evangelicals an epistemological method that answers the growing concerns within evangelicalism. His ST makes a considerable contribution to theological method as well as to the dialogue between science and theology.

5

Final Assessment of McGrath's Scientific Theology (ST)

THIS CHAPTER OFFERS A final assessment of Alister E. McGrath's ST. After a brief summary of chapters 1 through 4, this chapter will argue that McGrath's ST offers evangelicalism as an appropriate theological method. McGrath's ST does this by establishing dialogue between science and theology and shows how science can be used as the *ancilla theologia* (handmaiden of theology).

CONTEXTUAL SYNOPSIS

In chapter 1, this book offered a brief presentation of the relationship between theology and science in the premodern, modern and postmodern periods. There, it was argued that [NL 1–2]

1. Prior to the seventeenth century, theology and science were joined in a mutual quest to understand and explain reality

2. This situation changed significantly with the philosophical developments of modernity and postmodernity.

These are important matters of consideration since, as a result of these philosophical developments, the western world now finds itself in a state of epistemological unsettledness. Thus, chapter 1 sets the historical/philosophical backdrop for understanding McGrath's ST.

In chapter 2, McGrath's ST was explored and summarized to show how he develops a theological method in response to the epistemological problems of modernity and postmodernity. This chapter followed the headings of the three volumes of *A Scientific Theology: Nature, Reality*, and *Theory*. In volume 1 (*Nature*), McGrath offers a critique of the socially constructed concept of nature by showing how the concept has been variously understood by different groups throughout history.

For example, McGrath shows how the ancient Greek philosophers' understanding of nature included the idea of matter being eternal. In more recent history, nature has been portrayed a theater and as a mother. Thus, McGrath considers nature to be a highly ambiguous term that is beneficial for neither science nor theology. In its place, McGrath presents the Christian doctrine of creation as a viable alternative for both theology and science, by highlighting the implications of this doctrine for both disciplines. It is here that McGrath begins to unpack his important contribution to a revived and revised natural theology. The discussion of volume 2 (*Reality*) centers on the realism/anti-realism debate. Here McGrath defends and carefully distinguishes his realist approach from the classical foundationalist, postliberal coherentist, and postmodern anti-realist perspectives. McGrath does this by adopting Roy Bhaskar's critical realist understanding of a stratified reality. In this volume, natural theology receives further development, and McGrath ends by outlining his proposed theological method. In volume 3 (*Theory*), McGrath explores and defends the development and use of theories. He then defends the theological enterprise itself and explains how theology, like natural science, is an *a posteriori* discipline. According to McGrath, theology is an *a posteriori* discipline, since it is a response to divine revelation.

Some ambiguities relating to McGrath's ST were considered in chapter 3. With the doctrine of revelation, for example, McGrath draws from Karl Barth's position without clarifying how, if at all, he differs from Barth. As a result, McGrath's ST may be rejected by those evangelicals who are uncomfortable with Barth's doctrine of revelation. Furthermore, McGrath's suggestion that the Bible is not revelation in the proper sense of the word may cause concern among some evangelicals. Without clarification on these matters, McGrath's ST could be viewed with suspicion by evangelicalism. Nevertheless, evangelicals should not take McGrath as holding a non-evangelical view of Scripture, since he later explains how the Bible can be thought of as revelation in the more developed sense of the word, and he affirms the total trustworthiness and reliability of Scripture. Other ambiguities relate to possible connections in McGrath's ST to methodological naturalism as well as his use of natural theology. In each case, chapter 3 concluded that these concerns may call for further clarification or development. These concerns do not, however, call for the rejection of his ST since, upon examination, they either are not found to be problematic, or are not essential to his ST.

Chapter 4 offered an evangelical assessment of McGrath's ST and addressed three major areas where ST makes constructive contributions to evangelical theology. These areas include McGrath's use of Roy Bhaskar's critical realism (CR), the Christian doctrine of creation, and natural theology. As will now be argued, it is McGrath's contributions in these areas that allow for dialogue between science and theology and render ST commendable for evangelicalism.

OVERALL ASSESSMENT

After a careful analysis, it is concluded that McGrath's ST offers an appropriate theological method for evangelicals working toward the integration of science and theology. If McGrath is right (and this book concludes that he is), evangelicals may use science as the *ancilla theologia*. By adopting Bhaskar's CR, McGrath offers a theological method within a realist epistemology that avoids the dangers of modernity and postmodernity by steering a middle way between the two. Likewise, with his emphasis on the doctrine of creation, McGrath shows the ontological connection between science and theology and suggests that each discipline will be enhanced by dialogue with the other. Moreover, McGrath's ST recasts and reclaims natural theology as a legitimate and essential aspect of Christian theology. Here, he shows how natural theology gives Christian theology great explanatory power and apologetic viability.

Epistemological Value of McGrath's ST

The philosophical developments of modernity and postmodernity had enormous consequences for the relationship between science and theology, as shown in chapter 1. Moreover, as the western world moved from a modern to a postmodern perspective, absolute objective truth was denied and relativism became all pervasive. In this intellectual environment, neither science nor theology could claim to speak of truth. Now, at the beginning of the twenty-first century, however, philosophers and theologians are searching for an adequate epistemology. Indeed, as chapter 1 pointed out, some theologians and philosophers are already declaring the end of postmodernism and refer to the current epistemological setting as postpostmodernism. Within this context, critical realism is receiving attention as an epistemological perspective that offers a viable alternative to modernity and postmodernity.

Epistemologically speaking, McGrath's ST adopts a critical realist perspective for the development of an evangelical theological method. His approach is preferable to perspectives of modern classical foundationalism and postmodern relativism for a number of reasons. First, McGrath's ST affirms the existence of an objective reality that is independent of individual human minds, as well as the possibility of gaining knowledge of this reality.[1] As chapter 4 noted, these affirmations are necessary for human rationality, which explains why they have been assumed throughout most of history. Furthermore, these affirmations have been given substantial intellectual support by the success of modern science. As Benjamin Myers contends, "A basic assumption of both natural science and theology is that there is a reality independent of the human mind, which is intelligible in spite of the 'inescapable historicity' of the human subject."[2] In light of this understanding of reality, McGrath's ST affirms a correspondence theory of truth.[3] As he explains on multiple occasions, all theories and doctrines must be accountable to reality. A truth claim is not merely a matter of social construct, but is determined by how well a given proposition fits with reality. David Clark and John Searle suggest that these are basic assumptions of the human mind so necessary that they do not require validation.[4] Likewise, Alan Padgett and Albert Mohler have argued that these assumptions are central to the Christian faith.[5]

By affirming critical realism and a correspondence theory of truth, McGrath avoids the dangers of postmodernism that lead to relativism. On the other hand, he avoids the problems of modernism by rejecting classical foundationalism[6] and by acknowledging the mediated nature of knowledge, which is not to be confused with an affirmation of perspectivalism.[7] Here, McGrath recognizes the subjective factors that shape human understanding and explanation of what is apprehended. With

1. McGrath, *Scientific Theology*, vol. 2, 71–74, 199.

2. Myers, "McGrath's Scientific Theology," 11.

3. McGrath, *Scientific Theology*, vol. 3, xiv, 194.

4. See Clark, *To Know and Love God*, 354, and Searle, *Mind, Language and Society*, 9.

5. See Padgett, *Science and Study*, 36, and Mohler, "Truth and Culture," 59.

6. See McGrath, *Scientific Theology*, vol. 2, 20–38, and McGrath, *Science of God*, 97–111.

7. McGrath, *Scientific Theology*, vol. 2, 196.

this, McGrath avoids the naïve realism of the Enlightenment and shows how a critical realist navigates between modernity and postmodernity by accepting the valuable lessons of both periods, without falling prey to the dangers of either.

McGrath's ST is given additional strength by Roy Bhaskar's notion of a stratified reality.[8] This allows McGrath to affirm a unified theory of knowledge (UTK), while at the same time avoiding reductionism. Following Bhaskar, McGrath argues that there is only one reality,[9] even if this reality is multi-layered or stratified.[10] The oneness of reality requires a UTK, whereas its stratification means that each discipline will adopt methods and techniques appropriate for its object of study. In other words, given the ontological distinctions between different strata of reality, various methods and modes of investigation are required to properly study and understand the different strata.

By following Bhaskar's notion of a stratified reality, McGrath's approach is similar to, but better than, other theorists' in arguing for a UTK. As chapter 4 noted, although a number of philosophers and scientists recognize that the division of science and theology[11] in the modern period came with undesirable epistemological consequences and are now calling for a UTK, some develop a reductionist UTK at the expense of philosophy, theology, and a number of other important areas of human inquiry.[12] McGrath's approach is commendable to evangelicals, since it embraces a UTK while at the same time affirming the stratification of reality. Because of this, each discipline will develop its particular mode and methods of investigation in keeping with the nature of its particular strata of reality. In short, McGrath embraces a UTK that does not result in reductionism.

Finally, McGrath's critical realist approach is also favorable to a modern perspective because critical realism does not require certainty for a given belief to be counted as knowledge. As chapter 1 makes clear, the demands for certainty by modernism can now be seen as highly

---

8. See Bhaskar, *Possibility of Naturalism*, and *Realist Theory of Science*.

9. McGrath, *Scientific Theology*, vol. 3, 4.

10. McGrath, *Science of God*, 147.

11. Some categorize this more broadly as a split between science and the humanities.

12. Wilson is a case in point. See Wilson, *Consilience*, 9.

problematic.[13] Instead of accepting this assumption, McGrath proposes a balanced way of dealing with the issue of certainty by noting that one can gain varying degrees of closure (certainty) given the nature of the object under consideration.[14]

Because of these constructive aspects of McGrath's ST, it is argued that his theological method holds considerable advantages to theologies developed from a modern or postmodern perspective. This is an important consideration, since some evangelicals have been willing to embrace postmodernism or revert to a modern perspective. For example, in their rejection of Enlightenment foundationalism, Stanley Grenz and John Franke abandon a correspondence view of truth in favor of a constructionist view and believe that postmodernism is the catalyst for renewing evangelical theology.[15] Similarly, Carl Raschke seeks to reconcile Christianity with postmodernism, believing that this is necessary for Christianity to avoid becoming irrelevant.[16] Raschke is rightly concerned with the problems associated with modernity, but uncritically accepts the postmodern perspective as an appropriate epistemological perspective. Likewise, in an essay entitled "There's No Such Thing as Objective Truth and It's a Good Thing Too," Philip Kenneson suggests that the Christian is free to reject the objectivity of knowledge and the correspondence theory of truth.[17]

Douglas Groothuis, however, strongly disagrees, claiming that "the correspondence view of truth is not simply one of many options for Christians. It is the only biblically and logically grounded view of truth available and allowable. We neglect or deny it to our peril and disgrace. Truth decay will not be dispelled without it."[18] Mohler makes a similar point, suggesting that "postmodernists believe all truth to be socially constructed, [thus] all claims of absolute, universal, and established truth must be resisted. All meta-narratives—that is, all grand and expansive accounts of truth, meaning, and existence—are cast aside, for they claim far more than they can deliver."[19] J. P. Moreland and William Lane Craig

13. McGrath makes this point as well. See McGrath, *Doubting*, 24–25.

14. McGrath, *Scientific Theology*, vol. 3, 43–46.

15. Grenz and Franke, *Beyond Foundationalism*.

16. Raschke, *Next Reformation*.

17. Kenneson, "No Such Thing," 158.

18. Groothuis, *Truth Decay*, 110.

19. Mohler, "Truth and Culture," 59.

agree. They say, "In claiming that there are no metanarratives, postmodernists mean that there is no way to decide which among competing worldviews is true, and more importantly, there is no single worldview true for everyone. There are no metanarratives, only local ones."[20] The postmodern rejection of metanarratives is problematic for a number of reasons. Richard Tarnas notes the self-defeating nature of it when he says, "By virtue of that self-relativizing critical awareness, it is recognized that a quasi-nihilist rejection of any and all forms of 'totalization' and 'metanarrative' . . . cannot on its own principles ultimately justify itself any more than can the various metaphysical overviews against which the postmodern mind has defined itself. Such a position presupposes a metanarrative of its own, one perhaps more subtle than others, but in the end no less subject to deconstruction criticism."[21] Furthermore, Mohler contends that the postmodern rejection of metanarratives is contrary to the Christian faith itself since Christianity offers universal truth claims.[22] Thus, an uncritical acceptance of postmodernism is a dangerous path for evangelicals.

On the other hand, it seems that there are also problems with evangelicals reverting back to a modern perspective. As Tim Morris and Don Petcher point out, some evangelicals, in their avoidance of postmodernism, have reverted to a modern perspective. They say, "While some have gone too far in the postmodern direction, most Christians rightly recognize dangers of postmodern relativism. But many Christians, in their strong rejection of relativism, end up siding with modernism by default."[23] A few possible examples of this may be noted. In an essay entitled "The Premature Report of Foundationalism's Demise," J. P. Moreland and Garrett DeWeese argue that "the rejection of foundationalist epistemology is a serious mistake."[24] Likewise, claiming that the postmodern critique of modernity is overreached, Mohler suggests that evangelicals should retain a soft form of foundationalism.[25] Thus, by phrasing their epistemological proposals in modernistic language, these philosophers

---

20. Moreland and Craig, *Philosophical Foundations*, 149.

21. Tarnas, *Western Mind*, 401–2.

22. Mohler, "Truth and Culture," 59.

23. Morris and Petcher, *Science & Grace*, 6.

24. Moreland and DeWeese, "Premature Report," 81.

25. Mohler, "Truth and Culture," 68.

and theologians give the appearance that they have reverted to a modern perspective.

In fairness to Moreland, DeWeese, and Mohler, however, two points should be made. First, the concerns they raise with postmodernism are certainly valid and show the problems with this epistemological perspective.[26] Second, they are not necessarily advocating a return to the classical foundationalism of the Enlightenment.[27]

Nevertheless, the term foundationalism—whether soft or hard, broad or narrow, modest or strong—comes with philosophical baggage that evangelicals may not wish to carry. The term foundationalism, however it is modified, seems to suggest an affirmation of Enlightenment ideas that are now seen to be epistemologically hollow. This becomes even more problematic when and where evangelicals fail to show how their approach differs from classical foundationalism. In Mohler's case, for example, he contends for a foundationalist approach without discussing or acknowledging the social and subjective factors of human knowledge. In the end, his affirmation of soft foundationalism is not adequately distinguished from classical foundationalism. Thus, affirming a foundationalist approach without careful clarification and qualification seems to be problematic. As Morris and Petcher put it, "While Christians rightly believe that the postmodern 'anything goes' relativism is on the wrong track, combating postmodern relativism by simply reaffirming modernist convictions about scientific objectivism is not the solution."[28]

As this dissertation argues, McGrath's ST offers what appears to be a preferable epistemological alternative to the modern and postmodern perspectives. As Myers notes, this is because McGrath's theological method is "able to appropriate the valid insights of both Enlightenment objectivism and postmodern social constructivism, without capitulating to the one-sidedness of either."[29]

---

26. Moreland and DeWeese critique the postmodern rejection of (1) the referential theory of language, (2) the correspondence theory of truth, and (3) metaphysical realism. See Moreland and DeWeese, "Premature Report", 85–90. Mohler, on the other hand, offers a strong critique of postmodern antirealism. See Mohler, "Truth and Culture," 68–69.

27. See Moreland and DeWeese, "Premature Report," 90–93. Here they suggest that reliablism in some form may offer the key to a modest form of foundationalism.

28. Morris and Petcher, *Science & Grace*, 7.

29. Myers, "McGrath's Scientific Theology," 10.

Ontological Value of McGrath's ST

In addition to the epistemological strengths just mentioned, McGrath's ST also makes a significant contribution in the area of ontology. In volume 1 of *A Scientific Theology*, McGrath gives special attention to the Christian doctrine of creation and shows how it is not only essential to the Christian faith, but that it holds significant advantages for the natural sciences as well. He suggests the concept of creation is preferable to nature, since nature is a prime example of a socially constructed concept that is variously understood by different groups.[30] In his view, replacing the concept of nature with the Christian doctrine of creation is not only consistent with Christian theology, but also provides an ontological basis for natural science and the dialogue between science and theology.[31] To be sure, McGrath's preference for creation is more than just a mere exchanging of terminology. McGrath points to the ontological significance of positing God as the creator of the universe. That is, if God has created the universe, then one can expect the universe to possess a genuine rationality that is discernable by natural science and that also partially reveals the divine rationality behind it.

Chapter 4 noted three distinct benefits of McGrath's approach. First, from a theological perspective, McGrath's emphasis on the ontological implications of creation allows theologians to gain insights from creation in the development of doctrine. However partial or incomplete this revelation may be, theologians can affirm that creation reveals God to mankind since there is a correspondence between the works of God and the being of God.[32] Because of this, natural science—the study of God's creation—can serve as the handmaiden of theology. In addition to the common assumptions and methodologies shared between theology and science, McGrath thinks that natural science can be especially helpful to theology hermeneutically. That is, "natural sciences can be seen as offering a stimulus to Christian theology, to consider whether it has, in fact, achieved a correct interpretation of its foundational resources on points of importance."[33] Thus, McGrath believes that an emphasis on the

---

30. McGrath, *Scientific Theology*, vol. 1, 88, and McGrath, *Science of God*, 36–38.

31. McGrath, *Science of God*, 44–45.

32. McGrath, *Scientific Theology*, vol. 1, 193.

33. Ibid., 61.

Christian doctrine of creation reinforces the fact that theology can be informed by the natural sciences.

Second, McGrath suggests that there are also important benefits for the natural sciences in the doctrine of creation. McGrath notes how natural scientists assume certain things they cannot support without something like the Christian doctrine of creation.[34] That is, things like the rationality of the universe, along with humanity's ability to comprehend that rationality, are incredibly difficult for natural science to explain on its own. If the Christian doctrine of creation is posited, however, McGrath shows how natural science is given the ontological basis for some of these assumptions. Clark agrees with McGrath's approach, saying:

> Science can account for the operation of the natural world but cannot account for the fact that scientists value scientific knowledge of the operation of the natural world. To use an illustration, laws of nature that are stated in terms of physics and chemistry can explain the operation of individual parts of a machine. But these sciences alone can never explain the existence of the machine itself. Science must posit an intelligence in order to account for the information-dense boundary conditions that constrain the operation of chemical and physical laws in order that a purposeful end is achieved. While chemical and physical laws account for the operation of living systems, merely physical and chemical explanations do not account for the origin of these systems. Similarly, science explains the operation of natural processes, but it cannot explain why there are persons who could value the search for genuine knowledge.[35]

Like McGrath and Clark, John Polkinghorne also thinks that the Christian doctrine of creation is helpful to natural science. He says, "A metaphysical question such as why the universe is so deeply intelligible to us, with mathematics the key to the unlocking of its secrets, does not lend itself to knock-down answers of a logically coercive kind. The most we can require is an interpretation that is coherent and persuasive. Theism provides just such a response to the metaquestion of intelligibility."[36] By grounding natural science in a Christian understanding of creation, McGrath, like Clark and Polkinghorne, thinks that natural science is given an ontological basis for some of its most essential assumptions.

34. McGrath, *Science of God*, 59–71.

35. Clark, *To Know and Love God*, 268.

36. Polkinghorne, *Science & Theology*, 73.

Accordingly, as chapter 4 noted, McGrath's emphasis on the Christian doctrine of creation shows how theology and science can be mutually enhanced and encouraged by a dialogue with one another. Therefore, with the use of CR and the emphasis on the doctrine of creation, McGrath's ST offers the epistemological as well as the ontological basis for a UTK.[37]

Apologetic Value of McGrath's ST

McGrath's ST also makes a valuable contribution to evangelicalism with its reintroduction of natural theology as a legitimate aspect of Christian theology. To be sure, McGrath has done more than simply rehash the natural theology of the modern period, with all of its problems. As chapter 4 argued, McGrath's revised natural theology is quite consistent with a premodern approach that allows it to function within the Christian tradition[38] and emphasizes creation's ability to reveal the glory of God.[39] In fact, his natural theology might be seen as an extension of the doctrine of creation and its ability to reveal the creator.[40] Because of this, chapter 4 argued that McGrath's approach enjoys considerable biblical support.[41]

McGrath's approach has other advantages.[42] By repositioning natural theology within the Christian tradition, he abandons the foundationalist approach of the Enlightenment. During this period, philosophers and theologians used natural theology as the basis of justification for Christian theism.[43] In other words, one had to establish the existence of God before one was justified in holding to theistic beliefs, and natural theology was often used in an effort to accomplish this. Additionally, the Enlightenment approach demanded certainty from the arguments of natural theology. McGrath rejects this approach and argues that, histori-

---

37. McGrath, *Scientific Theology*, vol. 1, 21.

38. McGrath, *Science of God*, 113.

39. McGrath, *Scientific Theology*, vol. 1, 273–74.

40. Ibid., 297, and McGrath, *Science of God*, 72.

41. Chapter 4 gave special attention to Ps 19 and Rom 1:18–20.

42. Chapter 4 discussed at least six specific advantages, arguing that his approach (1) affirms creation as a source of divine revelation, (2) focuses on the laws of nature, (3) abandons classical foundationalism, (4) removes the requirement of certainty, (5) has great explanatory power, and (6) can be used as a point of contact with the nonbeliever. All of these points will not be rehearsed here. Instead, the most significant contributions are mentioned.

43. McGrath, *Scientific Theology*, vol. 2, 71.

cally speaking, natural theology is better understood as the "enterprise of seeing nature as creation, which both presupposes and reinforces fundamental Christian theological affirmations."[44] Thus, natural theology is not required to yield absolute certainty for Christian beliefs. Instead, it simply gives confirmation to an already existing belief. Therefore, in McGrath's approach, the unnecessary and impossible requirement of certainty is removed, allowing natural theology to play a significant role in Christian theology once again.[45]

Furthermore, even though it is allowed to function from within the Christian tradition—in light of an already present belief in God's existence—McGrath shows how natural theology has appeal to those outside the faith since it offers "both intra-systemic and extra-systemic insights."[46] He states, "Christian natural theology is a tradition-specific construal with universal applicability."[47] The universal applicability comes by way of natural theology's ability, according to McGrath, to give an explanation of the natural sciences as well as other religious belief systems. As chapter 4 argued, this aspect of McGrath's natural theology means that the Christian tradition has both explanatory power and a point of contact with the nonbeliever.[48] Thus, even though it begins within the Christian tradition and does not require absolute certainty, McGrath's natural theology has apologetic value for evangelical theology. Therefore, as Alan Padgett argues, "Evangelical theologians and church leaders would do well to reflect upon McGrath's defense of natural theology. In an important final section on 'natural theology as discourse in the public arena,' McGrath rightly points out that learned non-Christians will demand some Christian response to the natural sciences and to the ever-popular scientific atheists of our day. To be true to its mission, the church must contend in public for a Christian understanding of the natural order and of natural science."[49] McGrath's approach offers an acceptable way of doing this by reestablishing natural theology as a legitimate and helpful aspect of Christian theology.

---

44. Ibid., 73.

45. McGrath, *Scientific Theology*, vol. 3, 198; and McGrath, *Science of God*, 89.

46. McGrath, *Scientific Theology*, vol. 2, 76.

47. McGrath, *Scientific Theology*, vol. 3, 195.

48. McGrath, *Scientific Theology*, vol. 1, 303–4.

49. Padgett, "Scientific Theology," 110.

ISSUES FOR FURTHER STUDY

As with any book, the current study has been limited with what it could address. Chapter 3 discussed a few places in McGrath's ST where further clarification or development would be helpful. In chapter 4, an assessment of his ST was given in light of three important issues:

1. Roy Bhaskar's CR

2. The Christian doctrine of creation

3. Natural theology

Before concluding this book, however, something should be said about additional aspects of McGrath's ST that warrant further study.

One such area deals with the comparison of McGrath's ST with a premodern theological method. As noted several times throughout this book, there are significant similarities between the two. Millard Erickson notes several features of premodern thought, which includes beliefs in the rationality of the universe, the existence of metaphysical reality, God as the creator of the world, purpose within the universe, realism, and a correspondence theory of truth.[50] If Erickson's observations are correct, it is easy to see that McGrath's ST is quite similar to a premodern approach since he reaffirms each of these beliefs. The issue of natural theology provides an additional example of the similarities between McGrath's ST and premodern thought. John Hedley Brooke observes some differences between a premodern and modern approach to natural theology. While modern philosophers used natural theology to establish independent grounds for religious beliefs, he says, "By contrast, in premodern cultures, adherents of the monotheistic religions would scarcely have entertained a discourse of natural theology independent of that greater knowledge of God revealed in their sacred texts."[51] Because McGrath repositions natural theology within the Christian tradition, both James Keating and Benjamin Myers have noted the similarities of McGrath's approach to a premodern perspective.[52]

These similarities warrant further study on McGrath's ST. In particular, it would be interesting and valuable to give a more detailed juxtaposition of McGrath's ST and premodern theological method to see what

---

50. Erickson, *Christian Theology*, 160–61.

51. Brooke, "Natural Theology," 164.

52. Keating, "Natural Sciences," 134, and Myers, "McGrath's Scientific Theology," 6–7.

differences there may be between the two. This is important, since some fear a return to a premodern perspective will not properly acknowledge the valuable lessons of modernity and postmodernity. As Robert Greer points out, "Many Christians would prefer a backward move, since the highly venerated apostolic age is located in the distant past. Such a step backwards in time is wrought with much difficulty, though, because we cannot ignore the history that has transpired between then and now."[53] He then adds, "The context of our articulations cannot be presented with a philosophical or theological naiveté, as if modernism and postmodernism never existed. Any attempt to do so will not only betray our own worldview but also lack relevance to the worldview of our audience. It will cause us to drift into an intellectual ghetto."[54] Thus, in order to make the commendable similarities of ST to a premodern perspective clear, as well as the important distinctions, further study on this matter would be of great value to ST. This issue has been introduced in the current study, but has not received a full treatment.

A second issue for further study deals with McGrath's defense of the theological enterprise itself. This comes out most clearly in volume 3 of *A Scientific Theology*, where McGrath gives special attention to the issue of theory. Here, McGrath demonstrates the inevitability and necessity of developing theories in both science and theology (doctrine). He says, "Theory arises precisely because human beings are rational creatures, and feel impelled, both morally and intellectually, to give an account of things. The natural sciences and Christian theology are both rooted in human experience and culture; yet they also aspire to transcend the particularities of time and place to yield truths that claim a more universal significance."[55]

McGrath's defense of the theological enterprise is also seen in the fact that he clearly affirms and contends for an evangelical understanding of Christianity that is informed and guided by the Scripture. He says, "This work is written from an evangelical perspective, by which I mean an approach to theology which insists that theology must be nourished and governed at all points by Holy Scripture, and that it seeks to offer a faithful and coherent account of what it finds there. This task of rendering Scripture faithfully is, in my view, best carried out in dialogue with

---

53. Greer, *Mapping Postmodernism*, 22.

54. Ibid., 23.

55. McGrath, *Scientific Theology*, vol. 3, 9.

the 'great tradition' of Christian theology and in response to the challenges to the Christian faith which are raised by other disciplines—such as the natural sciences."[56] Because of this, Myers notes that the "entire *Scientific Theology* thus defends the possibility of a 'coherent systematic theology' which engages deeply with the working methods of the natural sciences."[57] In Myers' view, this is perhaps the most significant aspect of McGrath's work.[58] Likewise, Gregory Snyder says:

> Throughout this book, McGrath seems bent on the destruction of half-baked theologies which are constructed from bits and pieces of the Christian tradition and classic Christian theology. Instead, he advocates a bold defense of traditional Christian theology, *in toto*, while still seeing the need to go beyond this and allow for continuing development of theology and understanding through revelation. McGrath does not advocate an insular approach to Christian theology, but welcomes its interaction with other traditions that can stimulate its growth and development.[59]

Thus, in an age of under-emphasis or blatant opposition to doctrinal studies,[60] McGrath's insights may be of great value in showing the necessity of theology for the church. Therefore, further study on McGrath's defense of the legitimacy of doctrine itself may yield significant contributions to evangelical theology.

A third area for further study is McGrath's proposal for reestablishing metaphysics as an *a posteriori* discipline. Simply put, McGrath suggests that taking an *a priori* approach to metaphysics is illegitimate and must be abandoned. If, however, one practices metaphysics in an *a posteriori* fashion, then McGrath thinks metaphysics can once again be a legitimate practice. To make this point, McGrath suggests that the successes of the natural sciences lead to certain metaphysical conclusions. He says, "Metaphysical conclusions flow naturally and reasonably from scientific experimentation . . . physics cannot help but address metaphysical issues, whether its practitioners regard themselves as qualified to do so or not."[61] Adonis Vidu thinks that McGrath's proposal offers new

---

56. McGrath, *Scientific Theology*, vol. 1, xix.

57. Myers, "McGrath's Scientific Theology," 20.

58. Ibid.

59. Snyder, "Scientific Theology," 356.

60. McGrath, *Scientific Theology*, vol. 3, 24–25.

61. McGrath, *Science of God*, 239.

life to metaphysics. He says, "If metaphysics is conceived as an *a priori* discourse, before an engagement with experience and science, it should rightly be abandoned. But metaphysics could and should be undertaken as an *a posteriori* inference about the sorts of things that must exist in order that our experiences be properly explained."[62]

The issue of metaphysics is treated in the last chapter of volume 3 and is not fully developed by McGrath himself. Of the approximately sixty pages he devotes to the subject, the majority of space is dedicated to offering an overview of the history of metaphysics with little being said about how to do metaphysics in an *a posteriori* fashion. While his proposal seems to offer new life to metaphysics, it has only given partial consideration to the relationship between Christian theology and metaphysics itself. Nevertheless, since metaphysical claims are at the heart of Christian theology,[63] McGrath's proposal of how to reintroduce them is an important issue that most definitely warrants additional consideration by McGrath or others who adopt his ST.

A final issue that deserves further study is the relationship of particular scientific theories and theological doctrines. From the outset of *A Scientific Theology*, McGrath makes it clear that he limits his project to dealing with the assumptions and methodologies of the scientific and theological enterprises and does not focus on how the specific theories of the two fields interact.[64] Nevertheless, there are at least two places where the issue of theory relation comes to the surface in his work. This issue first arises when McGrath suggests that the natural sciences offer theology a helpful way of determining whether or not it has arrived at the correct interpretation of the Bible.[65] Simply put, natural science may offer a hermeneutical aid to theology. The issue also arises from the fact that McGrath accepts theistic evolution and views the earlier chapters of Genesis through Darwinian lenses.[66] Thus, one wonders what determines when a theologian should allow a given scientific theory to set parameters on his doctrinal claims. McGrath sets this issue aside, but it becomes clear that scientific theories are doing just this.

62. Vidu, "Scientific Theology," 274.

63. McGrath, *Scientific Theology*, vol. 3, 290.

64. McGrath, *Scientific Theology*, vol. 1, 45.

65. Ibid., 18–19. This issue is briefly discussed in chapter 2, but greater treatment in chapter 4.

66. McGrath, *Scientific Theology*, vol. 3, 273.

As noted, the purpose of McGrath's ST has been to consider the working assumptions and methodologies of theology and science, and not the relationship of their particular doctrines and theories. Nevertheless, the issue of theory relation is certainly important and even arises within McGrath's own work. While McGrath has made an enormous contribution to the dialogue between science and theology on epistemological grounds, it seems that there is still work to be done on the relationship between the particular theories of science and Christian doctrines. McGrath may choose to address this in later works. If not, this in an issue that would benefit from further attention by those who accept his ST.

CONCLUSION

Alister E. McGrath's ST—which is developed in *A Scientific Theology* and *The Science of God*—makes a valuable contribution to evangelical theology. Though very little has been written in response to his ST, the response so far has been quite positive. For example, Keating says, despite the areas "in which one could wish more exactitude, there can be no doubt that McGrath has moved the discussion over the theological value of dialogue with the natural sciences in a new and most welcome direction. In particular, he insists with clarity and sophistication that dialogue with the sciences must and can be in service of theology's ongoing quest to remain subordinated to God's revelation in Jesus Christ."[67] Myers concurs, saying:

> With immense learning and considerable sophistication, McGrath's *Scientific Theology* presents a theology of nature, a defense of the objectivity and knowability of the real world, and an account of the theoretical representation of reality. The whole work develops its argument through extensive engagement with the history of theology and the philosophy of science, while its most decisive formulations remain grounded in the witness of scripture. McGrath's passionate concern to integrate scientific and theological methods is balanced and enriched at every point by his concern to maintain the integrity of theology and by his commitment to an evangelical orthodoxy deeply rooted in the ecumenical faith of Christian tradition. What emerges is a uniquely sustained and wide-ranging demonstration of the methodological value of natural science as a dialogue-partner for and aid to theological reflection.[68]

67. Keating, "Natural Sciences," 149.
68. Myers, "McGrath's Scientific Theology," 19–20.

He later adds, "McGrath's *Scientific Theology* is one of the most sustained and sophisticated theological engagements with natural science yet produced, and one of the most important works on theological method to have appeared in recent years. Its nuanced critical realist vision of the nature and task of theology will offer a valuable stimulus to theological reflection in the future."[69] Likewise, Snyder argues that "McGrath's work in scientific theology and critical realism, in concert with the tradition of classical Christian theology, has much to recommend it. This approach opens up new avenues for study and discussion in Christian theology, without abandoning historical theology."[70] Finally, Edward Oakes says, "Taken together, the trilogy proves that McGrath can now claim to join the ranks of the most significant theologians of this new century."[71] Indeed, those who have considered McGrath's ST so far see it as an extraordinary achievement and valuable contribution to evangelical theology.

This book agrees with the overall assessment of these reviewers. McGrath's work stands out as a monumental achievement among evangelicals concerned with developing a theological method that takes the dialogue with natural science seriously. Furthermore, with the adoption of Roy Bhaskar's CR, McGrath's ST is better than theological methods that adopt a modern or postmodern perspective. Unlike these perspectives, McGrath's critical realist approach offers a balanced treatment of the objective and subjective aspects of human knowledge. In addition to this, it regains a UTK without yielding to reductionism. McGrath does all of this by observing the common epistemological assumptions and methods of theology and science. Based on these commonalities, McGrath brings theology and science back into dialogue and shows how they can be mutually enhanced by this renewed relationship.

McGrath's ST also offers important ontological insights for theology and science. By affirming that God is the creator of the universe, McGrath shows how creation gives theologians an important source of revelation. Likewise, McGrath's ST shows how the doctrine of creation provides the ontological basis for scientific investigation and demands a UTK.

---

69. Ibid., 20.

70. Snyder, "Scientific Theology," 356–57.

71. Oakes, "Scientific Theology," 200.

Finally, McGrath's ST recasts natural theology in such a way that it is once again allowed to function in a confirming role for Christianity. It is freed from the Enlightenment's stifling demands for absolute certainty and is now used to validate the prior belief that God exists. This, along with the fact that natural theology allows Christianity to offer an explanation of alternative belief systems, gives natural theology explanatory power and apologetic appeal.

Therefore, though there are areas that would benefit from further clarification or development, McGrath's ST offers evangelicalism an appropriate theological method and shows how science can be used as the *ancilla theologia*.

Bibliography

Abraham, William J. "Revelation and Natural Theology." In *Alister E. McGrath & Evangelical Theology*, edited by Sung Wook Chung, 264–79. Grand Rapids: Baker, 2003.

Adler, Mortimer J. *Truth In Religion*. New York: Macmillan, 1990.

Alston, William P. *Perceiving God*. Ithaca: Cornell University Press, 1991.

Aquinas, St. Thomas. *Summa Theologica*. Translated by Fathers of the Dominican Province. 5 vols. New York: Christian Classics, 1981.

Augustine. "Christian Doctrine." In *Nicene and Post-Nicene Fathers: First Series*, edited by Philip Schaff, translated by J. F. Shaw, 14, 513–97. Peabody, MA: Hendrickson, 2004.

———. *Confessions*. London: Penguin, 1961.

———. "The Literal Meaning of Genesis." In *Ancient Christian Writers: The Works of the Fathers in Translation*, edited by Johannes Quasten et al., translated by John Hammond Taylor, 42. New York: Newman, 1982.

Bacon, Francis. *The New Organon*. Edited by Lisa Jardine and Michael Silverthrone. Cambridge: Cambridge University Press, 2000.

Barbour, Ian G. *Nature, Human Nature, and God*. Minneapolis: Fortress, 2002.

———. *Religion and Science: Historical and Contemporary Issues*. San Francisco: HarperCollins, 1997.

———. *Religion in an Age of Science*. San Francisco: Harper & Row, 1990.

———. *When Science Meets Religion*. San Francisco: HarperCollins, 2000.

Barr, James. *Biblical Faith and Natural Theology*. Oxford: Clarendon, 1993.

Barth, Karl. *Church Dogmatics*. Translated by G. T. Thompson. 5 Vols. Edinburgh: T. & T. Clark, 1977.

———. *Die christliche Theologie im Entwurf*. Munich: Kaiser Verlag, 1927.

———. *The Epistle to the Romans*. Translated by Edwyn C. Hoskyns. London: Oxford University Press, 1933.

———. *The Gottingen Dogmatics: Instruction in the Christian Religion*. Grand Rapids: Eerdmans, 1991.

———. "No!" In *Natural Theology*, 67–128. Eugene, OR: Wipf and Stock, 2002.

———. "Schicksal und Idee in Theologie." In *TheologischeFrage und Antworten*, 54–92. Zurich: Evangelischer Verlag, 1957.

Barzun, Jacques. *From Dawn to Decadence: 1500 to the Present*. San Francisco: HarperCollins, 2000.

Beilby, James, ed. *Naturalism Defeated*. Ithaca: Cornell University Press, 2002.

Bernal, J. D. *Science in History*. 4 vols. Cambridge, MA: M.I.T. Press, 1971.

Bewkes, Eugene G., et al. *The Western Heritage of Faith and Reason*. New York: Harper & Row, 1963.

Bhaskar, Roy. *The Possibility of Naturalism*. New York: Routledge, 1998.

————. *A Realist Theory of Science*. New York: Verso, 2008.

————. *Reclaiming Reality: A Critical Introduction to Contemporary Philosophy*. London: Verso, 1989.

————. *Scientific Realism and Human Emancipation*. London: Verso, 1986.

Birkett, Kirsten. *Unnatural Enemies: An Introduction to Science and Christianity*. Sydney: Matthias Media, 1997.

Bloesch, Donald G. *Holy Scripture*. Downers Grove: InterVarsity, 1994.

Boyd, Richard. "The Current Status of Scientific Realism." In *Scientific Realism*, edited by Jarrett Leplin, 41–82. Berkeley: University of California Press, 1984.

Boyle, Joseph, et al. "The Reformed Objection to Natural Theology: a Catholic Perspective." *Christian Scholar's Review* 11:3 (1982) 199–211.

Bozeman, Theodore Dwight. *Protestants in an Age of Science*. Chapel Hill: University of North Carolina Press, 1977.

Brockman, John, ed. *Intelligent Thought: Science Verses the Intelligent Design Movement*. New York: Vintage, 2006.

Brooke, John Hedley. "Natural Theology." In *Science & Religion*, edited by Gary Ferngren, 163–75. Baltimore: Johns Hopkins University Press, 2002.

————. *Science and Religion*. Cambridge: Cambridge University Press, 1991.

————. "Science and Theology in the Enlightenment." In *Religion & Science: History, Method, Dialogue*, edited by W. Mark Richardson and Wesley J. Wildman, 7–28. London: Routledge, 1996.

Brown, Colin. *Philosophy & the Christian Faith*. Downers Grove: InterVarsity, 1968.

Brown, Hunter. "Alvin Plantinga and Natural Theology." *International Journal for Philosophy of Religion* 30 (July 1991) 1–19.

Calvin, John. *Calvin's Commentaries: Genesis*. Vol. 1. Grand Rapids: Baker, n.d.

————. *Calvin's Commentaries*. Vol. 4. Translated by Henry Beveridge. Grand Rapids: Baker, 2003.

————. *Calvin's Commentaries*. Vol. 19. Translated by Henry Beveridge. Grand Rapids: Baker, 2003.

————. *Institutes of the Christian Religion*. Edited by John T. McNeill. Translated by Ford Lewis Battles. Louisville: Westminster / John Knox, n.d.

Campbell, Douglas A. "Natural Theology in Paul? Reading Romans 1:19–20." *International Journal of Systematic Theology* 1:3 (November 1999) 231–52.

Carroll, Vincent, and David Shiflett. *Christianity On Trial*. San Francisco: Encounter, 2002.

Carson, D. A. *The Gagging of God*. Grand Rapids: Zondervan, 1996.

Case-Winters, Anna. "The Argument From Design: What is at Stake Theologically?" *Zygon* 35:1 (March 2000) 69–81.

"The Chicago Statement on Biblical Inerrancy," Article VI. Cited in Carl F.H. Henry, *God, Revelation and Authority*. Vol. 4. Wheaton, IL: Crossway, 1999.

Chung, Sung Wook. "Karl Barth's Evangelical Principles: Reformation Legacy." In *Alister E. McGrath & Evangelical Theology*, edited by Sung Wook Chung, 195–212. Grand Rapids: Baker, 2003.

————. "Preface." In *Alister E. McGrath & Evangelical Theology*, edited by Sung Wook Chung, vii–viii. Grand Rapids: Baker, 2003.

Clark, David K. "Postmodern Evangelical Apologetics." In *Alister E. McGrath and Evangelical Theology*, edited by Sung Wook Chung, 310–32. Grand Rapids: Baker, 2003.

———. *To Know and Love God: Method for Theology.* Wheaton, IL: Crossway, 2003.

Clark, Kelly James. *Return to Reason.* Grand Rapids: Eerdmans, 1990.

Cleobury, F. H. *A Return to Natural Theology.* London: James Clarke, 1967.

Clifford, William. "The Ethics of Belief." In *Philosophy of Religion*, edited by Michael Peterson et al., 65–70. New York: Oxford University Press, 1996.

Collins, C. John. *Science & Faith.* Wheaton, IL: Crossway, 2003.

Colyer, Elmer. "Alister E. McGrath, a Scientific Theology, Volume 1—Nature." *Pro Ecclesia* 12 (2003) 226–31.

———. "Alister E. McGrath, a Scientific Theology, Volume 2—Reality." *Pro Ecclesia* 12 (2003) 492–97.

———. "Alister E. McGrath, a Scientific Theology, Volume 3—Theory." *Pro Ecclesia* 13 (2004) 244–50.

Craig, William Lane. "Classical Apologetics." In *Five Views on Apologetics*, edited by Steven B. Cowan and Stanley N. Grundy, 26–33. Grand Rapids: Zondervan, 2000.

———. *The Cosmological Argument from Plato to Leibniz.* Eugene, OR: Wipf and Stock, 1980.

———. "The Kalam Cosmological Argument." In *Philosophy of Religion*, edited by William Lane Craig, 92–113. New Brunswick: Rutgers University Press, 2002.

———. "Natural Theology: Introduction." In *Philosophy of Religion*, edited by William Lane Craig, 69–81. New Brunswick: Rutgers University Press, 2002.

———. "Philosophical and Scientific Pointers to Creation ex Nihilo." In *Contemporary Perspectives on Religious Epistemology*, edited by R. Douglas Geivett and Brendan Sweetman, 185–200. New York: Oxford University Press, 1992.

Crombie, A. C. *Medieval and Early Modern Science.* 2 vols. New York: Doubleday, 1959.

Dampier, Sir William. *A History of Science and Its Relations with Philosophy and Religion.* Cambridge: Cambridge University Press, 1929.

Darwin, Charles. *On the Origin of Species.* Cambridge: Harvard University Press, 1964.

Davis, Edward B., and Michael P. Winship. "Early Modern Protestantism." In *Science & Religion*, edited by Gary B. Ferngren, 117–29. Baltimore: Johns Hopkins University Press, 2002.

Davis, Stephen T. *God, Reason & Theistic Proofs.* Edinburgh: Edinburgh University Press, 1997.

Dawkins, Richard. *The Blind Watchmaker.* New York: Norton, 1996.

Deason, Gary B. "The Protestant Reformation and The Rise of Modern Science." *Scottish Journal of Theology* 38 (August 1985) 221–40.

———. "Reformation Theology and the Mechanistic Conception of Nature." In *God & Nature*, edited by David C. Lindberg and Ronald L. Numbers, 167–91. Berkeley: University of California Press, 1986.

Dembski, William A. *The Design Revolution.* Downers Grove: InterVarsity, 2004.

———. *Intelligent Design.* Downers Grove: InterVarsity, 1999.

Denton, Michael. *Evolution: A Theory in Crisis.* 3d ed. Bethesda, MD: Adler & Adler, 1986.

———. *Nature's Destiny.* New York: Free Press, 1998.

Derrida, Jacques. "White Mythology: Metaphor in the Text of Philosophy." *New Literary History* 6 (1974) 5–74.

Descartes, Rene. *Discourse on Method.* Translated by Desmond M. Clarke. London: Penguin, 1999.

————. *Meditations on First Philosophy.* Translated by Donald A. Cress. 4th ed. Indianapolis: Hackett, 1998.

DeWeese, Garrett J., and J. P. Moreland. *Philosophy Made Slightly Less Difficult.* Downers Grove: InterVarsity, 2005.

Dillenberg, John. *Protestant Thought & Natural Science.* Nashville: Abingdon, 1960.

Dockery, David S., and David P. Nelson. "Special Revelation." In *A Theology for the Church,* edited by Daniel L. Akin, 118–74. Nashville: Broadman & Holman, 2007.

Draper, John William. *History of the Conflict between Religion and Science.* 7th ed. London: Henry S. King, 1876.

Dulles, Avery Cardinal. *A History of Apologetics.* San Francisco: Ignatius, 2005.

Dulles, Avery, SJ. *Models of Revelation.* Maryknoll: Orbis, 1992.

Erickson, Millard J. *Christian Theology.* 2d ed. Grand Rapids: Baker, 1998.

————. "On Flying in Theological Fog." In *Reclaiming the Center,* edited by Millard J. Erickson et al., 323–49. Wheaton, IL: Crossway, 2004.

————. *Truth or Consequences.* Downers Grove: InterVarsity, 2001.

Evans, C. Stephen. *Philosophy of Religion.* Downers Grove: InterVarsity, 1982.

Fackre, Gabriel. *The Doctrine of Revelation.* Grand Rapids: Eerdmans, 1997.

Feinberg, John S. *No One Like Him.* Wheaton: CrossWay, 2001.

Feinberg, Paul D. "Cumulative Case Apologetics." In *Five Views on Apologetics,* edited by Steven B. Cowan, 148–72. Grand Rapids: Zondervan, 2000.

Foucault, Michel. *Ethics: Subjectivity and Truth.* London: Penguin, 2000.

Frame, John M. *Apologetics to the Glory of God.* Phillipsburg: P & R. 1994.

Franke, John R. "Postmodern Evangelical Theology: A Nonfoundationalist Approach to the Christian Faith." In *Alister E. McGrath & Evangelical Theology,* edited by Sung Wook Chung, 280–309. Grand Rapids: Baker, 2003.

Fulmer, Gilbert. "A Fatal Flaw in Anthropic Principle Design Arguments." *International Journal for Philosophy of Religion* 49 (2001) 101–10.

Gardner, Paul, "What is Scripture?" In "Evangelicals Now." No pages. Online: http://www.e-n.org.uk.

Geisler, Norman L. *Christian Apologetics.* Grand Rapids: Baker, 1976.

————. *Systematic Theology: Introduction & Bible.* 4 vols. Minneapolis: Bethany, 2002.

Geivett, R. Douglas. "David Hume and the Cumulative Case Argument." In *In Defense of Natural Theology,* edited by James F. Sennett and Douglas Groothuis, 297–329. Downers Grove: InterVarsity, 2005.

Gerrish, B. A. "The Reformation and the Rise of Modern Science." In *The Impact of the Church Upon Its Culture,* edited by Jerald C. Brauer, 231–65. Chicago: University of Chicago Press, 1968.

Gilkey, Langdon. *Creation on Trial.* Minneapolis: Winston, 1985.

Gillespie, Neal C. *Charles Darwin and the Problem of Creation.* Chicago: University of Chicago Press, 1982.

Gingerich, Owen. "The Copernican Revolution." In *Science & Religion,* edited by Gary B. Ferngren. Baltimore: Johns Hopkins University Press, 2002.

Goldstein, Thomas. *Dawn of Modern Science: From the Ancient Greeks to the Renaissance.* Boston: Houghton Mifflin, 1980.

Gonzalez, Justo L. *The Story of Christianity.* 2 vols. San Francisco: HarperCollins, 1984.

Gould, Stephen Jay. "Two Separate Domains." In *Philosophy of Religion,* edited by Michael Peterson et al., 549–58. New York: Oxford University Press, 2007.

Grant, Edward. "Aristotle and Aristotelianism." In *Science & Religion: A Historical Introduction*, edited by Gary B. Ferngren. Baltimore: Johns Hopkins University Press, 2002.

———. "Science and Theology in the Middle Ages." In *God & Nature: Historical Essays on the Encounter between Christianity and Science*, edited by David C. Lindberg and Ronald L. Numbers. Berkeley: University of California Press, 1986.

Greer, Robert C. *Mapping Postmodernism*. Downers Grove: InterVarsity, 2003.

Gregersen, Niels Henrik, and J. Wentzel van Huyssteen, eds. *Rethinking Theology and Science: Six Models for the Current Dialogue*. Grand Rapids: Eerdmans, 1998.

Grenz, Stanley J., and John R. Franke. *Beyond Foundationalism*. Louisville: Westminster / John Knox, 2001.

Groff, Ruth. "The Truth of the Matter: Roy Bhasker's Critical Realism and the Concept of Alethic Truth." *Philosophy of the Social Sciences* 30:3 (September 2000) 407–35.

Groothuis, Douglas. *Truth Decay*. Downers Grove: InterVarsity, 2000.

———. "Truth Defined and Defended." In *Reclaiming the Center*, edited by Millard J. Erickson et al., 59–79. Wheaton, IL: Crossway, 2004.

Grudem, Wayne. *Systematic Theology*. Grand Rapids: Zondervan, 1994.

Gundry, D. W. "The Paleyan Argument from Design." *Church Quarterly Review* 151 (1951) 182–98.

Gunton, Colin E, ed. *The Doctrine of Creation*. 2d ed. New York: T&T Clark, 2004.

———. *The Triune Creator*. Grand Rapids: Eerdmans, 1998.

Gutenson, Charles. "Alister E. McGrath: A Scientific Theology." *The Princeton Seminary Bulletin* 24:1 (March 2003) 164–65.

Harbin, Michael A. "Theistic Evolution: Deism Revisited." *Journal of the Evangelical Theological Society* 40:4 (1997) 639–51.

Harris, Sam. *Letter to a Christian Nation*. New York: Knopf, 2006.

Hart, Trevor. "Revelation." In *The Cambridge Companion to Karl Barth*, edited by John Webster, 37–56. Cambridge: Cambridge University Press, 2000.

Hauerwas, Stanley. *In Good Company: The Church as Polis*. Notre Dame: University of Notre Dame Press, 1995.

———. *With the Grain of the Universe: The Church's Witness and Natural Theology*. Grand Rapids: Brazos, 2001.

Henry, Carl F. H. *God, Revelation and Authority*. 6 vols. Wheaton, IL: Crossway, 1999.

Hick, John. *The Existence of God*. London: Macmillan, 1964.

Hicks, Peter. *The Journey So Far: Philosophy Through the Ages*. Grand Rapids: Zondervan, 2003.

Hiebert, Paul G. *Missiological Implications of Epistemological Shifts*. Harrisburg: Trinity, 1999.

Hooykaas, R. *Religion and the Rise of Modern Science*. Vancouver: Regent College Publishing, 1972.

Hume, David. *Dialogues Concerning Natural Religion*. Indianapolis: Hackett, 1980.

———. *Enquiries Concerning Human Understanding and Concerning the Principles of Morals*. 3d ed. Oxford: Clarendon, 1975.

———. *The Natural History of Religion*. Edited by H. E. Root. Stanford: Stanford University Press, 1957.

———. *A Treatise of Human Nature*. London: Penguin, 1969.

Jaki, Stanley L. *Bible and Science*. Front Royal, VA: Christendom, 1996.

———. *A Mind's Matter: An Intellectual Autobiography*. Grand Rapids: Eerdmans, 2002.

———. *Miracles and Physics*. 2d ed. Front Royal, VA: Christendom, 1999.

———. *The Relevance of Physics*. Chicago: University of Chicago Press, 1966.

———. *The Road of Science and the Ways to God*. Chicago: University of Chicago Press, 1978.

———. *The Savior of Science*. Grand Rapids: Eerdmans, 2000.

Kant, Immanuel. *The Critique of Judgment*. Translated by J. H. Bernard. Amherst: Prometheus, 2000.

———. *Critique of Practical Reason*. Translated by T. K. Abbott. Amherst: Prometheus, 1996.

———. *Critique of Pure Reason*. Translated by J. M. D. Meiklejohn. Amherst: Prometheus, 1990.

Keating, James F. "The Natural Sciences as an Ancilla Theologiae Nova: Alister E. McGrath's A Scientific Theology." *The Thomist* 69 (2005) 127–52.

Kemsley, Douglas S. "Religious Influences In the Rise of Modern Science: A Review and Criticism, Particularly of the Protestant-Puritan Ethic." *Annals of Science* 24 (1968) 199–226.

Kenneson, Philip D. "There's No Such Thing as Objective Truth, and It's a Good Thing Too." In *Christian Apologetics in the Postmodern World*, edited by Timothy R. Phillips and Dennis L. Okholm, 155–70. Downers Grove: InterVarsity, 1995.

Kenny, Anthony. *A Brief History of Western Philosophy*. Oxford: Blackwell, 1998.

Klaaren, Eugene M. *Religious Origins of Modern Science: Belief in Creation in Seventeenth-Century Thought*. Grand Rapids: Eerdmans, 1977.

Köstenberger, Andreas, ed. *Whatever Happened to Truth*. Wheaton, IL: Crossway, 2005.

Kuhn, Thomas S. *The Structure of Scientific Revolutions*. 3d ed. Chicago and London: University of Chicago Press, 1996.

Kurtz, Paul. *Humanist Manifesto 2000: A Call for New Planetary Humanism*. Amherst: Prometheus, 2000.

Lane, David H. "Theological Problems with Theistic Evolution." *Bibliotheca Sacra* 151:602 (1994) 155–74.

Larson, Edward J. "The Scopes Trials." In *Science & Religion: A Historical Introduction*, edited by Gary B. Ferngren, 289–98. Baltimore: Johns Hopkins University Press, 2002.

Lawson, Hilary. *Closure: A Story of Everything*. London and New York: Routledge, 2001.

Lindbeck, George. *The Nature of Doctrine: Religion and Theology in a Postliberal Age*. Philadelphia: Westminster, 1984.

Lindberg, David C. *The Beginnings of Western Science*. Chicago and London: University of Chicago Press, 1992.

———. "Early Christian Attitudes toward Nature." In *Science & Religion*, edited by Gary B. Ferngren, 47–56. Baltimore: Johns Hopkins University Press, 2002.

———. "Medieval Science and Religion." In *Science & Religion: A Historical Introduction*, edited by Gary B. Ferngren. Baltimore: Johns Hopkins University Press, 2002.

———. "Science and the Early Church." In *God & Nature: Historical Essays on the Encounter between Christianity and Science*, edited by David C. Lindberg and Ronald L. Numbers, 19–48. Berkeley: University of California Press, 1986.

Lindberg, David C., and Ronald L. Numbers. "Introduction." In *God & Nature: Historical Essays on the Encounter between Christianity and Science*, edited by David C.

Lindberg and Ronald L. Numbers, 1–18. Berkeley: University of California Press, 1986.

Locke, John. *An Essay Concerning Human Understanding.* London: Penguin, 2004.

———. *The Reasonableness of Christianity.* Edited by I. T. Ramsey. Stanford: Stanford University Press, 1958.

Long, Eugene Thomas, ed. *Prospects for Natural Theology.* Vol. 25. Washington, DC: Catholic University of America Press, 1992.

MacKay, Donald. *The Clockwork Image.* Downers Grove: InterVarsity, 1974.

———. *Science, Chance, and Providence.* Oxford: Oxford University Press, 1978.

Mascall, Eric L. *Christian Theology and Natural Science: Some Questions on their Relations.* London: Longman, 1956.

McGrath, Alister E. "Alister McGrath." Interview by George Stroumboulopoulos. *The Hour* 68.

———. "A Blast from the Past? The Boyle Lectures and Natural Theology." *Science and Christian Belief* 17 (2005) 25–34.

———. *Christian Theology.* 4th ed. Oxford: Blackwell, 2007.

———. *A Cloud of Witnesses.* Eugene, OR: Wipf & Stock, 1990.

———. "Contributors: An Appreciation and Response." In *Alister E. McGrath & Evangelical Theology,* edited by Sung Wook Chung, 333–64. Exeter: Paternoster, 2003.

———. "Darwinism." In *The Oxford Handbook of Science and Religion,* edited by Philip Clayton. Oxford: Oxford University Press, 2006.

———. "Dawkins God: Alister McGrath Q & A." In "Christians in Science." No pages. Online: http://www.cis-centralsouth.org.uk.

———. *Doubting.* Downers Grove: InterVarsity, 2006.

———. "Engaging the Great Tradition: Evangelical Theology and the Role of Tradition." In *Evangelical Futures: A Conversation on Theological Method,* edited by John C. Stackhouse, 139–58. Grand Rapids: Baker, 2000.

———. *The Foundations of Dialogue In Science & Religion.* Oxford: Blackwell, 1998.

———. *The Genesis of Doctrine.* Grand Rapids: Eerdmans, 1990.

———. "Has Science Eliminated God?—Richard Dawkins and the Meaning of Life." *Science and Christian Belief* 17 (2005) 115–35.

———. "Intelligibility and Responsibility: The Christian Doctrine of Creation and Modern Science." *China Graduate School of Theology Journal* 37 (2004) 103–37.

———. "John Calvin and Late Medieval Thought: A Study in Late Medieval Influences upon Calvin's Theological Thought." *Archiv fur Reformationsgeschichte* 77 (1986) 58–78.

———. "Let's Keep Asking Questions." In "Evangelicals Now." No pages. Online: http://www.e-n.org.uk.

———. "On Writing a Scientific Theology: A Response to Ross H. McKenzie." *Perspectives on Science and Christian Faith* 56 (2004) 255–59.

———. "The Origins of A Scientific Theology." *Interdisciplinary Science Reviews* 28 (2003) 259–65.

———. *The Order of Things: Explorations in Scientific Theology.* Oxford: Blackwell, 2006.

———. *A Passion for Truth.* Downers Grove: InterVarsity, 1996.

———. "Profile: Thomas F. Torrance." *Epworth Review* 27 (2000) 11–15.

———. "A Rejoinder to Paul Gardner." In "Evangelicals Now." No pages. Online: http://www.e-n.org.uk.

————. *Science & Religion*. Oxford: Blackwell, 1999.

————. "Science and Religion: Developing a 'Scientific Theology.'" 2003. Online: http://users.ox.ac.uk/~mcgrath/lectures.html.

————. *The Science of God*. Grand Rapids: Eerdmans, 2004.

————. *A Scientific Theology*. 3 vols. Grand Rapids: Eerdmans, 2001–2003.

————. "Spiritual Information and the Sense of Wonder: The Convergence of Spirituality and the Natural Science." In *Spiritual Information*, edited by Charles L. Harper. Philadelphia: Templeton Foundation Press, 2005.

————. *T. F. Torrance: An Intellectual Biography*. Edinburgh: T. & T. Clark, 1999.

————. *The Twilight of Atheism*. New York: Doubleday, 2004.

McGrath, Alister E., and Joanna Collicutt McGrath. *The Dawkins Delusion*. London: SPCK, 2007.

McKenzie, Ross H. "Foundations of the Dialogue between the Physical Sciences and Theology." *Perspectives on Science and Christian Faith* 56 (2004) 242–54.

Meek, Esther Lightcap. *Longing to Know*. Grand Rapids: Brazos, 2003.

Merton, Robert K. "Science, Technology and Society in Seventeenth Century England." *Osiris* 4 (1938) 432–34.

Milbank, John. *The Word Made Strange: Theology, Language, Culture*. Oxford: Blackwell, 1997.

Mohler, R. Albert. "Truth and Contemporary Culture." In *Whatever Happened to Truth*, edited by Andreas Köstenberger, 53–73. Wheaton, IL: Crossway, 2005.

Moreland, J. P. "Science, Miracles, Agency Theory & the God-of-the-Gaps." In *In Defense of Miracles*, edited by Douglas Geivett and Gary R. Habermas, 132–48. Downers Grove: InterVarsity, 1997.

————. "Theistic Science & Methodological Naturalism." In *The Creation Hypothesis*, edited by J. P. Moreland, 41–66. Downers Grove: InterVarsity 1994.

Moreland, J. P., and William Lane Craig. *Philosophical Foundations for A Christian Worldview*. Downers Grove: InterVarsity, 2003.

Moreland, J. P., and Garrett DeWeese. "The Premature Report of Foundationalism's Demise." In *Reclaiming the Center*, edited by Millard J. Erickson et al., 81–107. Wheaton, IL: Crossway, 2004.

Morgan, John. "The Puritan Thesis Revisited." In *Evangelicals and Science In Historical Perspective*, edited by David N. Livingstone et al., 43–74. Oxford: Oxford University Press, 1999.

Morris, Tim, and Don Petcher. *Science & Grace*. Wheaton, IL: Crossway, 2006.

Murphy, Nancey. "Postmodern Apologetics, or Why Theologians Must Pay Attention to Science." In *Religion & Science: History, Method, Dialogue*, edited by W. Mark Richardson and Wesley J. Wildman, 105–20. London and New York: Routledge, 1996.

————. "Relating Theology and Science in a Postmodern Age." *The Center For Theology and The Natural Sciences Bulletin* 7 (Fall 1987) 1–10.

————. *Theology in the Age of Science*. Ithaca: Cornell University Press, 1990.

Myers, Benjamin. "Alister E. McGrath's Scientific Theology." In *The Order of Things: Explorations in Scientific Theology*, by Alister E. McGrath, 3–27. Oxford: Blackwell, 2006.

Nash, Ronald H. *Faith & Reason*. Grand Rapids: Zondervan, 1988.

Needham, Joseph. "Why Didn't China Give Rise to Modern Science." *Ching Feng* 17:2 (December 1974) 90–94.

Neurath, Otto. *Empiricism and Sociology*. Dordrecht: Reidel, 1973.

Noll, Mark. *The Scandal of the Evangelical Mind*. Grand Rapids: Eerdmans, 1994.

O'Donovan, Oliver. *Resurrection and Moral Order*. Grand Rapids: Eerdmans, 1986.

Oakes, Edward T. "A Scientific Theology: Volume 3: Theory." *Theological Studies* 67:1 (March 2006) 200–201.

Okholm, Dennis L. "'The Uneasy Evangelical: Alister E. McGrath on Postliberalism.'" In *Alister E. McGrath & Evangelical Theology*, edited by Sung Wook Chung, 90–112. Grand Rapids: Baker, 2003.

Oppy, Graham. "Paley's Argument for Design." *Philo* 5 (2002) 161–73.

Packer, J. I. "Inerrancy—Pros and Cons." In "Evangelicals Now." No pages. Online: http://www.e-n.org.uk.

Packer, James I. Foreword to *Alister E. McGrath & Evangelical Theology*, edited by Sung Wook Chung, xiii–xiv. Grand Rapids: Baker, 2003.

Padgett, Alan G. "A Scientific Theology, vol. 1, Nature." *Word & World* 23:1 (Winter 2003) 108–10.

———. *Science and The Study of God*. Grand Rapids: Eerdmans, 2003.

Paley, William. *Natural Theology*. Oxford: Oxford University Press, 2006.

Pannenberg, Wolfhart. *Systematic Theology*. 3 vols. Grand Rapids: Eerdmans, 1991–1998.

———. *Toward a Theology of Nature*. Edited by Ted Peters. Louisville: Westminster/John Knox, 1993.

Parker, James, III. "A Requiem for Postmodernism—Whither Now?" In *Reclaiming the Center*, edited by Millard J. Erickson et al. Wheaton, IL: Crossway, 2004.

Peacocke, Arthur. *Imitations of Reality*. Notre Dame: University of Notre Dame Press, 1984.

———. *Theology for a Scientific Age*. Oxford: Blackwell, 1990.

Pearcey, Nancy R., and Charles B. Thaxton. *The Soul of Science: Christian Faith and Natural Philosophy*. Wheaton, IL: Crossway, 1994.

Pelikan, Jaroslav. *Christianity and Classical Culture: The Metamorphosis of Natural Theology in the Christian Encounter with Hellenism*. New Haven: Yale University Press, 1993.

Penrose, Roger. *Shadows of the Mind: A Search for the Missing Science of Consciousness*. London: Vintage, 1995.

Peters, Ted. *Bridging Science and Religion*. Minneapolis: Augsburg, 2003.

———. *God: The World's Future*. Minneapolis: Augsburg, 2000.

———. *Playing God?* New York: Routledge, 1996.

———. Preface to *Cosmos as Creation*, edited by Ted Peters, 11–27. Nashville: Abingdon, 1989.

———. "Science and Theology: Toward Consonance." In *Science & Theology*, edited by Ted Peters, 11–39. Boulder: Westview, 1998.

Peters, Ted, and Martinez Hewlett. *Evolution from Creation to New Creation: Conflict, Conversation and Convergence*. Nashville: Abingdon, 2003.

Peters, Ted, et al., eds. *God, Life, and the Cosmos: Christian and Islamic Perspectives*. Burlington: Eerdmans, 2002.

Phillips, Timothy R., and Dennis L. Okholm, eds. *Christian Apologetics in the Postmodern World*. Downers Grove: InterVarsity, 1995.

Plantinga, Alvin. *The Analytic Theist: An Alvin Plantinga Reader*. Edited by James F. Sennett. Grand Rapids: Eerdmans, 1998.

———. *God and Other Minds: A Study of the Rational Justification of Belief in God*. Ithaca: Cornell University Press, 1967.

———. "Is Belief in God Properly Basic." In *Contemporary Perspectives on Religious Epistemology*, edited by R. Douglass Geivett and Brendan Sweetman, 133–41. New York: Oxford University Press, 1992.

———. "Methodological Naturalism." *Perspectives on Science and Christian Faith* 49 (1997) 143–54.

———. "Natural Theology." In *A Companion to Metaphysics*, edited by Jaegwon Kim and Ernest Sosa, 346–49. Oxford: Blackwell, 1995.

———.. "The Ontological Argument." In *Philosophy of Religion*, edited by William Lane Craig, 180–88. New Brunswick, NJ: Rutgers University Press, 2002.

———. "Reason and Belief in God." In *Faith and Rationality: Reason and Belief in God*, edited by Alvin Plantinga and Nicholas Wolterstorff, 16–93. Notre Dame: University of Notre Dame Press, 1983.

———. "The Reformed Objection to Natural Theology." *Christian Scholar's Review* 11:3 (1982).

———. *Warrant: The Current Debate*. New York: Oxford University Press, 1993.

———, ed. *The Ontological Argument: From St. Anselm to Contemporary Philosophers*. New York: Doubleday, 1965.

Polkinghorne, John C. *Belief in God in an Age of Science*. New Haven: Yale University Press, 1998.

———. *One World: The Interaction of Science and Theology*. Princeton: Princeton University Press, 1986.

———. *Reason and Reality*. London: SPCK, 1991.

———. *Science and Creation: The Search for Understanding*. London: SPCK, 2006.

———. *Science & Theology*. London: SPCK, 1998.

———. *Scientists as Theologians*. London: SPCK, 1996.

Poythress, Vern S. *Redeeming Science*. Wheaton, IL: Crossway, 2006.

Psillos, Stathis. *Scientific Realism: How Science Tracks Truth*. New York: Routledge, 1999.

Ramm, Bernard. *The Christian View of Science and Scripture*. Grand Rapids: Eerdmans, 1987.

Raschke, Carl. *The Next Reformation*. Grand Rapids: Baker, 2004.

Ratzsch, Del. *Science and Its Limits: The Natural Sciences in Christian Perspectives*. Downers Grove: InterVarsity, 2000.

Redhead, Michael. *From Physics to Metaphysics*. Cambridge: Cambridge University Press, 1995.

Reid, W. Stanford. "Calvin's View of Natural Science." In *In Honor of John Calvin*, edited by E. J. Furcha, 233–55. Montreal: McGill University, 1987.

Reynolds, John Mark. "Getting God Pass: Science, Theology, and the Consideration of Intelligent Design." In *Signs of Intelligence*, edited by William A. Dembski and James M. Kushiner, 80–89. Grand Rapids: Brazos, 2001.

Richardson, W. Mark, and Wesley J. Wildman. Introduction to *Religion and Science*, edited by W. Mark Richardson and Wesley J. Wildman, xi–xx. London and New York: Routledge, 1996.

Roche, John J. "The Scientific Theology Project of Alister E. McGrath." In *Alister E. McGrath & Evangelical Theology*, edited by Sung Wook Chung, 33–89. Grand Rapids: Baker, 2003.

Rorty, Richard. *Consequences of Pragmatism*. Minneapolis: University of Minnesota Press, 1982.

Ross, Hugh. *Creation As Science*. Colorado Springs: NavPress, 2006.

Russell, Bertrand. *A History of Western Philosophy*. New York: Simon & Schuster, 1945.

Russell, Colin A. "The Conflict of Science and Religion." In *Science & Religion*, edited by Gary B. Ferngren, 3–12. Baltimore: Johns Hopkins University Press, 2002.

Sarton, George. *Introduction to the History of Science*. 3 vols. Baltimore: William & Wilkins, 1948.

Scharff, Robert C. *Comte After Positivism*. Cambridge: Cambridge University Press, 1995.

Searle, John R. *The Construction of Social Reality*. New York: Free Press, 1995.

———. *Mind, Language and Society*. New York: Basic, 1998.

Sennett, James F., and Douglas Groothuis, eds. *In Defense of Natural Theology: A Post-Humean Assessment*. Downers Grove: InterVarsity, 2005.

Shea, William R. "Galileo and the Church." In *God & Nature*, edited by David C. Lindberg and Ronald L. Numbers, 114–35. Berkeley: University of California Press, 1986.

Shipway, Brad. "The Theological Application of Bhasker's Stratified Reality: The Scientific Theology of A. E. McGrath." *Journal of Critical Realism* 3:1 (2004) 191–203.

Singer, Charles. *Religion and Science Considered in their Historical Relations*. New York: Robert McBride, 1932.

Sire, James W. *The Universe Next Door*. Downers Grove: InterVarsity, 1997.

Sklar, Lawrence. *Theory and Truth: Philosophical Critique without Foundational Science*. Oxford: Oxford University Press, 2000.

Smith, R. Scott. "Language, Theological Knowledge, and the Postmodern Paradigm." In *Reclaiming the Center: Confronting Evangelical Accommodation in Postmodern Times*, edited by Millard J. Erickson et al., 109–35. Wheaton, IL: Crossway, 2004.

Snow, C. P. *The Two Cultures and the Scientific Revolution*. Cambridge: Cambridge University Press, 1959.

Snyder, Gregory A. "A Scientific Theology, Volume 2: Reality." *The Anglican Theological Review* 87:2 (Spring 2005) 354–57.

Spencer, Stephen R. "Is Natural Theology Biblical?" *Grace Theological Journal* 9 (1988) 59–72.

Spykman, Gordon J. *Reformational Theology*. Grand Rapids: Eerdmans, 1992.

Stahl, Steven P. "The Concept of Revelation In the Theology of Karl Barth." *Saint Luke's Journal of Theology* 23 (March 1980) 116–32.

Stark, Rodney. *For The Glory of God*. Princeton: Princeton University Press, 2003.

Swinburne, Richard. "The Argument from Design." In *Contemporary Perspectives on Religious Epistemology*, edited by R. Douglass Geivett and Brendan Sweetman, 201–11. New York: Oxford University Press, 1992.

———. *The Existence of God*. Oxford: Clarendon, 1991.

Tarnas, Richard. *The Passion of the Western Mind*. New York: Ballantine, 1991.

Taylor, Daniel. *The Myth of Certainty*. Downers Grove: InterVarsity, 1992.

Tertullian. "The Prescription Against Heretics." In *Ante-Nicene Fathers*, edited by Alexander Roberts and James Donaldson, translated by Peter Holmes, 243–65. Rev. ed. Peabody: Hendrickson.

Thorson, Walter R. "Realism and Reverence." *Journal of the American Scientific Affiliation* 38 (1975).

Tomlin, Graham. "The Scientific Theology Project of Alister McGrath." In *Alister E. McGrath and Evangelical Theology*, edited by Sung Wook Chung, 33–89. Exeter: Paternoster, 2003.

Torrance, Thomas F. "Divine and Contingent Order." In *The Sciences and Theology in the Twentieth Century*, edited by A. R. Peacock, 81–92. Notre Dame: University of Notre Dame Press, 1981.

———. *Divine and Contingent Order*. Edinburgh: T. & T. Clark, 1981.

———. *The Ground and Grammar of Theology*. Charlottesville: University of Virginia Press, 1980.

———. *Karl Barth: An Introduction to His Early Theology 1910–1931*. 3d ed. New York: T&T Clark, 2004.

———. "The Problem of Natural Theology in the Thought of Karl Barth." *Religious Studies* 6 (170) 121–35.

———. *Space, Time and Incarnation*. Edinburgh: T. & T. Clark, 1969.

———. *Theological Science*. Edinburgh: T. & T. Clark, 1969.

Van Doren, Charles. *A History of Knowledge*. New York: Ballantine, 1991.

van Huyssteen, J. Wentzel. *Alone in the World?* Grand Rapids: Eerdmans, 2006.

———. *Duet or Duel?: Theology and Science in a Postmodern World*. Harrisburg: Trinity, 1998.

———. *Essays in Postfoundationalist Theology*. Grand Rapids: Eerdmans, 1997.

———. *The Shaping of Rationality: Toward Interdisciplinarity in Theology and Science*. Grand Rapids: Eerdmans, 1999.

van Kooten Niekerk, Kees. "A Critical Realist Perspective on the Dialogue between Theology and Science." In *Rethinking Theology and Science*, edited by Niels Henrik Gregersen and J. Wentzel van Huyssteen, 51–86. Grand Rapids: Eerdmans, 1998.

Vidu, Adonis. "A Scientific Theology. Vol. 3: Theory." *Trinity Journal* 25 (Fall 2004) 272–74.

Wells, David F. *Above All Earthly Powers: Christ in a Postmodern World*. Grand Rapids: Eerdmans, 2005.

Wellum, Stephen J. "Postconservatism, Biblical Authority, and Recent Proposals for Re-Doing Evangelical Theology: A Critical Analysis." In *Reclaiming the Center: Confronting Evangelical Accommodation in Postmodern Times*, edited by Millard J. Erickson et al., 161–97. Wheaton, IL: Crossway, 2004.

Westfall, Richard S. "The Rise of Science and the Decline of Orthodox Christianity: A Study of Kepler, Descartes, and Newt." In *God & Nature*, edited by David C. Lindberg and Ronald L. Numbers, 218–37. Berkeley: University of California Press, 1986.

Westman, Robert S. "The Copernicans and the Churches." In *God & Nature*, edited by David C. Lindberg and Ronald L. Numbers, 76–113. Berkeley: University of California Press, 1986.

White, Andrew Dickson. *A History of the Warfare of Science with Theology*. 2 vols. New York: Dover, 1960.

White, Michael David. "The Function of the Doctrines of Revelation and Trinity In Karl Barth's Theological Method." ThM thesis, Southeastern Baptist Theological Seminary, May 2005.

Wilson, E. O. *Consilience: The Unity of Knowledge*. London: Abacus, 2006.

———. *Creation*. New York: Norton, 2006.

Wisnefske, Ned. *Preparing to Hear the Gospel: A Proposal for Natural Theology.* Lanham, MD: University Press of America, 1998.

Wood, W. Jay. *Epistemology.* Downers Grove: InterVarsity, 1998.

Wright, John H., SJ. "Theology, Philosophy, and The Natural Sciences." *Theological Studies* 52:3 (September 1991) 651–68.

Wright, N. T. *The New Testament and the People of God.* London: SPCK, 1992.